THE SPIRITUAL NATURE
OF THE UNIVERSE

THE SPIRITUAL NATURE OF THE UNIVERSE

THE ORIGINS, CHARACTER AND DESTINY OF THE SOUL

A Book of Chronicles, Revelations and Prophecies
Concerning Mankind's Relationships
with God and the Angels
from the Beginning, to the Present and
To the End

WILLIAM M. PLESS

Blue Dolphin Publishing

Published by Blue Dolphin Publishing, Inc.
P.O. Box 8, Nevada City, CA 95959
Orders: 1-800-643-0765
Web: www.bluedolphinpublishing.com

ISBN: 1-57733-079-X

Library of Congress Cataloging-in-Publication Data

Pless, William M., 1934–
    The spritual nature of the universe : the origins, character and destiny of
the soul / William M. Pless
        p.   cm.
    ISBN 1-57733-079-X
        1. Private revelations. 2. Spiritualism. I. Title.

BV5091.R4 P54 2000
248.2'9—dc21   00-046839

Printed in the United States of America

10   9   8   7   6   5   4   3   2

DEDICATION

To the Master, the Light of the World, the Prince of Peace,
Our Savior and Redeemer,
The Son of God.

IN MEMORIAM

To two extraordinary and wonderful people, my parents,
The Reverend David C. and Tyra Gunn Pless of Alabama.
They gave their all to the One to whom this book is dedicated
And to their children.

CONTENTS

PREFACE   xi

1. GENESIS OF GOD AND THE UNIVERSE   1

Prologue   1
The Beginning . . . and the BEGINNING   5
The Mystery of God's Origins   6
About the Father   7
The Beginnings of God's Creative Nature   8
Creation of the Archetypal Companion and a New Power   10
The Father's Creations Establish God   12
God Discovers Source of Truth and Law in His Own Being   13
The Father and Christ Create the Angels   16
God and the Angels Create the Universe   19
Early Activities of the Angels   21
How Angels Communicate   23
Does God Know Everything?   23
How Large is the Universe?   25
What Is at the Center of the Universe?   25

2. CREATION OF LIFE AND BEAUTY IN THE UNIVERSE   27

The Supreme Purpose of God's Creative Aspirations   27
God as a Trinity of Entities   29
The Angels' Capabilities for Creating Life   30
Creation of Life and Beauty Begins   32
Creation of Beauty   38
Creation of Life   39
Initiation and Development of New Life Forms   40

Angels Create Interactive Responses in Creatures   42
The Spiritual and Physical Domains of the Universe   45
The Biblical Story of Creation and the Relationship of Time   47
Interactions with Visitors to the Galaxy   48
Proud Lucifer Takes Keen Interest in Earth's Creation Activities   49

3. THE FALL OF LUCIFER AND THE ANGELS   51

The Father Responds to Lucifer's Disturbing Behavior   51
Lucifer Sees Possibility of His Own Kingdom Becoming a Reality   53
Passions are at the Center of Lucifer's Defiance   54
Lucifer Secures Earth as Base of Power   56
Lucifer Begins Expansion into the Galaxy   56
God Replaces Lucifer with a New Archangel: *GABRIEL*   57
Lucifer Claims Earth as His Kingdom   57
Some Angels Abandon Satan   58
God Yields Earth to Become Satan's Kingdom   59
Why God Gave Satan a Kingdom   60
An Impenetrable Veil of Darkness Encloses Earth   60
Reaction of Satan and the Angels to the "Veil"   61
Satan is Incapable of Ruling His Kingdom; the Angels Lose Hope   63
How Imperfection Came from Perfection   64
The Garden of Eden and Original Sin   67

4. GOD ESTABLISHES THE AGE OF REDEMPTION   71

The Time Is Right to Offer Redemption   71
Additional Conditions for Redemption   75
State of Mankind at Start of Soul-Sharing Phase   79
Angels Become Irretrievably Involved with Humanity
    and the Material Domain   81

5. THE AGE OF MANKIND— INTELLECTUAL AND SPIRITUAL DEVELOPMENT   83

Initial Conditions and Goals of the Early Stages   83
Satan's Continued Opposition to God   84
The Character of Holy Angels   85
How, Why Angels Infuse into the Human Body   88
Special Benefits and Gifts of Spirituality   90

The Growth of Spirituality in Mankind 94
The Ten Commandments 97
Moral and Natural Law 98
The Judeo-Christian Concept of God Is Right for the World 100

6. GOD'S GIFT OF CHRIST HIS SON TO MANKIND 103

Jesus Christ Came to Consummate the Age of Redemption 103
Insights into the Life Events of Jesus Christ 106
The Purpose and Manner of Jesus' Death 117
The Miracles of Immaculate Conception,
    Resurrection and Ascension 120
Christ and Women 123
The Church and Bible Preserve Knowledge of
    Jesus Christ and God 126
Jesus' Alternative Mission if Accepted as Messiah 130
The "Second Coming," the Return of Christ 132

7. ARTICLES OF SPIRITUALITY AND FAITH 137

Distinctive Relationship of Human and Soul 137
Spiritual and Human Purposes of the Holy Bible 138
Prayer and Forgiveness 138
The Spiritual Imperative for Forgiveness 145
Roles of the Mind and Soul in Becoming Saved 146
Who Sins, the Soul or the Human? 149
Unity of the Human and Soul 150
Baptism, the Way to Achieve Unity with God 153
Interactions of the Holy Spirit with Humanity 156
Belief and Faith 157
Letting God Have His Way 158
What is "God's Will"? 161
Achieving Life's Purpose for a Successful Life 162
Experiencing Death 165

8. THE AGE OF MANKIND—
MATTERS OF CURRENT INTEREST 173

The Human Perspective 173
Some Expectations for the Present Age 176

Behavior That God Abhors   179
Dishonoring God's Gift of Life   182
Spirituality and Religion   185
Worshipping God   187
Matters of Love and Marriage   188
Dealing with Diversity   197
Fairness and Justice   199
God Does Everything for Love and Truth   201

9. FROM NOW TO THE END OF
   THE AGE OF REDEMPTION   203

A View of Things to Come   203
The World in Moral Chaos   205
"Thy Kingdom Come, Thy Will Be Done on Earth . . . "   207
The False Prophet and the Beast   208
The Spiritual Battle of "Armageddon"   213
Armageddon Ends on the Eve of Christ's Millennium of Reign   215
Satan is Bound for a Thousand Years, Rules Hades in Terror   215
Christ Rules the Earth   216
The Millennium Ends; Fate of the Righteous   218
Return of the Unsaved to Life; Satan Is Unleashed   219
God Ends the Age of Redemption   220
A Summary of God's Acts of Redemption:
    He Has Done All That He Can Do...   221
The FINAL JUDGEMENT:
    God Brings an End to Satan and Hades   230
What Shall Become of Earth's Angels and Mankind?   232
The New Beginning   233
Death and Former Things in the New Heaven and the New Earth 234

EPILOGUE: A Message from Christ to the Souls of Mankind   239

PREFACE

The unique character of this book justifies a brief story as to how it came about. Any book requires a purpose for being, even if it is only to satisfy a simple dream to create a literary work that others may enjoy reading as much as you enjoyed writing it.

That relates to one of the unique factors of this book, for I began with no purpose whatsoever. I did not realize, at the beginning, that I was writing a book, or even what its themes would be. I knew only that I was writing messages given to me from an unseen Divine source that had been teaching me a strange new art for almost a half year. There were lesser entities before this who began the training and preparation for a year before this most exalted and Holy Being took me under his tutelage. Consequently, the messages in this book did not come from "spirit guides" or "angels," but from the Heavenly Father. *He is the only source.*

Nothing that is presented in this book came from any other source except for some scriptures given as examples. No historical accounts, no journals, no reference books, no carefully crafted opinions of learned philosophers, none of my own opinions or speculations, were used in the production of the basic draft of the book. It was a year or more after I began to write it that I was permitted even to read the Holy Scriptures. I was also permitted at that time to confer with some reference sources so that I could acquire certain information to round out and complete some of the ideas. This was because the more you know about a subject, the easier it becomes to understand unique truths that the Father provides, and the more precisely you can write about it.

I wrote the first draft of this book in July 1995. At that time, I had no idea what I was writing, why, or what avenues of knowledge or argument this activity would lead me into. Words came one at a time, sometimes as a phrase. As I labored through each sentence, each paragraph, I realized each included a message that was beyond my own learning or established thinking. I continued for several days while the words, even complete sentences, came more freely. I could now even grasp the complete thought of a paragraph before writing it. Yet, the words that were written were rarely the ones that had formed in my mind.

This process continued for three weeks until I had written about one hundred fifty pages of an astonishing document. I knew the thoughts, the expressions, were not mine because they did not generally portray *my* beliefs or understandings. I was the writer of these messages, but I was not the author! The author was an unseen guest, a quiet, patient *Presence* with whom I had already become familiar during an experience that had been ongoing for more than a year and a half.

Since the writing of that first draft, many changes and new sections have been added to the manuscript. I have gone through the manuscript numerous times to modify sentences, paragraphs and words to *ensure that what I had written is the message the Spirit had given me.* I finally realized that my editorial efforts involved a process directed from the unseen. The first stage was to write down all the basic information, then to fill out and round out the thoughts, then to expand and complete them, then to verify and assure their *truth,* then to make them *precise,* then finally to make them grammatically correct and literarily acceptable. *Truth and accuracy were demanded by the Unseen Presence and could not be compromised.* This required me to verify that *everything* I wrote or modified had the approval of this Divine Presence. All of this was done while my mind and soul were open and consecrated to this Spirit.

Through the use of a computer's word processing and storage programs, I was able to perfect these writings to a degree that *was not possible for the early writers of Divinely given messages.*

The experience began during the Fall of 1993 when I started to explore the world of spirits. I did this on my own without Divine guidance or protection, an activity that is extremely ill advised. After several months, I was in a very dangerous situation from which Christ rescued me from the brink of disaster upon my request contained in the *Lord's Prayer: "Thy Will be done on Earth as it is in Heaven."* I spoke these words from the depths of my soul and they released a power that saved and transformed me.

During this experience, I learned that the spiritual realm is a repository and source of unimaginable truth and wisdom and that it can be available to any person who enters and explores it in the right way. This realm exists because of the spiritual entities that abide there, and they are both good and evil. It can be a world of Light *or* of Darkness, but you cannot have both. The evil ones of darkness disdain Truth and Love and will do whatever they can to methodically corrupt and lead you away from truth, to betray those you love and destroy their faith in you.

A crucial lesson I learned in this is that without Divine guidance in this abstruse world that humans can neither see nor sense, evil spirits can come to dominate the activities through their skillful use of deceit and seduction. Through this they hold your interest and entice you to entrust your will to them. Their goal is to entrap you in shame and guilt and destroy any future hopes of fulfilling your good intentions. Doubt not that this is the reality of the world of darkness.

The realm of Light is different and I knew that it alone held the promise of fulfillment of my goals of exploration. Immediately following my rescue, I was determined to resume the explorations because of the potential for knowledge and spiritual rewards. I sensed that this would be granted. From this point forward, however, I would conduct my searches in the Light and with Divine blessing. I prayed that God would forgive me for my brash foolishness and that He would now guide and protect me while I toured this realm that *only my soul* could perceive and understand. But the soul and mind are not the same and, as I would learn, they each abide in two totally different "spaces".

God answered my prayer by sending two angelic spirits to serve as guides and trainers, and another to be my protector. With this arrangement, I began to grow in knowledge and understanding of this strange realm and to learn many basic methods to conduct my searches.

After a few weeks, I became aware that a very exalted angel had arrived. "He" took control and the angel guides left me after a few more days. Now my solitary teacher, this new angel began to teach me some very strange and powerful ways to communicate with him and how to find and verify the truths that I sought. He guided me for many months in the search for *truth* and in expressing truth in messages of astonishing and wonderful content. I began to look for purpose in his presence and his efforts to train me: *why* was he doing this? My mind began to fill with expectancy.

One day, months after his arrival, I realized that this angel was phasing out to leave me and a more extraordinary entity was replacing him. This new entity signified his presence by drawing the semblance of a wreath on my drawing pad. When I finally asked who he was, He identified himself as *the Heavenly Father*! From this point on, the Father alone worked with me and I entered upon a serious and deliberative phase of my search for spiritual truth. I knew now that nothing could stand between me and the truth that I sought about *any possible subject.*

He put into my mind the object of writing a book to express these truths and share them with all humanity. I didn't know what I would write! Then, one day I began to write the first lines of this book. For the last eighteen months, not realizing what was taking place, I had been led and trained to become a *messenger* for the Heavenly Father. When I realized this, I could not have felt any less qualified for the task. I was not a pastor, minister, priest, theologian or any other learned philosopher or practitioner of religion. I was a father and retired scientist who had fulfilled his life goals after spending his childhood as a preacher's son.

I had only to write the words that were coming to me, not to create them because I was not the author. The Author of this wonderful book is none other than the very source of Truth and Wisdom, *the Heavenly Father!* I learned to accept *only His words,* and not to mix any of mine with his. I would not be a mixing bowl to create bread from various ingredients, but a spigot to dispense only the pure water that came to me. He gave it freely because I had sought it and offered myself freely to his Will.

In the process of writing this book, my previous beliefs and thoughts about religion and spiritual matters were totally revised. These proved to be entirely inadequate to express what God is really like or to explain the nature and purpose of the relationship humans have with Him. The experience changed me profoundly, recreating me spiritually and intellectually. It infused into my mind a new wisdom that has made it all so clear. Now, it is available for all.

I could never have written this book because its messages are not mine. Everything in it came from the mind of God and He is the Author. He has given it to all humanity so that we may know him better, to understand our human and spiritual relationships through *new knowledge*, and to give us new faith and hope in his promises of salvation and eternal life. These things go beyond religious beliefs to reveal the foundation truths of those beliefs.

The result of this experience is a book that presents God in supreme majesty as the Creator of everything and the Source of all that is good. It displays him as absolute sovereign over the Universe, ruling it with Divine Law and Purpose that come from the powers of Love and Truth. The book presents the story of God, the angels and Mankind in distinctive content and relationships that are unique and far-reaching. It is a blend of chronicles, revelation and prophecy concerning things that were first revealed through our Judeo-Christian heritage. The story is told from the enlightened and authoritative perspective of the angels rather than from a humanistic viewpoint.

With an extraordinary perspective from beginning to end, the book provides a panoramic sweep of the activities of the Creator from his own genesis, through the creation of the angels and the universe, and the creation of life. It describes how the angels create life and beauty in worlds throughout the universe, including Earth, as agents of God's Will using themes that they conceive. It describes the development of opposition to God's Supreme Purpose by a deviant angel, humanity's innocent but crucial involvement with this, and God's concerns for the salvation and restoration of lost *souls*. In this setting, it discusses moral and spiritual issues that are extremely important for present society and why issues of right and wrong must be resolved soon. The book shows that sin and disobedience of God's laws belong to a temporary anachronism that is totally at variance with his nature and purpose and which will soon end forever, taking those who will not separate themselves from its attraction.

It reveals the identity of the soul as an angel, why humans have them, what the soul is trying to accomplish with its human host, and what the eventual destiny is of both souls and humanity. A clear distinction is made between the soul and the human. Mankind is challenged to establish a partnership with their souls to achieve God's Holy Purposes for the sake of them both.

This story of God and his relationship with humanity is given in *new* revelations that unite both traditional and nontraditional precepts of Christianity and Spirituality. These revelations will verify *some* things we already understand, will replace with *new understanding* some things we *thought* we understood, and will bring a new understanding of other things that we have *never* known. In this new knowledge, we are given a *new wisdom* that will strengthen our belief in God, deepen our faith in Him and bring us the peace of knowing finally the great purpose of our lives. Each human being is given a Holy Purpose before he is born and it is part and parcel of God's own purpose; this book will tell you how to fulfill that purpose by letting His Will become yours through the guidance of your soul.

The diverse messages in this book are presented in the broad expanse of Spirituality, as opposed to narrower religious standpoints. This is not the popular spirituality of psychics and astrologers, but is the Spirituality that is of and from the True God. Since these revelations came from the same God who gave us the Holy Scriptures, they have unity with the Bible, but unfold new perspectives and insights into biblical chronicles and prophesies. They reach beyond our religious beliefs to the very source of spiritual truth and give new meaning to many scriptures.

The Scriptures should not be used to validate these new revelations. The story is not intended to be an explanation or extension of Biblical teachings or religious doctrine. It offers a more comprehensive view of the Creator and his expressed Purpose to provide new knowledge and understanding through these revelations for Christians, Jews, Muslims and those of Oriental religions. The book is meant to have *universal* appeal to all people of the world, to all who practice religion as a means to seek unity with a transcendent Creator, the source of Truth, Love and Life. A hope of this book is to bring *all* religions in the world into *one* Spiritualism, with all sharing the *same* beliefs in the One True God and all advancing together in truth, love and peace.

ACKNOWLEDGMENTS

It would not have been an easy task to proceed with writing and promoting this unusual book without the genuine support of members of my family and certain wonderful friends. From the very start of this endeavor, my wife Yvonne and son William gave their full-hearted support through belief in what I was doing and faith in the Divine Source of the book's messages. My brothers and sisters inspired me to proceed and I particularly cherish the discussions with Mildred, James and George. Brother George quickly became an incredible supporter and verifier of the book's harmony with the Holy Scriptures, along with his daughter Elaine and grand-daughter Lisa. Then, two wonderful friends of extraordinary spiritual perception, Claire and Doris, sustained me through inspirational dialogues and Christian faith. I extend my unbounded gratitude to all of these for their faith and inspiration. Further, I thank my brother George and friend Claire for accepting my offer to be *trustees* of the book during the years it was being written.

I am deeply grateful to Mr. Paul Clemens of Blue Dolphin Publishing, Inc., for accepting the manuscript for publication and offering me the opportunity to publish it, and for involving me with the comprehensive activity of his staff to bring it about. Of particular note and of extreme importance to the integrity of the book, is Mr. Clemens' understanding agreement not to edit the text of the book, thereby helping me to ensure the purity and sanctity of God's Word presented therein.

May God bless you with his Grace and with eternal life with Him.

William M. Pless

1

THE GENESIS OF GOD
AND THE UNIVERSE

Prologue

There is One God, and He is *the one* who can be credited with Creation and all things that are good. He is *the only one* worthy to be called 'God' and to be worshipped by all to whom He has given life. He is the only god that is *omniscient and omnipotent* and who is also indestructible and eternal.

Yet, the world seems to worship many gods. Even those whose religion focuses on the One God do not know Him and cannot agree upon what He desires of all. People worship Him in ways that they perceive to be right, but some things are *not right* due to a lack of knowledge and understanding. Not *everything* they associate with God in worship is acceptable to him. Where is the truth and understanding that will enlighten their beliefs and creeds? It is evident that a transforming enlightenment will not come unless there is a new flow of Divine Wisdom.

God himself chose to be what He IS from many possibilities inherent in his being. Therefore, in his own development, He rejected many properties that could have defined Him differently. God *cannot* be all things to all people, for in this world He is a choice in matters of good and evil, light and darkness, life and death. Those who worship Him must also reject things that are not Divine because they can have no part in Him.

Many truths that support religious beliefs are incomplete, fragmentary and selective. The Holy Bible provides the basis for most of the truths for Judeo-Christian beliefs. Among the religions are many *interpretations* of the Scriptures and ideas that cause differences between worshippers. Yet, there is only *one* meaning that is true about anything God has done or spoken through his prophets. The way to Truth is straight and narrow. Truth is clear and distinct. In Truth there is no equivocation between alternative possibilities of meaning. Therefore, this book will give none. There is only *one way* that anything has occurred, only *one thought* for anything that was spoken. Disagreement, therefore, comes only from ignorance and misunderstanding. Enlightenment comes by one opening his eyes to the Light and his mind to the Truth.

It is said that *all things are possible with God.* The statement is true enough, but there is a condition associated with it that is never stated. All things that are possible must also be rational, that is, they must conform to God's spiritual and physical laws. These laws, which God must also obey, determine all that is possible. Therefore, *all possible things are rational.* All that is created, all that occurs as activity, must be rational. Irrational deeds are not possible, even with God. The adage is more accurately expressed as *all rational things are possible with God.* They may not all seem possible to humanity.

This book presents an account of some events performed by God that are significant to the present state of Mankind. It proceeds from God's own *genesis* to the present time and to the end of the Age that He has established for the enlightenment of humanity and the redemption of fallen angels. In this story one can learn truths that will increase his knowledge and understanding of God and his ways, and deepen his faith and acceptance of Him as the Creator and the Source of all that is good.

In the Scriptures, the Apostle John credits Jesus with saying: "*If* you continue in my word, you are truly my disciples; and you will know the *truth* and the truth will make you free…" (Gospel of John, chapter 8:31, 32; NRSV). Jesus' word was *truth.* No one can be his disciple without *accepting* the truth. The truth will free one from uncertainty and the pitfalls of wrong beliefs. Anyone can come to know the truths of which Jesus spoke. It comes from the very *Source* of truth and is unlimited and inexhaustible. Jesus informed us through his disciples that everything he spoke came from the Heavenly Father. Each person can turn to the Father and receive the enlightenment of which Jesus spoke.

When the Father began to reveal his Presence to Mankind many thousands of years ago, He attempted to teach humanity that He was Holy and that he should be approached through acts of uprightness and goodwill. This requisite was advocated through men and women whom He selected and inspired with divine wisdom through the Holy Spirit. Consequently, an awareness of the true God and a quest to know Him arose through the centuries.

God revealed himself to Mankind through his *prophets* and the priests, preachers and teachers who learned from them. They also knew Him through their *souls* because the soul is an angel of God who helps the person to develop a state of intelligence and spiritual awareness. Prophets can and have come in *any age* to impart God's truths to humanity. He led Abraham to begin the Jewish and Arabic nations through his descendants and He further developed the Jews to be recipients and teachers of his Word to enlighten the world.

The ancient prophets brought knowledge of God's laws and instructions for righteous living. When necessary, they brought praise and rebukes to teach people His ways. Their messages revealed God's perfect virtues while extolling his omnipotence, omniscience and praiseworthiness. Most prophets considered God to require only obedience and worship, not yet understanding that Love and Truth are the *basis* of all that He desires. God sent His Son Christ to live among humanity as a flesh and blood mortal to provide this understanding through his teachings. Men and women who accepted Christ's messages were transformed by their new beliefs. Many became apostles dedicated to taking his message throughout the Roman world to establish the foundations for his universal church. The intolerant guardians of the status quo who regarded the truths of the times to be *complete, perfect and inviolable* rejected Jesus *and* his messages.

In the times in which the apostles and prophets lived, the world was primitive and limited compared to any age since. God's messages were given to his messengers through mental processes of meditation or visions and competed with their own strong traditions, superstitions and unclear concepts of God. Their writings and proclamations were often spontaneous, uncorrected, and presented within limited consideration and outlooks. With few exceptions, prophetic pronouncements and Biblical events were seldomly recorded at the time they occurred. These were often passed by oral tradition from decade to decade, generation to generation, sometimes for several centuries before someone wrote them into permanent documents.

The legacy these people left to the world through the Scriptures is an awareness of God and His commandments, that we should do his Will and keep his Laws. These provide sufficient enlightenment so that everyone can know the path to righteousness and salvation. The Holy Bible stands as the ageless codification of Divine wisdom and the authority for righteous living. From the Scriptures, one can learn all he needs to know to find God, to live in ways that please Him and reject those ways that degrade humanity and devastate the soul.

A goal of righteousness is to ennoble and preserve Mankind, for as time passes it becomes more certain that humanity will perish in the destructive grip of iniquity if righteousness is not accepted as the way of life by all. When amoral ideas become the policy goals of nations and licentiousness becomes normal in styles of living, Mankind will fall into decay and death.

The Bible is a timeless treasure of God's recorded relationships with human beings that has had an immeasurable influence upon Mankind. Without the Bible and Christ's Church that has preserved and advocated it, the world would have become a Godless and hopeless quagmire of depravity and misery. Let *all* the world praise God for this gift of truth and love given for the sake of all humanity. Yet, people of modern times do not generally know enough about God to be completely firm in their faith or true to the religious creeds they embrace. The true nature and works of God have been obscured in mystery and misconception. There is a need in the present time for the deeper levels of truth that are provided in this *book*.

The writer is neither a *pastor* or a Bible scholar, nor a priest or a theologian. Indeed, very few of God's prophets and apostles of old were any of these. He is a *messenger* who was prepared and trained to qualify as the writer of these messages. He was born and raised in the Christian family of a preacher in which love and virtue prevailed and suffered the constraints of deprivation and hardship. He has an in-born desire for knowledge and inquiry into hidden truths. The discipline of science molded his manner of thinking and gave him insight into the laws of God. Science and religion were united in his mind into complementary aspects of his perception of God and the universe. As it was with Jeremiah the Prophet, God knew the writer before he was born, and just as surely, he came into life with a *purpose*.

In the manner of all Divine prophesies, the articles in this book came directly and completely from the Heavenly Father as messages communicated through the writer's receptive soul. The Spirit empowered the writer to transform these accurately and clearly into *human* thought. Angels guided the transcription of the messages into written documents. The writer carefully edited and revised the transcripts with angelic help and always with the Father's approval. The original text was expanded and perfected over a long period of concentrated and devoted labor. He read the document critically, time and again, to assure completeness of ideas, verify their truthfulness, and improve clarity of meaning. Knowing that this is God's book, he did not desire that a single line should be his own, but every one should be the Lord's because they *must* remain pure and true.

The writer humbly feels the awesome weight of presenting such revelations to a world in need of them. He understands the significance of these messages with respect to all that he believed beforehand and knows that they will change the reader as they changed him. He knows that the God who gave them as an instrument of his love will sustain and confirm him.

In this unprecedented time of choice and commitment for Mankind, these messages are given to all people of the world as a gift of the Father's love to fulfill holy purposes. They extend to everyone the objectives of God's plan which Mankind and the angels must achieve together to fulfill God's Will for the world. These messages come from the Fountain of Truth, pure and unchanged and untainted with human opinion and conjecture.

This book represents the story of God and Mankind in distinctive content and relationships never presented in previous sources. Never before has so much been revealed about the soul and its relationships to the human and to God. Never before has so much been given concerning the spiritual kingdoms of Heaven, Earth and Hades. Never before has so much been taught concerning the advancement of humanity brought about through the "spirit".

This book should remove much of the present obscuration. God will be revealed more for what He is and how He came to be. Human beings can have a greater understanding of what their relationship to God is, why He is concerned with us and how we should respond to Him. Through this new knowledge, the seeker will be able to understand and accept these things with greater faith and a more willing mind.

The Beginning . . . and the BEGINNING

The Holy Bible (RSV), Book of Genesis, Chapter 1:1, declares: "In the *Beginning*, God created the heavens and the Earth,"

There was a BEGINNING before God created anything that is in the heavens or on Earth, before the "beginning" disclosed in the first verse of the Bible. There was a BEGINNING before God existed. There was a BEGINNING before consciousness dawned upon the mind of he who would create *all* that has come to be. The BEGINNING lies beyond the reaches of the Consciousness of the Creator and cannot be known, even to the Father of God!

The following sections provide an account of the course of events in the great void that God eventually came to occupy and made into His own abode, which we call HEAVEN. This message will, in part, fill the blank spaces in our awareness that lie beyond "...the Beginning," and since "...the BEGIN-NING", before God was fully formed. The Father has given these truths so that we may share in the mystery and know that ALL that EXISTS has come from Him.

The Mystery of God's Origins

In the BEGINNING..., there existed only the Father, utterly alone in a great void. In total peace and isolation, the Father began to contemplate his existence and origins of being. This posed great mysteries to Him because he had no knowledge of a beginning or memories beyond a dawning of aware-ness. All that He has come to know of Himself and the ability to exercise his great powers has come from nothing except the Father's basic substance, since nothing other than He was in the void.

The Father has no memory or knowledge of his own beginning or when "time" began for Him. His development was like that of a child who was seemingly born without parents, left alone to live and grow under its own care and tutelage. Similarly, the earliest stage was a period of "beginnings" for the Father.

First came *awareness*, an awakening without knowledge or understanding during which he became mindful of his existence. Then *learning* began to take place from his consciousness and He began to visualize Himself with great interest and wonder, as when a child becomes curious about itself. Eventually, with a growing sense of inquiry He began to wonder *what* He was. A sense of the circumstances of this "place" led Him to question *where* He was. With increasing knowledge and wisdom, He realized that He was a "personality" and began to explore his identity, wondering: *Who am I?* Finally, in great perplexity and a growing need for *purpose*, He asked: *Why?*

His experiences could provide no answers to these questions and there was no one to ask. So, the Father has no conscious knowledge of either the nature, time and place of his origins or his fundamental identity. The Father knew only that He was a shining sea of consciousness and intelligence without vocation or purpose; yet, this is the beginning of the great spiritual Mind of God.

In suggesting such queries as What? Where? Who? and Why? for the sake of presenting this dilemma in human terms, we have greatly oversimplified the quests of this powerful and unfathomable mind. We cannot know the progressions or the substance or directives of thought that proceeded through this mind to unceasingly create knowledge through rational thought alone. And we cannot know what moods and sensations arose from loneliness, desperation, yearnings, hope, and peace to compel this mind to seek persuasive answers to its most intimate and profound concerns.

The accumulation of knowledge soon began to produce an identity for this mind and would proceed to manifest a being of supreme intellect and consciousness. God did not yet exist, but He would emerge from this Mind and discover all the intrinsic powers that made Him supremely omnipotent and divine. This waif from a void of mystery increased in wisdom and absolute power to become the Creator of our Universe and of Life, the storehouse of all knowledge and understanding, and the unique Source of LOVE, TRUTH, LIGHT and LIFE. In our universe there was and is none but HE, and all else that IS issued from Him!

WRITER'S NOTE: Curious about the mystery of His origin, I asked if perhaps the Father had been created by another being in a higher level of existence than Himself. The answer was that He had no awareness of a Being either higher or equal to Himself, that He alone inhabits the void. So, a mystery full of the most profound and fundamental questions of existence remains to engage the curiosity *even of God.*

About the Father

The Father is a Being of supreme power and intellect who is capable of thinking, knowing, feeling, doing and interacting with his internal self. There is nothing outside himself with which he can interact, so that ALL that he knows and does comes from within and is directed from within. His great Intellect and Consciousness are not abstract quantities, but are actually "spiritual" substance for which humans have no concept. His space is a spiritual space of many dimensions, existing within a three-dimensional void.

The Father is all-powerful, apparently with infinite capabilities and total command of his abilities and actions. The interactions between his Intellect and Consciousness produce an essence of mind that is rational and all knowing. Like a human body, he is aware "instantly" of conditions and "sensations" that affect any part of him, even though the distance covered is of enormous cosmic magnitude. The whole of him is maintained in integral unity by an attractive energy that is commanded by him and usable for any purpose that he wills.

The basic substance of his Being is subject to his control and is available and usable for creative purposes conceived in this Mind. He can create products from elements he selects from His Intellect and Consciousness. He can move or expand any small or large part of himself and create changes in the products of his substance. He can concentrate his tremendous internal energy to compress, expand, move, combine, coalesce, or disintegrate any portion of his basic or created substance to accomplish whatsoever he desires.

The Father's abilities and actions in exercise of these abilities are not arbitrary or whimsical or irrational. All that he does within his domain follows inviolable laws that arise from the nature of his being and *which He must obey.* All creatures of spirit and material form that he has created must, like him, also obey these laws. All that He creates represent absolute reality composed of truth, and nothing can exist outside this reality. All that He does is accomplished through the exercise of his perfect intellect, so that *everything is logical and rational.* Even his most perplexing mysteries, when analyzed thoroughly, will reveal a perfect and purposeful logic.

In his great loneliness, the Father discovered Love and saw that consciousness is not worthwhile without love; therefore, He developed Love to the extent of a basic power and incorporated it into all of his intellectual pursuits. Thereafter, everything was created from Truth, and all life was created from Truth and Love. He applies his laws to life in a manner to infuse and express love and to assure its fulfillment and perpetuation.

Although we speak of the Father and God using masculine names and pronouns, we could just as well use feminine terms. Sexual references are completely irrelevant. But our language demands a simple, unencumbered, personal way of addressing him. You may think of him as either sex as you wish or any color as you please; it will neither offend him nor describe him. He is both the Mother and the Father of all that exists. The angels who populate Heaven, whom He created in his likeness, created all forms of life distinguished by unique characteristics having purpose and importance.

The Beginnings of the Father's Creative Nature

The Father of God knew that his consciousness was the essence of his Being and that it contained an infinite capacity for intelligence. He had learned that he could manipulate the elements of his intelligence either as a passive or a deliberate endeavor. This led him to begin amusing himself by combining various random elements of intelligence. By manipulating these elements of substance further, he discovered that "strings of information" could be produced then expanded into "structures" having interrelated hierarchical levels of detail. Specific meanings could be associated with each structure.

He soon learned that two basic types of information strings could be produced. One string form seemed to be complete in itself and contained only pure thought, or "knowledge". The other form seemed to be incomplete or inconclusive. In examining ways to bring the second string forms to completion, the Father found that, by using his intrinsic energy, he could "compress" the logic strings and form them into shapes of high substance density. Furthermore, these shapes had definite and specific characteristics depending upon the intelligence elements used to create the logic strings. Also, during compression, the inherent energy within the strings was stored within the shapes and served to give the shapes a capacity for certain actions. These shapes can be called "creation precursors" and "condensed logic structures".

The Father realized that by choosing any combination of intelligence elements to form the information strings, he could produce an unlimited, infinite variety of strings of each form, either "knowledge" or "creative precursors". Elated over this new awareness, he began to expand his thoughts to extend over his total Being, visualizing the creation of structures that could be displayed throughout the great void, and which he could manipulate and change at will.

But *something* was missing: for *what purpose* would he create any of this other than to his own amusement and pleasure? A great yearning began to grow within him, a feeling to share all of this with another Being who could appreciate it and rejoice in all that it offered. He wanted a companion. The Father began to realize that none of his achievements, no matter of what magnitude or splendor, would satisfy him or have meaning unless he could share it freely with another appreciative being. He wanted to present all that he could do to another similar being for its joy and benefit and receive in return only its gracious esteem and commensurate response.

He began to look about, searching the great void in hopes of discovering such a Being, but none could be found. Yet his dream would not leave him, and his failure left him in grief.

This was the beginning and discovery of "love". Powerful yearnings began to fill the Father's bosom and became an obsession. In the failure to fulfill these longings, he experienced other feelings such as disappointment and sadness. These newfound qualities of his personality pressed heavily upon him, but served to point him in a new direction and kindled a new concept of himself.

With no other Being within the great void, the Father began to reassess his former creations to see if he could discover a purpose that would yield a fulfillment for his yearning, or "love", to make his existence and achievements worthwhile. In his meditations, it occurred to him that each part of his great Being was complete in itself and that possibly he could form a companion by using part of himself, separated from his central Being.

The Father concentrated his thoughts upon this new idea. He soon decided that he could produce such a new Being in the same way that he had produced the two forms of information strings, except that he must also give it a share of his Essence to endow it with awareness and sensitivity. With this capacity, it could respond to him and feel the same things that he felt. He also wanted it to be a restricted replica of himself, yet independent and distinctly different. To affect this, he could extract certain intelligence elements from the portion of himself that he used to create the companion, being careful to use the elements that were necessary to achieve the ideal.

The Father gave careful thought to the creation of the companion Being because he wanted it to be exactly as he desired without having to change or destroy it to begin over once it was created. He knew that he may wish to create still other Beings after successfully creating the first one. He would now create the first Being as a model and proceed on the basis of its success.

Creation of the Archetypical Companion and a New Power

In accordance with his plan, the Father separated a small part of the substance of his Being having both consciousness and intelligence. He isolated it from himself and removed the unwanted intelligence elements so that it would not be a precise replica of himself. Then he formed suitable information strings, manipulated these into the arrangement he wanted, then infused it with consciousness to enervate the creature and bring it to life. Its conscious essence was fully representative of the Father, so that the new Being had an immediate affinity for him and responded to his love.

The Father was extremely pleased. He knew from this result that he could now create any number of such Beings, each different from himself and from each other. There could be a great multitude of unique Beings, depending upon how much of his own substance he wished to expend or how many he simply desired. He anticipated that this creature and all that would follow could now mature into an equal, complementary companion with a sovereignty of independence and action.

The Father wanted to fully know the new Being and show him all that he had done and could do, sharing with the creature his own delight over his powers to create whatever he desired in the great void. The creature responded to all that the Father shared with it and proved to be just the companion the Father wanted. When he revealed his ideas to possibly create additional new Beings each with their own individuality, the companion responded excitedly and joyfully and encouraged the father to proceed with it. Together they roamed the great void contemplating the Father's plans to fill the void with imaginative structures. Along the way, the companion began to offer ideas of his own, adding to the Father's pleasure and joy.

The time came when the Father desired to send the companion alone into the void so that it could learn to think independently from the Father and arrive at its own ideas, growing intelligently and consciously in its own way. He did this desiring and expecting his young companion to develop into an entity equal to himself with whom he would have an enduring mutual attraction in love and sharing all things. So, the companion departed and went alone into the void, as the Father desired. Then the creature began to feel lonely and sad, all of which increased as the separation widened. There came a point when it felt completely alone and dejected and desired to go no further or be away from the Father for another moment. It began to writhe as if in intolerable anguish.

Seeing that something was terribly wrong, the Father brought his beloved companion back to himself and consoled it. The companion was immediately relieved and restored to happiness. He began to interrogate it and to contemplate the answers along with his own awareness of things. The Father then realized that his companion could *not* live apart from him, that it must always abide *within* him. He understood that this applied to *all* life created from the substance of his being because there is nothing outside of himself to nourish or sustain another being. Because the substance of his being is the source of life and the nourishment for life, nothing that he creates can exist *outside or apart* from him. Whatever he creates of spiritual or material form must always remain within as *part* of him. Consequently, he will always be *One* while composed of *everything* that can exist as a result of his acts of creation.

Outside in the void, the beloved creature could not feel a connection with the Father and they could not *communicate* in thought or love. Without a connection, the companion could not grow in the powers of intellect or love.

This caused the creature to miss the Father. In the unpleasant separation hopefulness turned into anguish and failure. This companion and all future creatures must live within the Father as *subordinate* beings. There could be no separate, equal companions produced from his substance. Yet, he desired that all entities be free and independent while forever being an integral part of the whole. This requires that *every entity must conform to the intrinsic laws and live harmoniously with all*, while each grows by partaking from the infinite resources of the Father.

The Father realized that to establish and maintain this plan of independence and conformance, each creature would need direct access to his intellect to accomplish acts of his Will and to conduct their own activities *in harmony* with it. So that all their activities in the Heavenly space would be done in amity and grace, each would also need to share love with the Father and all creatures. This capability must be readily available to all spiritual entities wherever they may be in the wide expanse of the Father's being.

From this perception, the Father devised a way to combine the power of his intellect with love and to project the combination into all the Heavenly space so that wherever the companions dwelled, they could still feel a closeness and connection with the Father. Thus was born a new power composed of the Father's love and intellect and which could be directed by the Father as a means for his creature to perform in accordance with his Will anywhere in the Universe. This was essentially a new entity that would later become known by all his angels as the *Spirit of God*, or the *Holy Spirit*.

Since all angels that the Father planned to create later would be independent creatures, they could have no direct connection with him or have access to his intellect without the Holy Spirit. Connection through the Holy Spirit would empower them to perform all things authorized by the Father, including all the creations that they would come to produce in the universal void. The Holy Spirit would also guide the intelligent minds of material life, giving insight into abstract ideas that come from the spirit.

The Father's Creations Establish God

At this point, the Father had created the first model companion and the Holy Spirit so that three distinct entities now existed in the great void.

The Father had created the first companion after lengthy and careful exercise of his great intellect, not wishing to make a single error in its creation.

Consequently, the Father was greatly pleased with the result. He filled the creature with the essence and consciousness of his own Being. He taught it all that he knew and told him of the structures he desired to create in the great void. Yet, by rational constraint, the creature remained a restricted replica of the Father. Then, after sharing all that the Father could give him, the creature acquired the experience of being completely apart from his creator in the void. This is of great significance because he was the only such entity the Father ever created who felt the unbearable anguish of being totally disassociated from the Father's love, which proved the necessity of Love for all created life. From this unpleasant experience, the Father conceived the need to create the Holy Spirit that would become a source of power and authority for accomplishing his Will. The Father himself had experienced the great loneliness and despair of having a love that could not be shared until he created his companion.

Because of these things, the Father gave him an exalted place among his great creations: to be principal above all the angels and living entities that would be created. He would be the alpha and omega of God's creations. The Father would call this creature his "son" and name him "*The Christ*", or simply "Christ".

Now, the three distinct entities in the great void, each serving essential and grand purposes, the Father over all, together formed a unity bound within the Father's love and dominion. This is the trinity we have come to know as God, and He is the supreme Master and Creator of His Universe and all that is in it. There is no other God in this Universe.

From this point, God began to create all the entities from His own substance, to be called angels, then to create the structures of the physical universe. Once the universal structure was in place, attended by the angels doing His Will, God set them to creating life and beauty on planets about stars distributed among the galaxies. The universe filled with the presence of God is *Heaven*.

God Discovers Source of Truth and Law in His Own Being

From the earliest times when the Father began to create either pure-thought or condensed logic structures using elements of his intellect as starting points, the result always depended upon the specific elements he used and the process used to create them. If he started with the same elements each time and processed them in exactly the same way, he always got precisely the same results. On the other hand, if he varied either the input elements or the process, the results would be different. He therefore recognized that *there were inherent inviolable principles involved with whatever he did.*

Later, when he began to combine elements of consciousness with either form of creation to produce "living" entities, somewhat the same thing occurred, but these having very distinct differences from the non-living entities.

To understand this, it is necessary to delineate the four types of creations the Father had produced:

- Type One) "pure-thought" structures produced from elements of intellect alone; these are "truths" or elements of *knowledge;*
- Type Two) condensed logic structures produced from elements of intellect alone; these are the *basic building blocks of the material worlds;*
- Type Three) "pure-thought" structures produced from combining elements of intellect and consciousness; these are *spiritual entities;* and
- Type Four) condensed logic structures produced from combining elements of intellect and consciousness; these are *living material entities of the plant and animal kingdoms.*

Type One creations always had the form of "statements" of knowledge that can be referred to as "truths". These truths never varied whenever the input and processing conditions were exactly the same. They were also permanent and could be destroyed or disassembled only by God's unique powers of will and control.

Type Two creations had the form of physical structures of various densities and characteristics and can be identified as the nuclear, atomic and molecular constituents of material structures. These also never varied whenever the conditions were the same.

Dramatic differences in form and character existed between Types One and Two, so that the Father found it necessary to consider each of them to be entirely separate categories. Type One creations can be regarded as "spiritual", and the Type Two creations "physical" or "material". It is extremely important to note that *both Type One and Type Two creations were derived from the Father's own substance!* This is also true for Types Three and Four. Thus, *all truth, all spiritual beings and all "living" and lifeless material forms are part of Him!!*

The Type Three creation had very special properties and abilities because it possessed consciousness, or "life," and was very much like the Father. Since the Father had wanted this creation to be a limited replica of himself, he had anticipated its requirements for input of intellectual elements and thus had composed it with a vast array of "truth" structures. "Life" enabled this entity to act either independently or interact in concert with the Father. At this time, the Father had made only one such entity.

Because this type of entity could project power to affect other creations, it was necessary to identify all the principles that affected the entity and its actions based upon the truths incorporated into the entity. Therefore, the Father decided that the principles governing all actions of the entity would be based strictly upon those inherent truths and that the entity could be fully conscious of those truths. The entity could then understand the relationships of its interactions with other beings. The Type Three entities are all spiritual beings, the first of whom was Christ, His son.

The Type Four creations, of which the Father had made many of various kinds, were material structures which had also been given the property of "life" and were constructed from the Type Two building blocks. Of these, he made two general types: one type consisted of living structures which had no self-awareness and could not deliberately interact with other entities; the other type were living structures which did have self-awareness and could act independently to interact with or respond to anything in its environment. The latter type may be called "animate" structures and includes humanity; the former type may be called "inanimate" and includes all vegetable life.

The characteristics and capabilities of any living structure of either kind were strictly dependent upon both the intellectual elements and the con-sciousness elements selected to create them. Furthermore, Type Four *animate* creations were subject to the inviolable principles that governed the physical category enhanced with principles of intelligence. Type Four creations charac-terize all the animate and inanimate creatures appearing upon the planet Earth at a much later time.

The principles relating to all activities that the Father could perform in the great void seemed to be infinite in number. Yet, he saw that some principles were associated with a defined general category of activities or ceations, and not with others. Through direct association and inference, the Father eventually identified all the principles that applied to his activities in the great void.

He saw that these had nothing to do at all with the void itself, but *only to his own Being*. Therefore, these principles became *his truths*. He had recog-nized that all truths would not apply equally to either the physical or spiritual categories or to the four types of creations, but would be divided as appropriate to each. Since *these truths governed all actions and interactions related to his creations,* they had the strength of *laws* to which all must involuntarily conform. *Absolute truths form the inviolable laws of the Universe,* and both issue from the substance of God the Father.

It is obvious that nothing can take place anywhere in this universe, whether performed by God, an angel, man or by any created thing, without being subject to inviolable principles which are derived from God's discovered truths, which were created from God's Intellect and Consciousness. If an attempt is made to apply or violate any such principle, there will be an inescapable result, which may be intentional or unexpected, good or bad, great or infinitesimal, permanent or fleeting, instant or delayed.

So *God Himself must obey His own laws,* which He did not create, but which were inherent within His Being and which He discovered in the course of His diligent and ceaseless work. The Father himself cannot *change* nor revoke any of these laws in either the physical or spiritual realms. Therefore, all reality is constrained to be rational by inviolable and invincible laws.

Wisdom comes from seeking Truth and following His Laws in all things. *From this comes all that is possible.*

The Father and Christ Create the Angels

The Father and Christ wandered in the great void contemplating and discussing all the possible creations that the Father had imagined. Great shining structures of strange beauty and inhaled power would range freely within defined bounds in this place. The Father would create multitudes of new spiritual entities, not much different from Christ, and they would be dispersed throughout the defined space. The space would be filled with the Holy Spirit, radiated from the center to all reaches, even outside the space if there were cause to go into the void. All the spiritual entities could then feel attachment and association with the Father, for whatever purpose they shared with his Will. This place of creation would be their Heavenly home forever.

Before the Father created any of the Heavenly entities, including his firstborn Christ, He examined all possible forms that would characterize their appearance. Out of the many, He selected the best of all possibilities. This choice would result in companions of magnificent beauty and grandeur. Because they would be brought forth in Love, He conferred upon each of them a unique persona that would portray his highest vision of Beauty. He also chose the characteristics they all would possess that would make each of them an equal companion of the Father, capable of performing any act of his Will and sharing all of Heaven's amenities.

Now He and Christ were set to proceed with the Father's plans, and both were filled with happy anticipation. It was time to create the new Type Three entities, from henceforth to be known as God's Holy Angels, or simply angels. Thereafter, they would create the physical universe with all the new angels assisting in the work, to provide an eternal home for them all, a place in which the angels would for evermore adorn worlds with magnificent creations of beauty and resplendence.

The Father rested himself in peaceful repose, with Christ lying upon his bosom like a cherished child. Then, he began to expand the substance of his Being into an ever-growing sphere so that it would eventually reach the bounds they had decided upon. He did this in order to define the scope and boundaries of his Universe and to determine the places where he would create groups of angels, because angels would be created for specific structures at various locations. This was a decisive point because the distances between the planned structures would be so vast as to preclude moving angels to them from a central assembly area. Therefore, the angels were to be created in congregations near the structure that would be their permanent home.

Having made these determinations, the Father began to bring the required amounts of substance from his Intellect and Consciousness to the many various locations, converting the substance into Type One elements. From these, he began to form individual angels and give them permutations of intellect so that each angel was unique. Because the Father is all knowing and all-powerful, he could create angels at all locations at once. Angels could then be produced individually in quick succession at each location. Not all locations received the same number of angels because his purposes for each structure would require varying numbers, some small in number, some great. Also, certain locations, because of the Father's special plans, would require angels having specialized or exceptional faculties.

Thus, the Father produced all of his angels. The Holy Spirit acted as "godmother" for each angel as it was produced and christened each with the Father's Love and Truth. As they were created, Christ projected his own personality into the locations to welcome each new angel into God's home and "threw" his cloak of love around it. At once, each angel came to know Christ as its Master. Christ would be their teacher and servant and they would associate with him as his "brothers" and "sisters."

A vast kingdom of new angels, each a companion of the Father and Christ, now populated the space that was already Heaven before the material domain was made.

The Father had made the angels so that any two of them could become *complementary pairs*, in the manner of male and female, so that each one would attract another in love for creative purposes. Angels do not have male or female properties in the material sexual sense, but the characteristics that distinguish complementarity in the angels are also present in the spiritual nature of human males and females. All of the angels thus made to be the creators of their heavenly home would serve directly under Christ as the Master Creator. Creation would be a process in which all angels could discover and share the truths that emanate from the Father's mind.

The Father needed other angels endowed with versatile and special powers to serve him directly as envoys and his representatives for exceptional projects. Therefore, he created angels for this purpose, and they would be known as *Archangels*. Archangels serve the Father directly and do not report through Christ. The archangels are very powerful entities among the Heavenly hosts, but the Father gave Christ greater power and authority to speak and act in His name than was given to them.

Of the creative angels serving Christ, some 4.5 trillion were created for the entire Universe, distributed at the locations of galactic structures. He created only seven archangels, including Lucifer and Michael. Of the archangels created in the beginning, only these two have human names because *they are the only ones who would later become associated with Mankind.* Each angel has been given its own *Heavenly name* which reflects the distinctiveness of its personality and conveys the uniqueness of its identity. No angels have human names.

The Father has no Heavenly name by which the angels may call him. The Father, not knowing "who" he was, did not know what to call himself. He is so supreme in every respect that no one can know him. Consequently, the creatures made from his own Intellect and Consciousness do not know who he is and cannot describe him. The Holy Angels refer to him in terms of his gifts of Love and Truth. In recent times, Mankind has called him by many names, which include "The Heavenly Father", "God the Father", "Almighty God", "The Creator", "Jehovah", "Yahweh", "Allah" and other names. When Moses wondered, "Who art thou, Lord?" the Father replied, "*I Am Who I Am!*". This may be as good as any depiction for "someone" so supremely powerful, great and good that no one can know or describe him.

As the time to begin creation of the physical universe approached, Christ set about teaching all his angels about the Father's plans and the structures desired at their locations. Angelic songs began to ring through Heaven from the heart of every angel, in anticipation and praise of the coming creation and this awesome show of God's unlimited Power.

God and the Angels Create the Universe

Before the angels were created, the Father and Christ had determined how the physical universe would be created and what resources within the Father's substance would be required for structures as well as certain contributing factors. They calculated the energy needed to assemble and compress vast quantities of Type Two creations that were to serve as basic components. They also determined the functions the angels would serve in the creation process. Certain processes would be too vast and energetic for the angels' powers and the Father would control these himself. During the early phases when stars and planets were forming, the angels would serve mainly to monitor the processes and assist in the combination and permutations of the physical entities, namely the atoms. A major work of the angels in this period would be to study all that the Father had created, initiate the precursors of life for Type Four creations and begin as soon as possible the creation of life and beauty on planets about stars in the galaxies.

The Father began to create and prepare the physical elements from which the universal structures would be created. From every place within his "body," which was now an expanded sphere within the void, he created vast numbers of Type Two entities having the desired properties. These entities can be considered to be atoms of helium. Once a sufficiently vast number of such atoms were created, he began to transport them from near and far reaches of his inner being toward the center, assisted by the angels. The accumulation began to form a huge mass within him. Constantly increasing energies were required to compress the ball, assisted by its internal attractive interaction. Finally, the Father succeeded in squeezing the great mass into a ball having the critical size, storing all the applied and created energies within it.

The Father, in his great wisdom, had determined beforehand that helium atoms alone would not suffice to cause combinations for new atoms during the expansion and consolidation of solid bodies. The atoms needed something to assist them. Since each atom is an independent entity, a way is needed for them to interact coherently. For this purpose the Father created particles that could transport excess energy away from atomic processes in the void of space and balance the energy between interacting atoms. He created other entities with the capacity to transfer, convert, and dissipate energy in short span atomic and nuclear processes. All atoms, particles, processes and interactions are strictly governed by the laws of God, which come from His Truths. Through these special entities, the desired processes could proceed entirely on their own to form the structures of His universe.

Now, all the angels of Heaven were poised awaiting the explosive expansion of the mass of compressed helium, an awesome spectacle the likes of which had never before been witnessed and never will again. The Father released his energy. A flash more brilliant than the mind could imagine preceded the enormous outward rush of glowing, chaotic tides of matter. Having some resemblance to the "Big Bang" concept in our science, starting at the point where hydrogenous nuclei are generated in the theoretical explosion, the conceptual expansion from there on is fairly descriptive of the one produced by the Father.

The frothing gas rushed outward, forming tremendous swirls of particles ever growing in size and particle density as it moved through radiant space. The great swirls separated even further into smaller swirls, which would eventually settle into galactic masses of interacting matter.

Where were the angels during the explosion and its mighty onrush of primeval dust? They were still in the galactic locations where God had created them, safe in their dimensions of spirit-space, impervious to harm as matter waves rushed past their "bodies." For aeons, they observed this cosmic display of grandeur that the Father had prepared from his own substance and power.

After great spans of "time," the galactic masses would coalesce into stars, planets, other material bodies and clouds. Once planets formed and stabilized, the angels could begin their assigned tasks of creation of life and beauty on and about them. The Father allowed the angels complete freedom to experiment and create their worlds, involving vast arrays and variations of Type Two and Type Four creations, both living and non-living.

The Father authorized the angels to develop their own themes of creation for each galaxy, wherein one or several themes could be used separately or blended. In time, the angels proved to be almost as creative as the Father, not surprising since He had created them to be limited replicas of himself. The Father was very pleased with all that he and Christ and the angels had accomplished in bringing about the universal galaxies, which contained the stars, planets, and all the worlds of beauty and wonder within them.

One of the galaxies thus formed was one that Mankind has named the Great Milky Way galaxy because of the white filamentary swarms of distant stars that can be seen from his Earthly home. On a thin, narrow strand far out on one of the galaxy's starry limbs is the Solar house of the planet Earth, a beautiful and unique speck chosen by the angels to be one of the laboratories of life for the galaxy. The Planet Earth, the daughter of a small star within an apparent grouping of stars so beautiful and compelling that galactic observers at certain vantage points constantly view it in inspiration and wonder. The Planet Earth, the site of a conflict now being waged with one who arose to deny, defy and corrupt God's Laws of Love and Truth. The Planet Earth, the home of Mankind, a place of spiritual desolation, despair, hope, salvation and joy. The Planet Earth, a temporary gateway for the return of lost angels to God. The Planet Earth, soon to be restored to its place in God's Heaven.

Early Activities of the Angels

What were the angels doing during the enormous expanse of time before the galaxies and the stars and planets formed? How did they use this Time? Be assured, there was no "devil's workshop" of idleness in Heaven.

All angels were very busy examining all that God had created, learning the profound relationships of and absolute necessity for Truth and Love for ALL created things. They studied, analyzed and tested all conceivable aspects of God's Type One and Type Two creations and experimented with the unlimited combinations and relationships among them.

Some angels studied the truths and knowledge that formed and issued from all Type One creations and examined their relationships to all things possible in the Universe. They learned that *with Truth anything is possible* and that nothing is possible without Truth. They learned that *Truth establishes Law* and that *Law without Love is unfit for Life*. They learned that *Love makes all things worthwhile* and that without love all meaning and purpose for Life vanishes.

Other angels studied and experimented with the physical entities of Type Two creations, which included atoms and molecules. They learned that these basic elements of all physical structures could be combined and compounded to produce a large array of atoms each of which had its own distinct characteristics. They learned that atoms could be combined to create many unique basic substances and a vast array of different substances having multitudinous possibilities.

From these they created such things as crystals, liquids, gases, acids, hydrocarbons, proteins, amines, enzymes and all possible families of substances. They learned which of these could be combined with Consciousness to create living entities and which atoms are most suitable to create and sustain living tissues. They studied how life and matter interact to give a physical entity a sovereignty of action and self-control. They learned how various types of living structures could possess either active or passive relationships with their environment; how living structures can use and extract substances from their environment to promote and sustain life; how some living tissues can "break down" certain substances; how some can absorb, store or transfer life-sustaining elements or compounds; and how some tissues can create substances of its own which benefit or control other tissues. They learned how some tissues can feel stimulation and transfer "messages" to other parts of the entity; how some living tissues can possess "awareness" or has the ability to learn, remember, and make rational associations. The angels knew that only God, that is, the Father and Christ, can incorporate Consciousness into the tissues of life to create living entities.

From studies, experiments and developments such as these, the angels became capable of creating all the substances and structures that make life—in all its aspects—possible for both animal and vegetable entities in all possible conditions. They created cellulose, chlorophyll, photo-sensitive tissues, the organs of living bodies, blood, cerebral matter, nerve systems, skeletal structures—all the different things that are seen in Type Four living bodies, not just on Earth, but throughout the Universe. They devised the associative and supportive systems within living bodies and all the forms and combinations of matter that give life its capabilities and adaptabilities.

God gave the angels power to create anything imaginable *using* Type One and Type Two creations; yet He limited their own creative abilities to Type Four creations. The angels cannot produce Type One and Type Two creations, for this is the province of God only. The angels are likewise prohibited from creating Type Three spiritual entities, because from this all the angels are created and God will not allow the angels to create likenesses unto themselves or to change their own beings. *God* is the creator of all angels, all spirits, all souls; yet each one of these can alter their "personalities" through their own efforts and experiences to become unique entities. The angels' experiences can *change* them.

How Angels Communicate

The spiritual entities that the Father created were given an extraordinary ability to communicate with each other and all Hosts of Heaven. The angels, widely dispersed throughout the Universe, must be able to convey messages about conditions and events, and their own thoughts and emotions. Messages must be exchanged in close proximity or across wide expanses of separation. An angel can transmit its message openly so that any angel can receive it, or direct in confidentiality to a specific desired angel. The message must convey the angel's thoughts with absolute fidelity, painted with whatever emotions it wishes to impress upon it. The angel conceives the thought and transmits it rapidly to the recipient with perfect articulation.

The angels do not have or need a language, so they do not communicate in words or sentences. They make no sounds. They communicate by generating the message internally and emitting it in the form of *pure thought*. There is no transformation into another form, such as verbalization. The message is transferred with incredible speed to its recipient, wherever he may be, and the recipient responds instantly, if desired. So rapid is their thought generation and transfer that a body of information equivalent to an entire book can be exchanged in about three seconds of time.

Messages travel at a speed that greatly exceeds light, in a medium composed of the Father's own substance which is dispersed throughout the Universe. This enables the Father to know "instantly" everything that is taking place in the Universe, whether physical or spiritual. He has constant contact, if desired, with any angel, spirit or soul. Spirits and souls have the same capabilities and use the same methods of message generation and dispersion as the angels in Heaven.

Does God Know Everything?

God's store of knowledge, or Truth, is bound up in all that He has made in the four types of creations now in His Universe and in all acts He has performed. There is knowledge derived from the understanding of the relevance of all his created truths and from application of the principles that apply to the use of his powers. There is knowledge about Himself that did not come from His creations, but from a Mind striving to know itself. There is knowledge arising from this Mind responding to its awakening, and its first stirrings of curiosity and questioning which led to the extraordinary store of knowledge and understanding that illuminates the Universe.

Before the Father's "beginning", there was no repository of knowledge or truth in the void where he lay awakening. All knowledge he has acquired since that time has been created through his own endeavors that required *consumptive transmutations* of the substance of his being.

We have seen that all of the creations were derived from the substance of His own Being, using only the elements of His Intellect and Consciousness and the energy of their interactions. In all that He has yet created in this manner, He has consumed only a small part of Himself. All the truths that He created as "pure-thought", which is the body of His Truths, has so far used a small portion of the substance of His Intellect. In total, the Father has used only about one-eighth of His substance to make all that exists.

Actually, God could use as much of Himself as He desired to fill the universe with the four types of creations, as long as He retained a portion sufficient to maintain His full identity and powers as God. This implies that there are unlimited volumes of truths and knowledge that He has not yet created from His substance, which He could create. There are so many ways that the elements of intellect could be combined to produce uncovered knowledge, that there is still an infinite volume that have not yet been created and discovered. The potential for new knowledge that could be produced by Him is unimaginable.

Since He has not yet created this knowledge, God does not know what truths lie in these unopened volumes. Therefore, God does not know everything, but He has the power to attain this state as He wills. *God is the unique source of all truth in the Universe and the sole proprietor of the storehouse of knowledge.*

Herein lies unlimited potential for the universe and Heaven to evolve through one age to the next in panoramic change of enormous scope and wonder. Already, God has changed and added truths, while angels have produced new themes through the aeons to evolve Heaven and Earth and the universe, which will continue forever. Heaven never remains constant, but moves purposely from one magnificent stage to another in unbroken sequence. No human or angel, not even God Himself, can imagine the things that are possible to be, because He hasn't and cannot develop every possibility of His Infinite Intellect.

Surely a certain portion of His created Truths is nonsensical or has become irrelevant to His purposes in the Universe. In such cases, God has the power to reduce these truths to their basic elements of intellect, thereby destroying them as truths. Then they will no longer exist. The elements that composed them are part of God and cannot be destroyed, but are returned to His substance where they may be used again.

How Large is the Universe?

The great void that God and the Universe inhabit is a three-dimensional space whose boundaries seemingly extend to infinity. We cannot intellectually define such a space because we cannot presume to know what God only may understand about the void. Scientists can argue as to whether the space is "Euclidean" or "non-Euclidean," but such matters are irrelevant to this discourse.

It is an absolute fact that our universe exists in this indeterminate void. Does the universe in its present or future state extend to the limits of the void? The answer given is, "NO! The universe has boundaries, but the void does not."

How do we visualize the finite universe in an infinite void? The answer lies in the truth whose source is God's Intellect. God, desiring to create a universe of purposeful dimensions, extended Himself within the void as far in all directions that He thought prudent and necessary to achieve His goals. The *bounds of His own Being firmly establish the bounds of the physical universe,* either now or whenever its final size is attained. The universe is the material component of God's Being, created as Type Two and Type Four creations. Where God ends, the universe ends; where the universe ends, God ends. Therefore, the physical universe forms the shape and material substance of His body. *The universe and all its physical structures and Mankind and all living creatures are part of God!*

Heaven knows of no God but He, and of no Universe but this one that He created. Beyond the boundaries of the Universe is an absolute nothingness that extends forever and forever. The human mind cannot visualize it, for only the Mind of God can comprehend an infinite emptiness without boundaries!

What Is at the Center of the Universe?

The center of the universe coincides with the center of universal expansion where the expansive forces were minimal. The center is a region devoid of galactic structures and material forms. In this region swirls the primal dust of unformed matter, in perfect isolation from all but its own effects.

From the center, the *Essence of God* radiates into all the Universe. At the center stands a throne upon which No One sits, not even God, for God has distributed Himself throughout His Universe. God consecrated the throne a monument to Love and Truth, without which neither Christ, nor the Holy Spirit, nor the angels, nor the universe, nor Mankind, nor anything that He has made would have been created. God turned over His Throne for Love and Truth to sit upon it, *for these powers made everything possible and gave meaning to every thing.*

Behold God in His Firmament: God, a shining sphere of such brilliance within a greater void of total darkness so that He may be seen from one end of infinity to the other, where He has been ALWAYS and where He shall be forever and FOREVER, honoring TRUTH and LOVE like royalty and giving it freely to ALL He has and will ever create!

2

THE CREATION OF LIFE
AND BEAUTY IN THE UNIVERSE

The Supreme Purpose of God's Creative Aspirations

God has a purpose for all that He has created and for his very existence. This is the Supreme Purpose that underlies all things and gives meaning to life and to everything that humanity and the hosts of Heaven aspire to do.

The Father and his precursive mind existed for unimaginably long aeons before He formed the trinity of God with Christ and the angels and the Holy Spirit. They created the material universe together, which provides the only evidence from which Mankind can speculate about the character and age of the universe. No one can speculate about the age of God. God has been in the Universal void for so long, first as a solitary mind developing and maturing in knowledge and understanding, then as the Father driven by truth and the power of love to create Christ and the angels, then the physical universe. An eternity has already come and will come again, without interruption or end, because *God and his creations are everlasting.*

Throughout all this *He has ruled Creation through his Supreme Purpose.*

In its primal search for meaning and purpose, the Mind of God examined all possible avenues for framing and establishing his Heavenly abode. As this mind increased in knowledge and understanding, He realized that the substance of his being was everlasting and that He had the powers to establish the nature of himself in any way He desired, that is, He could create himself to be of whatever personality and likeness He chose. This mind had discovered that the laws inherent within the processes and interactions of his substance were rational and predictable, but that unlimited possibilities lay within the associations and "structures" that could be formed from them.

He realized that He must give complete and careful thought to each and everything that He created from his substance and this must always be done before any action was initiated to commence the project. Neglecting to do this could introduce into the structure causes for failure or imperfections that could lead to degeneration, chaos, or discord. To be worthwhile, the plan must be perfectly conceived and perfectly executed to achieve the most desirable state of existence. This precept became an unalterable principle of action for this Mind.

He also realized that any enterprise must have a purpose, which renders it meaningful, worthwhile and achievable. He examined all possible purposes that could motivate his creations. From this, He decided that only three qualities would be worthy of an everlasting Heaven filled with the Life that He had envisioned.

Since nothing can exist without *Truth*, the purpose for any endeavor must include the search for and discovery and application of truth, which includes the knowledge and understanding needed to accomplish the task. Since creation seems pointless without other beings sharing in the creation and its benefits and displaying veneration and gratitude, and the yearning for such beings comes only from love, then *Love* must be a fundamental part of the Purpose.

From the power of love and through acts of love, Life would be created for Heaven and material worlds. He discovered through his own yearnings, that life needs to enjoy blessings other than mere existence, including pleasure, joy, and serenity. Such blessings could be provided through *Beauty* that could permeate all things created in Heaven and "Earth."

Therefore, before any worlds were made, even while He *planned* the Universe, God decided that a single purpose would direct all that He would ever do in his Heaven, and *this purpose would be founded upon and composed of Truth, Love and Beauty*. These would be the pillars of his *Supreme Purpose*. All things to be created, including the Heavenly angels, the Heavenly "spaces," the material universe, all worlds with Life, all material life and their "spaces," would derive from the Supreme Purpose; nothing more, nothing less, nothing else.

God established the Heavenly Universe as his *eternal* home and sanctuary. It is a "place" where love, beauty, happiness and peace abound, that offers countless challenges in the search for truth and wisdom, infinite resources for creation, timeless pleasures for mind and spirit, unending joy in sharing all things that come through his Purpose, where perfection guards against deterioration and corruption.

All of this derives from a Mind that decided that He could not languish forever in a lethargy, unchallenged, not knowing his possibilities, not fulfilling his visions and not sharing all that He created through love. Any tendencies to do so had been defeated in the early dawn of this mind's search for meaning through the power of its Will, which is invincible. He thereby came to recognize the necessity of Will and the benefit of autonomy to choose to do as wisdom directs; but Will exists to constrain the quests that are fulfilled in God's great Purpose. The Purpose directs him always to follow the paths that He has chosen, which are the best of all that were possible.

God as a Trinity of Entities

The Holy Trinity is perceived to consist of the Father, the Son and the Holy Ghost. These entities should never be considered to be *separate* from each other or from the Father. They are as One, united in God.

Yet, God is too complex to be regarded as a *trinity* of entities. The idea of a Trinity can be viewed in *other* aspects different from those of Father, Son and Holy Ghost. These aspects define who God is in a basic sense and what He has become due to pursuit of his aspirations. They include the spiritual and material components that He has created from the substance of his Being as well as the vast part of him that remains to the present time as *pure Mind.* All living and non-living material in the physical universe constitutes one aspect of the Trinity. The angels, including souls, and the body of Truth which God has created constitutes the second aspect. The third aspect includes the overwhelming portion of him that has not been consumed in creations and remains as pure Mind.

The unification of the first two of these aspects can be referred to as the *Universe.* The Universe includes *all* spiritual and material creations and the physical laws that control all processes in the physical universe and the great reserve of Truth that advances and sustains the Universe. These are not separate from God, but are immersed *in* him and are *part* of him as a result of his deliberate and purposeful acts. *All* that exists as the three aspects constitute God. He is All and in all.

Do not think of God as an old man of some sublime human form seated on a throne amidst a similar world of his creation. This idea is wrong and it limits him to being one of his own creatures. God is *everything* absolutely. The pristine part of God is Mind and Energy that, working harmoniously to-gether, has unlimited potential for expression, action and creation. Knowing the possibilities for this potential, God realized that He must always act with discipline and use his powers with responsibility. He knew that He could become whatever He wanted to be, but that He must be pleased with the consequences for eternity. Therefore, with great thoughtfulness, He decided upon the best of all possible outcomes. To achieve this outcome and direct him forever toward it, He devised his Supreme Purpose that serves as the charter that governs all his acts and decisions to act.

In strictly following the Supreme Purpose, God has become all that He is and has created everything from Truth as expressions and objects of Love. He adorns himself with the Beauty of the Universe, which the angels refer to as Heaven. Heaven *is* the Universe, which consists of all that God creates. And with all that He is concentrated and directed with Purpose, the Universe progresses forever with *new* truths and *changing* beauty that will never grow stale. God is who He is because He chose to be the best of all possibilities, derived from the best constituents of his Being. This assures all creatures that He will forever be the infinite source of Truth and Love from which come his gifts of Life and Beauty. Since nothing else is acceptable to God, all who seek him *must be justified in these things.*

The Angels' Capabilities for Creating Life

The Heavenly Father, having created the angels, gave the angels capabilities and personal resources to enable them to share with Him in the creation of a Universe of resourceful progression. The Father created each angel using a vast array of "truth structures" which endows them with an enormous store of knowledge, including all of his laws that pertain to them. Incorporating consciousness elements into their makeup gave them life and imparted awareness and understanding of their innate knowledge. Consciousness provided high intelligence and a capacity for learning so that an angel is sufficiently knowledgeable and intelligent to perform as an independent agent in Heaven.

Through sharing the Father's "essence", they also have an intrinsic love for the Father and a complete awareness of his Will. Connected through the Holy Spirit the angels constantly feel the Father's love for them, which gives them peace and absolute faith. The Holy Spirit also connects them with the higher level of awareness and understanding which issues from the Father's Intellect. The Spirit gives them access to Heaven's "culture" which is the sum of the Father's and angels' wisdom. The Father empowers them through the

Holy Spirit to create life and life processes by providing access to the Father's unique power of Life. In the absence of the Spirit, no angel is capable of endowing life or changing the basic nature of life characteristics and processes.

Each angel is equipped with the means to monitor animate life. Such life must be independent and self-regenerative, capable of thriving in its environment and interacting with other life under changeable conditions. This requires an adequate level of intelligence and consciousness and an ability to sense and respond to environmental factors which are important to it.

An angel is able to infuse special appendages of its own "body" into any living thing by which it can sense physical and emotional feelings and monitor the intellectual and neural processes. In this way, the angel can monitor and evaluate the creature's "state of life" and the sensitivity, intensity and characteristics of its responses to stimulation of any kind. Because the angel is a spirit, infusion into the creature's body is not physically intrusive, destructive or even detectable by the creature, and infusion produces no physical effects in the creature.

One angel can infuse its appendages *simultaneously* into two or more individual creatures to monitor the interactive responses in pairs or the group. In this way, the angel senses and monitors the causes and effects of stimuli created within the group to which members respond individually, in pairs or collectively. This capability enables the angels to evolve animal response characteristics to achieve an ideal response to such things as *personal* or *social* interests or threats. The capability involves the ability to make biological, physical and mental changes that alter the response in a way to benefit the creature in the context of its peers and environment.

Christ is the Master of Creation. All creation angels perform their functions under his charge. The angels establish themes for creation and are free to use their own genius to create animate and inanimate life. The nature and diversity of life forms result from the angels' imaginations applied to selected elements of truth defined in the theme. Certain "laws of life" which emanate from the Father's Will pertain to their work. These laws are never violated in the creation of life. The angels strive to express the magnificence of love and beauty, even mystique, in living entities produced through their resourcefulness. In the course of any project, the angels are rewarded with new revelations of truth and understanding derived directly from pursuit of the work. This establishes the real catalyst for creating life.

Angels do not create for the sake of creation. Their creations are only the end result of *a process performed to discover and express truth and to share these experiences in love.* In the process of creation, they discover new truths and laws that issue from the Father's own great Being. This helps them to understand him and all things. Discovery of truth leads to greater sharing of the power and majesty of the Father and esteem for the magnificence of his creations. Of greater value to the angel is the personal benefit each receives from their quest. As the angel discovers new truths or shares in new knowledge from others, these are added to his inventory or truths, available henceforth in his repertoire for application to creation. Since the angel is constituted *from truth*, the angel therefore grows in a sense that a material child grows from the nourishment of food.

Like the Father, angels share their creations with other angels because they desire to share all they do with other appreciative and responsive beings. In displaying their creations to other angels, they enjoy explaining the new associations of truth structures they discovered or developed in bringing forth the creation. This is their joy. *Love and Truth both empower the angels and are the powers they wield* to create things of beauty that pleases and bring edification to themselves and others.

All aspects of God's Will are derived from his Supreme Purpose. In all their endeavors, the angels work to assure that the integrity of his Will is maintained in all that is brought forth or performed in the spiritual and material domains.

Creation of Life and Beauty Begins

THE UNIVERSE TAKES CARE OF ITSELF WHILE ANGELS CRE-ATE LIFE AND BEAUTY ON WORLDS THROUGHOUT   A significant and interesting period for the angels occurred when the swirling galactic masses began to produce stable stars and planets. This meant that the angels could begin to select the planets on which they would initiate their own creations in accordance with God's plan and the themes the angels had selected for each galaxy.

Great numbers of galaxies came into being, each different in some respect. Some were circular or spherical, some oval spirals, some were solitary, some grouped, some bedded in great clouds of gas and dust, some in collision with others. Much of the variation was deliberate to achieve a purpose, while some of it was "accidental". Natural processes can produce distinct conditions and evolve to bring forth life on worlds throughout each galaxy.

God created the physical universe to function in a manner that is completely independent of his Heavenly powers. He has given the universe all powers, energy and resources to run perpetually forever on its own. All that occurs within the universe conforms to his Law which came from the Truth that he created, and all activity is energized through a multiplicity of powers derived from his intrinsic energy. All physical processes from the birth, life and death of stars, planetary motions in star systems, geological actions that change and renew worlds, and biological systems that create and sustain life can proceed on their own without help from the Heavenly hosts.

The worlds differ in the preponderance of various elemental materials and the amounts and forms of matter that are produced from them. This unquestionably causes variations in the internal dynamics of material worlds with dependence upon their environment in space. Unrest caused by internal forces becomes manifest in the external or surface features and the natural activity that may take place on any one of them. Earth is a complex and lively world where forces and material forms interact to produce continuous changes throughout the surface regions. Inhabitants often witness such changes in awe and fear, knowing that they are powerless to prevent or control even the smallest act of nature.

On worlds such as Earth where *all forms of life are interdependent and interactive*, life begets life, nourishes life, sustains life, and consumes life. In each world, every life form takes nourishment from a common source which life shares through cycles of birth, death, decay and regeneration. When a life form is born it begins to absorb nourishment from living life forms and substances which contain the residue of decomposed life forms. Continuance of this practice produces an ever growing entity that maintains its character as a discrete collection of material forms.

A life form matures by taking nourishment from sources outside itself through scavenging or absorption. When the entity dies, it decays to give it all up to the sources from which it came, which then nourishes the continuation of surviving life forms. Thus, *death nourishes life, and life returns to life through death*. The cycle is consummate and perpetual.

Nothing of the residue of decomposition is ever lost, rejected or wasted within the Earth's natural systems, whether the system is land or water, rain forest or desert. The material results of decomposition are compatible with the elements and chemical compounds of the Earth's soil, air, water and life forms. Materials of decomposition are either taken directly into living life forms or are received into the soil, water or air where they become available as nutrients. These natural processes maintain the storehouse of basic substances of Earth and benefit all life forms. All creatures, including humanity, share these common substances.

If all life lived forever without dying, the materials meant to sustain life would eventually become stored in living tissues. Then newly born life could perish unless the Heavenly hosts intervened to replenish the supply. In that event, physical worlds would not proceed independently from God. In this universe, God does not supply manna to all. Physical processes, whether they occur in galactic or stellar levels or in the smallest form of life, proceed in harmony with God's inviolable laws. No one, not even the angels, can change or stop them. All such processes have actions and reactions, causes and effects. Any act performed to intervene is itself a cause that will have its own effect.

Yet, *God has given the angels the authorities and powers* to monitor the processes, to incorporate their themes of creation and to assure that everything conforms to his Supreme Purpose. The angels also incorporate new Truth that God creates from the substance of his Being. Because processes are usually not static and proceed progressively and because angels change themes and add new truths, most worlds exhibit panoramic stages of geologic and biologic change. The Father has commissioned the angels to care for the physical universe and establish worlds where life and beauty may flourish and evolve. Such worlds are like tiny points that radiate the Light of love and truth through the dark spaces of the void.

DEPLOYMENT OF ANGELS IN GALACTIC SETTINGS   God had not intended for angels to attend to the evolution of all galaxies. Indeed, approximately one-twentieth of the galaxies is not attended by the angels and they are left to evolve on their own by purely physical cause and effect. This was deliberate to see what would become of them under a range of conditions with no influence from God. Seemingly, this is experimentation, but we cannot know the purposes in the mind of God. The Universe is still young and its evolution will never be complete. Experimentation by angels provides new themes for use in galaxies and worlds in distant futures yet to come.

Most galaxies have little creation activity occurring within them. Some of these are used mainly as gigantic heavenly "classrooms" where angels learn about unusual physical processes in stars and other bodies or study aspects of God's Being. Some angels study new combinations that can be used to create products from any of the four types of his creations. Some study the evolutionary effects of introducing entirely new Type Four creations into existing worlds. Type One and Type Two creations are particularly interesting subjects for many angels. Some experiment in creating new truths and study the effects of introducing them into the changing Heaven. Such strange objects and experiences proceed from these activities to fascinate and baffle the most astute minds!

The greatest number of angels is deployed in galaxies where there are centers of creation for life and beauty. There are a number of such galaxies, all of them having at least thousands of worlds where life exhibits advanced intelligence. The Milky Way galaxy is one of these. Intelligent beings inhabiting these worlds throughout the Universe are the material complement of the Heavenly hosts. The Holy Spirit guides the development and ensures that progress toward their evolutionary destinies suits God's Supreme Purpose.

The Milky Way galaxy has millions of worlds supporting life in some form. Many tens of thousands have very intelligent life, most far exceeding the intelligence of Earth's humans! The Milky Way galaxy was given one of the largest angel populations: approximately two and one-eighth billion angels. The Father's wisdom has justified that unusually large number to accomplish his dreams for evolving the Universe.

The planet Earth, being a tiny world within this galaxy is unique from several aspects. First, it was selected by the angels to be a laboratory for life forms of animate and inanimate types. The results of this work are used elsewhere in the Galaxy. Secondly, relatively few worlds in the universe display such an extreme diversity of animal and vegetable life. The earth supports varied families of higher life forms including mammals, birds, fish, reptiles, insects and others, including such minute forms as to be virtually invisible. Among all species there exists variations ranging from the grotesque and absurd to the sublimely graceful and beautiful. Some are created to be highly specialized, others greatly adaptable. All exist in a world of interdependence and interaction. Some experiments determine how long a species can survive upon the changing earth among a wide range of diversity and life interactions.

The Earth and its mother, the Sun, and the sister planets are relatively young heavenly bodies. They were formed from extensive swarms of matter that moved sufficiently close to each other to accrete into a protostar, which eventually developed into a star with evolving planets. Other galactic stars and worlds are billions of years older than Earth and the Sun. In these other worlds, beings do not have angels as souls and have developed intelligence through natural evolutionary processes without direct nurture from souls. These minds may exceed Mankind's intelligence by tens of millions, even to billions, of years. Mankind cannot imagine what wealth of erudition and creativity these minds have produced!

CREATION AS AN EXPRESSION OF TRUTH SHARED IN LOVE
Creation is an expression of truth conforming to God's inviolable laws, brought forth in material form. The existence of Earth's extremely broad range of species and variations of animate and inanimate life demonstrates the possibilities for the application of Truth. Is truth restricted? No! Count the many different forms of life; or consider the many ways that processes or actions can accomplish the needs and aims of life.

How many ways can life be conceived or regenerated among the various life forms? Most of Earth's life forms, including humans, are regenerated either through seeds or roots. How many types of seeds are there? How are the seeds generated? Are the seeds internal or external? How are the seeds made available for germination? How is life initiated within the seed? Does germination need counter partners or is it self-initiated? How is life incubated after germination? How is life given birth? Count the many different ways that life is brought forth and consider the many processes that are available in which this is done. Think also of the many different environments available on Earth to which some creature has adapted uniquely or comprehensively to provide all needs of life.

Consider also the many ways that life may use to transport itself from place to place. Most of Earth's higher forms of animate life have four limbs with which they accomplish a wide range of physical activities. Most animals have four legs, used for walking, running, standing, leaping, climbing, clutching, catching prey, tearing food, or perhaps digging the ground. Humans prove that only two legs are sufficient, at least, for transportation, leaving two arms and hands free to perform activities ranging from simple needs to extraordinary skills. Still, some insects have six, eight or scores of legs. The snake proves that legs are not needed at all: undulations of internal ribs and rhythmic body motions are sufficient to propel them on land or water, and that even arms and hands are unnecessary for other needs, such as catching food or climbing. Like humans, birds have two legs used for perching, standing, walking, leaping, or catching prey; yet, their principal means of transportation is through the use of wings which frees them from the need to contact the ground. Fish do the same without legs in the medium of water, using tail and body fins. Some birds can "fly" to great depths under water, and some fish can sail in the air for short distances.

In all of these many ways, the creation angels have proven that God's unlimited truth can be applied in myriad ways to accomplish essentially the same objectives. Is one way fundamentally better than another? To any specific creature, his way is best of all!

One may view *each form of life as a unique, harmonious, self-sufficient embodiment of truths expressed in love and beauty from the mind of the creation angels.* Once this is understood, it becomes easy to see how the Earth operates as a laboratory. It is a world in which a creation angel can select compatible elements of truth and combine them into a harmonious whole to enable the resulting creature to thrive in one of Earth's environments and interact symbiotically and, perhaps, intelligently with other creatures while each creature seeks its own benefit. Through this, the angels increase their understanding of the Father's boundless resource of Truth for which they exalt Him in love and praise with their own gifts of beauty and uniqueness.

EARTH'S CREATION ANGELS AND THE INSOLENT PRIDE THAT INTERRUPTED THEIR WORK   In the Earth laboratory some fifteen million angels once worked to develop life forms adaptable to other galactic worlds. Some one and one-half million additional angels were at work elsewhere in the Solar system. Most other worlds in this galaxy which support life are older than Earth by billions of years. These are advanced sufficiently to take care of themselves and need relatively few angels to guide them. Activities of Earth's creation angels have gone on for many geological ages since the Earth became a suitable place for life. Themes of creation have changed through the ages, affecting both animal and vegetable life.

Several hundred thousand years ago a strange aberration of God's purpose, a diversion of His Will, took seed among some angels on Earth, initiated by a powerful angel whose concept of truth became perverted through self-centered ambition and pride. This angel began to use the great powers that the Father had given him to establish and pursue his own purposes, abdicating the responsibilities and purposes given to him through the Grace of God. In depraved willfulness he started a movement among Earth's angels and spread it like an ill wind through much of the galaxy. He deceived many Heavenly angels into forsaking God's Will and joining his escapades of abuse and corruption. God's creative processes on Earth were thereby interrupted and diverted from Holy purposes. *This cycle of disobedience and insolence shall soon end and Earth will be returned to its former Heavenly status.*

Creation of Beauty

In the realm of Heaven, *Beauty* is a creative resource of the angels and is always used to express the feelings angels have about their relationships with the Father. Such feelings are as varied and intense as are the endless ways that Beauty can be expressed. Beauty can be applied to anything God has ever ordained to be created, whether physical or spiritual, animate or inanimate. Beauty is the manner in which all the hosts of Heaven and all created life with intelligence share Love and Truth with all others.

In the natural state, Beauty is established upon certain orders of the Father's inherent truths and physical laws. Intelligent creatures in the material worlds can discover the principles of Beauty's orderliness for whatever aesthetic or practical uses they can make of them. Yet, intelligent creatures cannot appreciate Beauty in the way that angels do, who create to express their intense feelings in which love and truth are associated in praise of the Father. The intelligent creatures of Earth, the collective body of Mankind, have been enabled to appreciate Beauty in a spiritual sense because an angel, or soul, resides in each of them. Thus, the angel souls can share with human minds the feelings they have for the One who created them both.

Throughout the worlds of the Universe, *physical beauty* is expressed and displayed in terms of form, pattern, color, texture, harmony, balance, brilliance, softness, subtlety, sweep, depth, splendor, magnificence, and majesty. *Spiritual beauty* comes from expressions of love and truth and is difficult for humans to describe for they cannot translate it into physical associations; humans can detect it emotionally and intellectually when it emanates from other humans or from scenes of natural beauty.

Beauty has been created in the physical heavens through the random distribution of stars and galaxies, clouds of dust and matter, and other celestial bodies. These shining bodies immersed in a totally dark space present patterns of dreams to intelligent minds throughout the universe. Such displays of beauty inspire awe and worship for their Creator.

In the planets, beauty is produced in the distribution of both living and inanimate creations. Seas, lakes, streams, landmasses, rocks, mountains, vast mosaic stretches of plain and forest, snow and ice, are distributed creatively to produce captivating beauty and majesty. Beauty is created in varieties of forms and colors of the largest to the smallest of the subjects of creation; it is given in the sweeping landscapes of mountains, deserts and seacoasts; it is given in the tiniest flower and in snowflakes. Transient displays of beauty are displayed in glowing forms and colors of sunsets, sunrises, drifting clouds, weather and rainbows.

Intelligent minds can drink it in and create beauty of their own once they discover its essential nature and learn to express it. Beauty is a product of love that brings peace and joy and engenders the craving for more and a yearning to know its Creator. Without Beauty, there would be only the starkness of Truth and love could be shared only through the intellect. Then *wisdom* would be the basis of God's greatest commandment to Mankind. Because beauty can be perceived as a blessing to be shared, expressions of love involve *beauty* combined with *thoughtfulness*. A gift of beauty conveys the grace and devotion of the one who shares it.

Such beauty is displayed in the angels of Heaven that each of them seems to be a monument to a single facet of the Father's Being. The full beauty and splendor of an angel can be "seen" only within the domain of spirits, for it is not visible in physical space. On Earth, Beauty is displayed in the faces, lives and deeds of humans who have allowed their souls to freely express the Will and love of the Father. Such beauty is seen not only with the eyes, but also with the mind and soul.

Beauty is also generated within the angel in thought and song. Music is an important form of expression of love, praise and inspiration to the angels, used often to acclaim the magnificence, profundity and gravity of their experiences. Angels habitually sing in praise of the Father and their Master, songs of love, adoration, beauty, grandeur, accomplishment, honor of other angels, truths newly discovered, and success of their endeavors. There are also songs of things gone wrong, of anger, of fear, of horror, of death, of loneliness, of separation from companion angels, and of memories of things long past. An angel can enwrap the full range of its emotions in expressions of song and Beauty.

Creation of Life

Before stars were fully formed, the angels created and distributed precursors of life forms to float through the space of galaxies seeking resting places that may nurture life. Once life begins, the angels can inject the laws of their creative themes to give that element of life a determined direction. From the precursors, life is conceived on all worlds where conditions are favorable to it, and is inhibited where conditions are unfavorable. The types of life that are compatible to the conditions can then arise. A life form can thrive within the possibilities that have been given to it uniquely.

Even in galaxies that are not attended by the angels, life begins on its own and seeks its own direction and development. These are monitored by the archangels where they appear in the heavenly realm assigned to the archangel. What strange forms of life arise when angels do not guide them! What monstrosities, freaks, or formless globs of life that are formed by opportunistic, unimaginative CHANCE! What bizarre, irrational behavior in these life forms that manage to develop intelligence! Where angels apply their love and grace, guided by God's Will, such sublime contrasts to the unattended come forth!

The angels are given complete freedom to create material life forms of plants and animals as they may envision. Angels rarely work alone. The smallest work unit consists of a pair of complementary angels whose unique characters unite to produce creative power and imagination. Love binds them like shimmering "chains of gold", each giving to and receiving from each, striving to induce in the other the highest pleasure from what they can offer in creativity. Angels also work in groups, both large and small, as the activity warrants.

The angels dream of presenting their creation to the Father to show Him the beauty and uniqueness of the creature and demonstrate its powers to live in and interact with all in its environment. What joy they receive from the Father's satisfaction! The angels love to share happiness over their progress with fellow angels. There is no envy among them, but there is often a competitive spirit and they all join in to celebrate and praise anyone of them when success is achieved.

Initiation and Development of New Life Forms

Life is produced within a *perpetual and everlasting process* that involves resources on every material world. The *resources* are the imperishable elements and compounds that constitute and sustain living organisms. The *process* is formulated from the components and effects of the fluctuating environments. Whenever appropriate resources are amalgamated to initiate a species of life, it is then infused with consciousness to produce a unique living entity. *This principle is the foundation of life creation in material worlds.* Any given species is an *object of expression* of this principle.

No species is everlasting, but the principle that underlies life processes *is* eternal and immutable. By this principle new species of life are generated, then transformed through the creatures adaptation to cyclic alterations in the processes. The importance of any species on Earth does not transcend the thematic purpose guiding the creation angels. Thus, a species may change or become nonexistent in time, but the resources and processes of life creation are perpetual, assuring that other species can emerge.

Whenever the angels initiate a new life species, they usually start with a tiny life form already existing among many that are always available on planets that support life, such as Earth. These may be microscopic or larger creatures already existing as a defined creature. The angels can mutate these to some other form that will serve as their starting point for the new species. Speciation occurs whenever one root species begins to branch into two creatures with distinct genetics.

Whenever a change is made in a life form, there are always two or more alternative mutations from which they can select. The angels select the alternative that will take the creature in the direction for evolving into the desired end result. If there is no angelic guidance, the dominant mutation, if favored by the natural *process*, will usually prevail. There is no way to predict the final result of thousands of mutations occurring through random Chance and Fortune.

In contrast, the angel can always select the options that will lead to the creature he had visualized. *This is divine creation*, yielding the emergence of Earth's marvelous beasts and creatures of the sea, sky and forest, and of human beings. These are not the result of chance mutations of the strong and fortuitous, but of *the mind and purpose of God*.

Aeons of time may be required to develop or evolve a given species to perfection. Many things are involved to achieve the ideal. All material life is temporary and consumptive. Out of love the Father gave life the powers of healing and renewal so that distress could be overcome.

The angels must assure that the species can resist death, deterioration, and weakness. To accomplish this, the angels have introduced, in all galaxies and planets, organisms such as bacteria, germs and viruses. Bacteria and other primal organisms benefit a species by helping to break one substance down into others such as in the digestion of food, decomposition of the dead or conversion of one substance into another. Germs are introduced simply to eliminate weaknesses, to build strength into the creatures' internal defense structures. Viruses do a similar thing, but work within the cells to help them build strength and immunity. Such organisms, often seen as the nemesis of Mankind, are agents used by the angels to help their creatures tolerate and adapt to incompatible interactions and environments. Mankind, and indeed all life on Earth, are still a ways from the angels' ideals and must, therefore, continue to suffer from disease, illness and deterioration. Strength and perfection are continually increasing in the species of Earth through the process that is both helped and hindered by Mankind's own efforts.

Life is more than the functioning of biological and anatomic systems that enable life to exist and thrive. Animate life must be satisfied with its well being. Life having advanced intelligence is capable of anticipating and projecting its sense of well being to others with which it shares life and into future times. Feelings of attachment such as love and devotion, the search for intimacy and understanding, a perception and desire for improvement, a belief in the capability for achievement and advancement, the power to affect change fostered by belief, faith and hope become part of their sense of well being. God instills these things into intelligent life through his Spirit and gives them the sovereignty to affect their own welfare. There is no other power from which this can come regardless of the degree of material intellect. Without such things, life could not be content with existence.

If there are those who think they can create life, can they also create its spirit? Can they create Consciousness and Intellect? Some can *change* life, but only God can create life and instill the things that make it worthwhile.

Angels Create Interactive Responses in Creatures

APPLICABILITY OF RESPONSE   It isn't enough just to create the life forms. A coherent, practical way must be provided for creatures to respond to and interact with each other and deal with factors in their environment over a great range of conditions. A primary concern of all creatures is the survival of self and the species, either consciously or instinctively. Such responses come from Consciousness, which provides awareness and sensitivity. The capabilities of creatures to react to all things in their environments and to have meaningful relationships with others of their kind and some not of their kind require creative input of tremendous scope and complexity.

Reactions to stimuli that affect interrelations must be rational, consistent, personal, versatile and adaptable. Those that affect survival must arise from a perceived need to protect and nurture the self, the young and the family, and to defend the home and the territory. Those that affect the quality of life arise from an awareness of adequacy of conditions that promote or enhance the enjoyment of life and personal comfort. Stimuli can be presented to a creature singly or compounded, as threats or attractions, and as subtle or powerful. Each species will react in its own way to any stimulus, either reacting appropriately or ignoring it. Response is a product of the angels' creativity and is profoundly complex.

Response to stimuli is the key to interaction and interdependence. Creatures and agents in the environment continually assault other creatures which results in tendencies to alter the life form. Such changes can be beneficial or harmful, but the life form cannot respond favorably in all interactions. In material worlds where life is interactive and interdependent, all creatures are constrained in behavior to enable their survival and propagation. This principle is manifested in roles of attraction and intimacy, mastery and submission, pursuit and evasion, tactics of offense and defense and other practices that require cognizance of stimuli and a capability to respond appropriately. The desires and instincts to prevail or survive feed equally the hunter and the prey, the loving and the loved.

THE ANGELS' INVOLVEMENT   Angels do not attend a species intensively once it is well developed, such as now the case of most all species on Earth. They have given all species the power of self-propagation, maintenance and perpetuation. To accomplish these goals through use of these powers, the creatures must regenerate, feed and protect themselves, satisfy their urges or yearnings, optimize their life conditions, achieve their functions and purposes of existence, and enjoy the success of living.

To some creatures of limited mental powers and physical capabilities these powers are given and controlled through "instinctive" responses and activities. Instincts are built-in programs of behavior wherein a given response is automatically triggered by an external or internal stimulus. Higher forms of creatures that possess mental powers of varying degrees, also exhibit some forms of automatic response. Even humans respond "instinctively" when confronted with a sudden life-threatening danger.

Higher forms of mental and physiological response are more difficult to develop in the creatures, but relatively easy to evolve to an optimum state once it is developed. This involves inducing into the creature an assured process of responding to the stimulus that interests or threatens it. The process must possess properties to allow sensing the stimulus, evaluating it, and making a decision on whether to respond and what the response will entail. For each type of creature there are a wide variety of stimuli to which it must at least acknowledge and respond appropriately as warranted.

The angels must build into the creature the capabilities to sense the stimuli, identify it and respond to it. Such a process is very complex and involves so many variables that Chance could never have successfully brought a single one into existence. Such wonders can be produced only by angels that have access to God's Intellect through the Holy Spirit and apply devoted care through aeons of dedication.

HOW RESPONSIVE BEHAVIOR IS CREATED   Let us see how the angels might develop the responses that lead to sexual love in any creature, using the human as our example of a mammal. First, there must be male and female, each of which possess half of a mutually compatible reproductive system. Secondly, coming together they provide a complete system for sexual love and the reproduction of young.

The creative problem for the angels is, how do you get them together to reproduce? First, the male and female must be aware in some manner that either of them alone is insufficient and they need each other. Then, there must be a way to get them to notice each other, then to attract each other, then to stimulate each other's desires, then to assure that they complete the sexual union.

This is not an easy problem to solve. For example, what characteristics in one would attract or provide interest in the other? The angels give "male" characteristics to one and "female" characteristics to the other. They may bestow "attractiveness" to both male and female, seductive behavior to the female and aggressive or masterful behavior to the male. But these do not automatically trigger an appropriate response in either one. The response to these characteristics must be built-in by the angels. Sight of the female form must produce attraction in the male and not cause him to feel hunger pains or run away in fright.

The angels must create all responses at the earliest time of development, and measure the appropriateness, sensitivity and intensity of these responses in order to optimize them. As the creature evolves, so must the characteristics that cause interest and attraction. The angels created the partition in complementary reproductive capabilities and the attendant sexual attraction and behavior for the specific purpose of giving each species the power of self-generation and to provide a means to bring the creatures together as families. It was a very effective and ingenious approach to achieving these purposes.

The angels develop these responses through a deliberative process of trial and error: the angel produces a prototype mutual response capacity in both the male and female, then infuses itself into both of them simultaneously and waits until there is "contact" between the two creatures. Is one attracted to the other? If yes, is the response appropriate and is it sensitive and sufficient? Is attraction mutual, of equal power? If no, what is wrong and what can be done to correct it? The angel, through direct sensing and monitoring all responses to stimuli that involve the two creatures, can eventually initiate and develop the correct response and fine tune the sensitivity and intensity to achieve an ideal mutual response.

Sexual attraction is only one of the many response-stimuli capabilities that must be built into a human or any creature. They are all very complex and require intensive, constant, and devoted attention from the creative angels. Many distinctive responses are developed simultaneously.

All members of a developing species need not be monitored in this manner. A pair of complementary angels will select typical male-female pairs of a species and develop the whole range of responses as they encounter their life experiences. Then they can incorporate the results of their progress into others not monitored. And there may be many pair of angels working with many pair of creatures at the same time. Because of inherent variations in individuals of a species, variations in degree of induced response-stimuli capabilities will likewise exist.

The Spiritual and Physical Domains of the Universe

Much will be said throughout these chapters concerning the movement of the angels through the galaxy and in the vicinity of Earth, and the simultaneous infusion of an angel into several humans or creatures. These acts involve capabilities that do not seem possible within human knowledge and understanding. Certainly, they do not seem to be possibilities for humans since they defy Mankind's understanding of the physical world. Although this conclusion is correct, these acts do not take place in the physical domain familiar to humans: they are performed within the domain of spirits.

Humans cannot apply their understanding of the physical domain to spiritual affairs. The Universe is divided into two distinct domains which we may regard as *physical or material* space and *spirit* space. These immiscible spaces have their own distinctive characteristics, operational laws and concepts appropriate to the unique entities which inhabit them. The differences between the two spaces and their inhabitants are incomprehensible to the human mind, which has no capability for observing or evaluating the peculiarities of spirit space.

So vast is the whole of Space and "Time" that Mankind can rationally sense only his immediate environment in these spheres. The concept of "distance" has very different meanings in the two domains. The distance between two points in three-dimensional physical space is not at all applicable to spirit space. The manner in which humans are accustomed, indeed, compelled to travel between points on Earth provides no clue to understanding how angels can travel so incredibly fast over vast distances in their own space. Angels must have such capabilities in order to perform their activities in the heavenly Universe, where they definitely do not have the disadvantage of immobility. Humans, under their own power, are "Earth-bound" because of the effects of gravity on material bodies and their unalterable dependence upon the life sustaining environment of this world.

The concept of "time", or what appears to be time to the human mind, presents another profound difference between the two spaces. In physical space, time apparently begins at the present instant, then appears to flow linearly and relentlessly from the present into the past. In physical reality, neither past time nor future time actually exist. Neither the human nor any Earthly creature can venture into the future or the past, and all material creatures are locked forever onto the present instant. Providentially, the mind has the ability to remember the past and anticipate the future, powers that enable Mankind to live and thrive progressively in his world.

One can construct a "time-line" of human or geological history, beginning at the present and projecting "backwards" to the bounds of recorded or evidential experience. In such a display, the flow of time is shown to be linear and continuous. In spirit space, the flow would not appear to be linear; rather, the time-line would flair into curving "planes" and even "solids" of conical or cylindrical shapes. Time would not flow with constant increments, but would undulate with slow and fast phases and appear to make attempts to change direction. Time exhibits these paradoxical traits in the spirit world because of its multi-dimensional structure and due to the extraordinary mobility of the angels in their world and their ability to project their presence into several locations at any moment. Mankind could never attain the intellectual orientation to comprehend "time" in spirit space, though it seems to behave well for his own use in physical space.

Angels are familiar with the conditions in both spaces and can act appropriately in either space. The angel souls, though presently intimate companions of every person, do not attempt to illuminate the human mind with such awareness because the mind does not possess the capability for this understanding. Let the reader be aware that the properties of spirit space allow angels to perform acts that appear impossible and incomprehensible to the human mind.

The Biblical Story of Creation and the Relationship of Time

The story of God creating the universe, as told in the Book of Genesis in the Holy Bible, is beautiful and has for thousands of years given Mankind the knowledge that God made everything, this is His world and He requires obedience to his laws. The author, understanding the story only from a human viewpoint, attempted to demonstrate this magnificent power of the Creator and that everything in the universe are the creatures of the Lord of Heaven and Earth.

The writer set the story in terms of a work week so as to show Mankind's kinship to God's own ways. The story is full of spiritual symbolism not discerned by the writer. The symbolism of "day" was poorly chosen, for it has confused and misled Mankind through the ages. Either "cycle" or "phase" would have been more appropriate, avoiding the confusion. Would God, in his eternity, be in such a rush to complete any phase in a short day, between the two successive appearances of the Sun in the Earth's sky, and that before the Earth was even formed! The concept of a twenty-four-hour day, seven-day week exists nowhere else in Heaven other than on Earth. God has no watch or calendar and He doesn't work according to schedules in anything that He does. Complete fulfillment of purpose marks the end of a project in Heaven, not the arrival of a predetermined day and time as man provides in his plans.

The concept of Time is important and useful to Mankind. Yet, Time is not a real physical process in the Universe. More tangible is the inverse of time: frequency, repetitions, periods or cycles. *Frequency* changes the material world. The number of cycles and how quickly they come and go is important to processes of creation and the evolution of all things. A cycle is a period that can be defined by specific properties that may change in an evolutionary manner. The cycle ends when the properties have changed sufficiently to give the entity a new or different character or purpose. In Earth times, a cycle can be a day, a season, a year, an era, an epoch, the reign of a king or dynasty, the period of an empire and so on.

Variations within a cycle impart evolutionary changes or mortality: one cycle is not precisely the same as the one which preceded it, so the entity improves or degrades, strengthens or weakens, increases or diminishes, lives or dies. Thus a human's days are numbered. The life of a star is limited. But all the material that composed these entities remains to begin new life again, followed by death; then a new cycle begins.

Eternity is composed of cycles. Time is only its *sensation*, though it is not a physical sensation. The sensation is produced by something beyond the understanding of humankind. Yet, Mankind has devised a means to use this sensation for his own benefit: he *invented* Time.

Time is of little concern for God and the angels and they are hardly conscious of "time". They do not relate their activities to Time but to cycles. Thus, questions such as When was God "born"? When did he begin to "think"? When did he create Christ? or the Holy Spirit? or the angels? or the Universe? have no meaning in Mankind's perception of Time which is based on the motions of a young Earth. Scientists can calculate when the physical universe apparently began from their theory and other physical evidence. They have arrived at a reasonable "ball park" age for the Universe. Yet their calculation is much closer than those who use misinterpretations to guess the age to be only a few thousand years.

God is not a deceiver. He has put nothing on the Earth to deceive Mankind, but to enlighten and challenge him. God does not attempt to make fools out of those who seek Truth, but gives it gladly to the earnest seeker. Humans can discover God's laws that govern the physical universe and use them to gain knowledge and understanding of it and thereby improve his condition. The soul can teach humanity that these laws are Divine and should be used to help him live in harmony with all created things and to use his exalted wisdom and abilities to fashion a world of sublime progression.

Interactions with Visitors to the Galaxy

Any angel may have the need or simply the desire to communicate with Christ, his Master, from any place in the Universe. This is especially important in creation activities since he is the Master of Creation. His wisdom helps the angels to conceive and perfect their assignments, as well as inspire them to achieve the greatest and most magnificent of their dreams. The angels feel his presence at all times. Occasionally, Christ comes bodily into the galaxy to visit with each angel. He always shows concern for their well being and the fulfillment of their aspirations and asks them what he can do for them. Christ is so full of Life and Love, it is a great inspiration for him to be near.

Occasionally, in the past, the archangel Lucifer also came to the galaxy, since the Milky Way was in the region of the Universe under his purview. This, too, was always a big event because the angels liked Lucifer. He was so warm, likeable and smooth. The archangels are not rivals for Christ because they all have distinctive powers and functions that affect angels differently.

Proud Lucifer Takes Keen Interest in Earth's Creation Activities

Thus we find the angels assigned to the very interesting laboratory of life on the planet Earth engaged in developing and improving both animate and inanimate species of enormous variety. The Archangel Lucifer was very proud and fond of this place, since it was in his realm of the Universe. The Earth was a very beautiful, captivating world! And Earth's heavenly environs are compellingly beautiful when observed from distant vantage points. The Earth was a place of prestige, pride and wonder for the angels working here and, indeed, for the entire galaxy.

Lucifer became very interested in the processes of development of response-stimuli. It fascinated him to observe the creatures responding to each other or to dangerous threats or stalking and killing another for food. He keenly observed the angels as they monitored and assessed these responses while they were infused into the creatures. He saw how the angels enjoyed some of these responses and delighted in the joys and pleasures produced in the creatures, for the angels can feel precisely what the creature feels. Lucifer began to lose sight of the fact that the angels always engaged in these activities as a necessary and beneficent stage of creative development of a species. He began to fantasize that the angels did it for their own pleasure and not just to accomplish the Will of God.

Thereupon, Lucifer began to spend more time in the vicinity of Earth, neglecting God's business in other galaxies of his realm. He had finally decided that whatever was good for these creation angels, was good for him too. Lucifer had begun his Fall that would eventually cause him to become, in his own limited way, the opposite of God: a dissenter, a deceiver, an anti-God.

Lucifer developed this viewpoint approximately 351,000 years before the present time. At this point, Mankind was only a mammal who had developed an intelligence superior to his fellow animals and had only learned to use very simple, naturally occurring tools to help him accomplish the basic tasks of life. Lucifer was about to affect Mankind's ways and distort his interactions with fellow humans and many other animals of Earth.

3

THE FALL OF LUCIFER
AND THE ANGELS

The Father Responds to Lucifer's Disturbing Behavior

The Father was aware that something was amiss on the planet Earth and He asked Lucifer to explain it. Lucifer, already getting the hang of deception, lied to the Father. The Father was not deceived, for he already knew exactly what Lucifer was doing. He wanted to hear about it in Lucifer's own words. Now, Lucifer had not only disregarded God's Will, he was now trying to deceive the Father by distorting and withholding the truth.

The Father then called the Archangel Michael and, in the presence of Christ, informed them both of the problem. Then he dispatched Michael to the Milky Way galaxy so that he could observe Lucifer. He wanted Michael to be a witness on behalf of the angels. Meanwhile, the Father shielded Michael so that his presence there would remain a secret.

Michael saw all that was going on: angels were kept from attending to their projects while they helped Lucifer experience the passions of animals, including those of humanity, in various activities. Lucifer seemed especially fond of the sexual acts of humans and certain other animals and he insisted that the angels participate with him in experiencing their acts of passion. Archangels were forbidden to engage in such activity. Causing angels to pervert the creative processes and to engage in unlawful behavior through deceitful means was definitely corruption of high order unprecedented in God's Universe. This could not be condoned!

Michael informed the Father and Christ of Lucifer's deeds. Then the Father asked Michael to make himself known to Lucifer and confront him with the knowledge of his misdeeds, and he did so. The smooth Lucifer tried to convince his colleague that there could be nothing wrong with what he was doing since the angels did the same things in the course of their work. He invited Michael to join him.

Michael, knowing God's laws and putting Love and Truth above all else, refused to consider joining him. He pled with Lucifer to cease doing these things and return to doing God's Will. Lucifer "smiled" slyly, indicating that he would do as he pleased in his own realm. Michael then left him to return to the Father's heart.

After Lucifer refused to heed the advise of a fellow angel of equal standing, Christ took it upon himself to visit Lucifer to determine the cause and extent of his insolence and confirm God's love and respect for his misbehaving archangel. Lucifer was not responsible to Christ; but Christ was in charge of all other angels, some of whom were now being deceived by Lucifer. Lucifer was disrespectfully and unlawfully crossing boundaries of propriety and authority. Yet, Lucifer would not repent before Christ or indicate that he had any misgivings about his behavior. Christ departed from Lucifer and returned to the Father.

Christ was saddened and angered that his angel charges were being led from doing the Father's work to pursue perverted acts that abused the creatures they had created. He was sorely disappointed that a fellow angel having exalted power and honor in the Father's kingdom would deceive the angels into performing corrupt acts that only gave them pleasure. He tried to understand the motives and the eventual consequences of such acts that defied the Father's Will.

When Christ arrived, the Father was already grieving over Lucifer's entrenched waywardness. He explained to Christ: "I created Lucifer and whatever has become of him has come from that. I gave him some elements of consciousness that has proven to be a mistake. I will not destroy Lucifer, but will offer him a remedy that will transform him. We must do all we can to save him." In saying these things, the Father acknowledged that he had erred and He took responsibility for the mistake and sought immediately to correct it. The Father thereby set an example for his angels to follow.

The Father offered Lucifer the remedy, but Lucifer refused, saying, "Why do you want me to give up something that I started, and which gives me pleasure while I go about doing good?"

The Father replied: "You should stop because it corrupts my processes of creation. It corrupts the angels and diverts them from their tasks. It heaps abuse upon the creatures you are draining your pleasure from. It diverts you from your assigned work. And it is an end in itself that serves only to give you pleasure. No good at all comes from it."

Lucifer, recognizing the truth but resisting the admission of any wrong-doing, had no reply except to reject the Father's pleas and turn his back. He had now become disrespectful, arrogant and disobedient. Thereafter, Lucifer continued his unlawful activities and began to broaden them to more animals, including sampling all their passions: sexual pursuits, rage, killing, fighting, fear, dying, envy, and all else that he had discovered in the animals' interactions. He also involved more and more angels to assist him and join his activities. He had established solid bonds with many angels who did as Lucifer asked without question.

Lucifer's activities had become intolerable! The Father once again dispatched both Christ and Michael to plead with Lucifer. Lucifer listened to their entreaties, then scoffed. Seeing that Lucifer was not in a cooperative mood, Christ told him that the Father had promised to transform him into the most perfect and powerful angel in Heaven if he would only cease his lawless activities and make amends. Lucifer's power would then be equal to Christ's own power. Lucifer considered this for a moment and nearly accepted the offer. But Lucifer was thinking that he was already perfect enough in his own eyes. Nothing would suit him better than having his own kingdom that he could rule supremely and do as he pleased. Once more, Lucifer turned away from the highest in the Father's kingdom. There was nothing more to offer Lucifer that could possibly change his determined disobedience.

Lucifer Sees Possibility of His Own Kingdom Becoming a Reality

Lucifer's wrongdoing was greatly disturbing, particularly since he had set himself against the Will of God. Not only had he broken God's law, but he persuaded thousands of Holy Angels to do the same. He seduced the trusting angels with promises of wonderful things and deceived them with claims that his activities were right and would become acceptable to all of Heaven.

He told angels who had reservations about joining him about his dreams for making the entire galaxy his own Kingdom wherein anything they desired to do would be acceptable. He argued that he was convinced that the Father, out of his love and grace for all angels, would eventually turn the galaxy over to his sovereignty.

Lucifer was under no delusions about his relative standing with the Father. He had no argument with the facts that the Father had created the Universe and all the angels, was all-powerful and was the possessor of all knowledge. The Father had created him as one of the most powerful angels, but he was still like a small animal in comparison to Him. Yet, he truly believed that he could persuade the Father to turn the Milky Way galaxy over to his rule to establish forms of creations to suit his own purposes. After all, there were countless other galaxies in the Universe, some of which were not even attended by angels. Why could not just one be given over to his form of experiments?

In disobedience and defiance toward God, Lucifer had abandoned his commission which had been assigned to him as one of the highest creatures in Heaven and had self-exiled himself from God's presence. Having great pride and giving up great powers and exalted fraternity with the Heavenly hosts, Lucifer felt lonely and unessential. This drove him to compel other angels to join him and he proceeded to build up a company of adoring, compliant angels. Since these angels were deeply loyal to the Father and Christ, their Master, and were unaccustomed to following any motives other than those found in truth and love, Lucifer knew that he must deceive them about his own actions and motives from the very outset. Therefore, he found ways to cover his activities with a veneer of truth and false sanction that would hide their real intent to give them the appearance of acceptability while leading the angels into accomplishing his wishes. He seduced them with promises of reward and honor from a gratuitous Father.

To build support among the angels, he persuaded more and more of Earth's angels to join his activities and involved them ever deeper into his perverted activities. At the point wherein they would come to realize their error, the angels would be too stained with corruption to face their Master unashamed, an unprecedented situation in Heaven. They would find solace and comfort in Lucifer, who would claim to intercede on their behalf with the Father, while actually strengthening his defiance. He would lie to the angels about the Father's response and minimize any of God's concerns about the perverseness of their activities. Thus Lucifer broadened his following and power, while his pride and self-importance grew apace.

Passions Are at the Center of Lucifer's Defiance

The central purpose of Satan's defiance directed against God's Will was to develop the enjoyment of animal passions to such extent that it could replace God's love and grace in his kingdom. The most sought after of these passions were those associated with sexual activities, violence and death. Satan controlled and offered opportunities for participation as prizes for loyalty and service to him.

The human animal was their favorite for sexual activities, because the human had the capacity to fantasize, anticipate and fan his desire for fulfillment. He displayed envy and greed which, when mingled with sexual desire, could produce dramatic behavior. The human ability to premeditate about violence and death, whenever associated with rage, hatred and envy, were also highly valued for exploitation.

Other animals were valued for various passions. For example, the horse was valued for its love and pursuit of freedom and its capacity for dramatic sexual activity and propensity for foreplay. The dog was valued for its fierceness, rage and violence in fighting, chasing and killing and for its insatiable, orgiastic mating habits. Other valued animals, for various reasons, included cattle, sheep, mountain goats, bears, felines, elk, caribou, rabbits, chipmunks, and others.

The corrupted angels became fond of temporarily infusing with any of these animals, or several of them who were sharing as mutual partners or as perpetrator and victim. They could experience simultaneously both sides of the act, the passions generated in *both the active and the passive member*.

These angels loved to infuse with humans when they went on the hunt for food, to experience their passions of excitement, courage, fear, anticipation, killing and satiation. Human passions, though more varied and calculated, paled in comparison with those of the lion, tiger, cheetah and any of the felines when they were on the hunt. First were pangs of hunger to prompt the cat to leave its den, perch or resting place; then the slow, deliberate prowl in search of prey; then the adrenaline-fed excitement when quarry was sighted; then the stealthy, quiet, smooth stalking to bring the cat within striking distance; the tense moment of stillness and quiet awaiting the quarry to fall into vulnerability; then the swift, violent ambush, the chase, the fateful pounce, and the death struggle; then the triumph when the quarry lay warm and limp beneath him, the body giving its final, faint spasmodic twitches; and finally the flow of still warm blood and satiation of hunger. The infused angel could experience it all from both participants.

The angels infused into both the hunter and the hunted to experience both sides of the triumph and the agony of this survival ritual. One beast would triumph and survive, the other would lose and die. Such dramas were played constantly in the forests and grassy plains of the world, an endless arena of pleasure for the angels, who often were able to intensify the passions within the beasts. The angels could experience the emotions both of triumph and utter defeat without suffering the slightest injury or loss to themselves or giving any benefit to the creatures.

Lucifer Secures Earth as Base of Power

Lucifer sought first to secure his own position on Earth before embarking on the much larger galaxy. This decision was made about 350,000 years before the present time on Earth. He set himself and his converted angels to winning as many as possible of those angels now working on Earth and its environs, about 16.5 million in all. At last, he firmly won all but about 5.5 million. Those angels who refused to join him were too strong in their love and loyalty to Christ and the Father to believe and accede to Lucifer's guile. These would remain on Earth to attempt persuasion of the fallen to abandon Lucifer. The creative work on Earth virtually ceased.

Lucifer Begins Expansion into the Galaxy

With the Earth won, Lucifer put princes in charge of Earth's fallen angels and went into the galaxy, taking many loyal angels with him to begin converting other angels. Normally, God's angels are always ready to give devotion and adoration, and poise in reverent awe whenever one of the powerful archangels enter their presence. Filled with the power of love, the angels trustfully accept their messages, certain that they issue from the Father. Lucifer loved the adoration that his presence elicited; but, his character was different from the other archangels. Many angels fell readily into the sway of the suave Lucifer, who could persuade almost anyone that excrement is the same as milk and honey.

Now, Lucifer had approached them for his own purposes, not those of the Father. Under his persuasive deception, countless angels began to leave their assignment wherever he spread his message. Some followed to help recruit others, some journeyed directly to Earth to join his growing kingdom.

God could have stopped Lucifer at any time, but He would have been faced with a malicious, unrepentant archangel with the problem of having to deal with him. There were also millions of the galaxy's angels who offered a different problem. These angels had been deceived and seduced into joining him and thus were innocently following and proclaiming the merits of his kingdom. Lucifer's actions were deliberate and calculated. If God stopped Lucifer and the angels, He would have to force them unwillingly back into His kingdom still nurturing the corrupted ideas adopted from Lucifer. The corruption could then spread like an untreated disease and Lucifer would at least have his way, if not his desired kingdom.

God had given the angels total freedom, including the freedom of will and choice, although they had never been faced with choosing between God and an anti-god. God will never force any angel to choose Him or Heaven against their will, for that is not where their "heart" and loyalty is. Therefore He must abide with them in love and patience while He attempts ways to win back their own love and loyalty.

In the meantime, God began to obstruct Lucifer's inroads into the Galaxy. The resistance became so difficult for Lucifer that he turned back to Earth taking most of the angels he had won. This is the visionary conflict with the angel Michael spoken of by Saint John (Revelations 12:7-9). Some of his angels remained in the galaxy to continue enticing others to come.

God Replaces Lucifer with a New Archangel: *GABRIEL*

Lucifer had plainly demonstrated his stubborn disobedience and disrespect for God's appeals. Now, he would openly defy God and aggressively expand his activities. In this way Lucifer hoped to demonstrate his own strength of leadership and power to rule his kingdom.

Consequently, God decided to take away Lucifer's powers as archangel. At this point, God called one of His angels from another part of Heaven who had been given extraordinary faculties. God promoted and transformed this chosen angel to the position of Archangel, empowering him to take over Lucifer's realm, replacing him as one of the seven. Heavenly angels gave the new archangel the human name of *Gabriel* for he shall help the fallen angels to redeem their sins against humanity and Earth's creatures and to triumph over Lucifer's defiance and deception.

Lucifer Claims Earth as His Kingdom

Arriving upon Earth once more, in the company now of hundreds of millions of angels but stripped of his Heavenly powers, Lucifer declared that the Earth and all around it, namely the Solar system, was his kingdom. He also declared that he would henceforth be called by a name of his own creation, that of Satan, giving up the name that God gave him at his own creation in Heaven.

Angels continued to come to Earth in fewer and fewer numbers. God's loyal angels on Earth were overwhelmed and greatly saddened over the fall of Earth and the unlawful activities now taking place there. God's processes of creations had been completely abandoned and Earth's creatures were at the mercy of corruption and unbridled lusting. God's loyal angels left Earth and took positions outside its environs as a means to persuade Satan's converts to turn back to their Heavenly tasks. Few did so.

By the time of approximately 332,000 years before the present time, there were no new recruits arriving. Some of Satan's most devoted angels continued to travel into the galaxy to proselyte, without much success. God had taught the other angels how to resist and counter Satan's deceptive arguments. Satan and his angels continued to project communications into the galaxy to persuade companion angels to come to Earth. But no more of God's angels would be receptive to Satan's entreaties.

Now there were approximately 740 million angels who had joined with Satan on Earth. This number was nearly a third of all angels in the Milky Way galaxy and most all of these came from only half the galaxy which Lucifer nefariously pillaged. There was no angel in this part of the galaxy who had not lost a beloved partner or companion to Satan's attack. Songs of sadness and lamentations rang mournfully throughout the galaxy.

Some Angels Abandon Satan

Meanwhile, the Father and Christ and their loyal angels never ceased in their efforts to win the wayward angels back to God's love and to doing His Will, while Satan continued to press for a perceived right to rule the galaxy. After much time had passed, some angels had become disillusioned and repentant and desired to go back unconditionally to God's work. These numbered about 15 million angels. God's angels ushered them out of Earth's realm into other galactic locations.

Seeing that some had left Earth, Satan was angered and his pride deeply hurt. Consequently, he gathered a large squad of powerful, very zealous angels to hinder and repel any others who attempted to leave and punished those who did so. He set up a cordon around the Earth to repel any angel attempting to leave. He had taken the first step in becoming a tyrant rather than a leader.

Many other angels considered returning to Heaven if God would grant them certain conditions once they returned to His assignments. God would grant no conditions because this would allow willfulness to be taken back into the galaxy, which could then spread like a virus to corrupt others. The galaxy would eventually become a place dominated by disobedience and racked with contention, possibly spreading to other galaxies. The security and sanctity of Heaven were threatened.

God Yields Earth to Become Satan's Kingdom

Finally, God decided to give Satan his own kingdom, knowing that Satan would not be able to rule it to benefit himself or the angels. God said to Satan: "You may have Earth as your kingdom, but *that* is all that you will ever have. You may rule it any way you see fit. I shall withdraw my presence and my own angels from your kingdom and it shall be all yours. But you will never be able to come back into My Heavenly Kingdom without fully and unconditionally repenting of all you are doing, and remedying any injury and damage you have done to the angels who followed you, or Earth's creatures whom you are desecrating, or to the Earth itself. You can no longer come before my face or use the power of the Holy Spirit. All power to rule the Earthly realm will come from you."

Satan would have to establish and rule his own kingdom without access to Heaven's powers. So great was Lucifer's fall from Heaven's Grace!! While in Heaven, he wielded the considerable powers of an archangel. Now he is stripped of those powers and God has denied him even the use of the Holy Spirit. The lowliest angel in Heaven now towers over him. His domain of Divine cognizance once included a region of the Universe that included many *galaxies*. Now his domain is only a "speck of dust" in a remote locality of *one* of those galaxies. He calls *this* his "kingdom" and he is the "king" to whom many yield and serve, and some worship! Even a human does not have to follow him *unless* that is his desire. Is Satan really *worthy* of you?

Why God Gave Satan a Kingdom

God's purpose for allowing Satan to have the Earthly realm in which to establish his own kingdom was to demonstrate to Satan and all the angels who chose to be with him that he has no Divine power of his own, he cannot rule without God, and his angels can do none of the things that the Holy Spirit had previously empowered them to do. Satan and his angels will have power to do only those things in which they broke God's laws so that they may see the bankruptcy and shame of endlessly doing something without holy purpose. Once they see the truth in the errors of their ways, the angels can repent and remedy their sins. Total, sincere repentance and remediation will be required for restoration of any fallen angel to Heaven's grace.

Following God's decision to yield the Earthly realm to Satan's control, His angels began to inform all the fallen angels, including Satan, of the conditions that would soon be imposed within the realm. This was in the form of a warning so that those who had an inclination to return to doing God's Will could do so while there was still time. Sadly, all the angels who were strongly drawn to God's entreaties had already departed from the realm.

Most fallen angels ignored God's warnings. Many others refused to believe that God, because of His infinite capacity for love and grace, would withdraw and impose the hardships portrayed in the warnings. These would remain in the realm, either to conscientiously serve Satan's wishes or simply to challenge God's resolve. Yet, some angels, few in number, loved God and their fallen companions so greatly that they elected to stay in the realm to help them to know the truth and to overcome their mistake.

God had never before had a reason to display to His angels another part of His Love: the offer of Mercy. But mercy is not appropriately given until the doer of sins has seen a reason to repent and asks for God's Mercy and surrenders to His Will. The time will come when many of the fallen angels will be motivated to do so.

An Impenetrable Veil of Darkness Encloses Earth

After relinquishing the Earth to Satan's power, God withdrew His angels, the Holy Spirit, and His own Presence from inside the Earthly realm. Then using a mighty host of His angels, He enclosed the Solar system within an impenetrable shield, through which no angel and no angelic communications could pass without his authority.

This shield would come to be called a "veil of darkness" by both God's angels and the angels enclosed within. The veil was placed around the Earthly realm about 225,000 years before the present time. Now, the realm was made a separate place from Heaven, sealed off and isolated. The angels began to call it Hades, the Kingdom of Lost Angels.

God did not withdraw completely, for he left a tenuous opening so that He could have dialogues with Satan to persuade him to repent, and occasionally to let Satan feel the love that He still had for His lofty creature. A faint "glow" of God's Presence remained within the Earthly realm so that all fallen angels could, at times of meditation and reflection, feel the appeal of His Love and Grace. They would not forget Him.

Because of the veil of darkness, no view of Heaven from the Earthly realm has been possible from the time it was placed. This affected only the angels, not humans or animals, because Heaven is spiritual and Earth and the universe are physical. Humans can see only the three-dimensional physical heavens with its stars and galaxies. A view of God's Heaven, if it could be seen, would confuse humans because of its six-dimensional space and the strangely beautiful and shimmering displays of light and darting rays resulting from angelic activity. Christ's golden glow would captivate, possibly blind them, as he draws near. Humans would be amazed by the spectral glow of archangels, displayed in personalized hues.

Heaven is a sight to behold, but not for human eyes! Humans and animals are unable to see Heavenly scenes because the natural laws of God have separated the material and spiritual worlds. Material beings cannot see spiritual things, but angels, including the soul, can "see" both. To angels, Heaven is even more beautiful with the overlay of the physical galaxies and worlds onto the spiritual forms of the Universe. Angels and spirits can move from the spiritual realm into the physical realm, and return. When in the spiritual realm, they are impervious to matter; when in the physical realm, they can affect matter for various purposes to do God's or Satan's will.

Reaction of Satan and the Angels to the "Veil"

When Satan saw that he could no longer see into Heaven or feel the presence of God he became greatly dismayed. When his angels perceived these things they were shocked; fear and trepidation filled them. They rushed this way and that about the Earth and in the outer reaches of the realm. Many angels rushed toward the barrier, beyond which was only darkness. None could get through the barrier and they could not discern what was causing it. They could not "speak" with angels beyond the barrier or even see them. They called out to Christ and the Father, but no reply came back to them. These factors prompted a general state of fear. What has happened? What is becoming of them?

Meanwhile, Satan tried to calm the situation and he sent his elite followers out to the barrier to bring those back who were trying to get out. Finally he began to get their attention. He told them what God had done: the Earth had been given to him as their kingdom and he would begin to rule. He told them that everything would be fine as long as all obeyed him and his laws, just as they would be required to obey God and His laws if they were still in Heaven. He would now be their god, and pleasure would soon replace the love that God had withdrawn from them.

Satan told them that he would see that all were taken care of and rewarded according to their loyalty and service to him. He charged them that, since there was no place for them to go, all should now be content to obey and please him. He promised that the angels would begin to change the Earth's creatures to increase their passions in all things so that the angels' pleasure could eventually match God's love. The angels had already caused such perverted changes in many species by influencing selective breeding habits to enhance their pleasures and passions. New creatures could even be created having very special capabilities, he said, and many more things that bring enjoyment to the angels. His new kingdom would be one all the angels would like and enjoy.

Realizing that there was nothing they could do, the angels began to accept their lot. They would go back to doing as Satan had enjoined them before the "veil". The initial shock and confusion that swept over the angels were giving way to disillusionment and anger at Satan and their own decisions to join him. Many of the angels began to show indifference to him and ignored his commands.

Seeing that he was losing control, Satan devised more tyrannical methods laced with a system of reward and punishment. He brought around him the most zealous, loyal, and competent of his angels and organized them into a powerful, elite cadre to enforce his will on all. He put them under the command of his most feared prince, whose name was Amal. These became the professionals of service and control for his kingdom. They became so power-ful, ruthless and merciless in their methods of controlling and punishing disobedient or disloyal angels that the angels called them "beasts". The cadre came to appreciate this name and adopted it as their own.

The reward-punishment system involved a highly controlled rationing of the animals most favored for enjoyment of passions. Humans were at the top of the list. Since there were now approximately 725 million angels and only a few million adult humans, only the most loyal and cooperative of angels were accorded the privilege of exploiting the humans. Other favored animals included the horse, cattle, the felines, dogs, rabbits, caribou, wildebeests, and several others. Exploitation of these was controlled through Satan's cadre of "beasts". The uncooperative angels would have to fight over those not controlled or do without. Occasionally Satan would allow one of these angels to experience the passions of favored animals, including humans, so that they could know what they were missing by not bowing to his wishes.

Satan also directed harsh measures through the beasts for any angel daring to disobey or disappoint him. Any command, expression of desire or suggestion, however slight, must be obeyed immediately and without any equivocation, or they would suffer some undesirable consequence.

As a result of all this, the angels came to exhibit emotions within themselves and exhibit behavior that had never occurred in Heaven. These included greed, lust, envy, hatred, deviousness, stubbornness, disobedience, terror and all the passions of darkness that disgrace and devastate the soul of Mankind today. The angels began to put their own self-interests above those of others. They stopped sharing love, envied those who were given generous rewards, despised those who mistreated them or excluded them from the rewards that were given to some, and generally adopted Satan's tricks of deception, deviousness and meanness to get their way.

Satan is Incapable of Ruling His Kingdom; the Angels Lose Hope

Now Satan's kingdom, the kingdom of Hades, was in chaos. Hordes of angels engaged in lawless, ruthless, ravaging behavior, while the innocent valued creatures of Earth suffered from rape and violently distorted passions. Dissatisfied, compassionate angels began to fall away from these activities, to ignore them, and seek solace in observing and admiring the beauty and wonders of the planet Earth. It became their sweet reward to drink in the tranquility and magnificence of this world. Many desired to return to their assignments in Heaven and would do so without any condition. But how could this be done?

Meanwhile, Satan ordered the angels to begin creating characteristics that would expand and improve the most cherished animal passions. Angels attempted to do this, but soon learned that they no longer had a capability for creative accomplishment. This power had been taken away when God withdrew the Holy Spirit. God would not permit them to continue the desecration and abuse of these creatures that had been produced by Holy Angels through Love and Grace. The angels began to realize the extent of loss that their disobedience had brought them. Many were appalled and filled with despair.

Satan began to reflect on the conditions that now prevailed in his kingdom. First, most angels had become disillusioned, disloyal and uncooperative. He saw that he had no real power over most of them except through fear and tyranny. Only harsh, tyrannical methods could compel them to comply with his will. Secondly, he realized that other than this, he had no real power to achieve the things that he had desired and he could neither control nor improve his kingdom in a progressive way. Thirdly, he knew that God had withdrawn His own power and that it was not available for creation or other profitable endeavors.

Satan wondered how long these conditions would endure before the kingdom collapsed in a rebellion of its own. Yet, his pride was too great to admit to wrongdoing and return to God's Kingdom, submitting to God's Will. He would hold his position in stubbornness, resenting the Father and Christ and Gabriel who replaced him as Archangel, seeking ways to build his power to resist God and make his kingdom succeed.

Since Satan intended to rule the Earthly kingdom in rejection and defiance of God's Will, he would have to do it entirely on his own. God would not grant any avenue of help to him. Any angel or person who sets himself on such a course, however modest, will experience the causes and effects of his own willfulness. God cannot help those who replace His Will with their own.

How Imperfection Came from Perfection

Those things that Satan brought forth to defy God and corrupt the angels are imperfections because they are all destructive and out of harmony with God's Will and *undermine the foundations of a perfect Universe.* These work in opposition to the Virtues that derive from God's Spirit.

Since God is the Creator of all in the Universe, both spiritual and material, his mind possesses essentially limitless knowledge and all wisdom to use the knowledge in the most advantageous way for any purpose. There are no limits to what He can perceive or conceive. Such an intellect knows all the possible ways that anything can be produced. From his perception at the beginning of Creation that an *eternal* Universe could not contain the seeds of its own destruction or present any lasting tribulation to life, *God made everything perfect.*

Truth and the infallible operation of his laws are consolidated in the most infinite of his creations, such as the Universe, and in all things ranging to the infinitesimal, such as the components of the atomic nuclei. All is made perfect through his infallible laws for truth and life.

How, then, did the imperfection of sin come out of something that was absolutely perfect? The answer underlies another question: Does Satan actually exist? Do some say "There is no Satan!", that he is only a make-believe character whom humans blame for the world's ills, including their own imperfections? Certainly it is evident that sin, which is opposition to God's Will, does indeed exist throughout the world. This is an indisputable truth, although some have invented innocent-sounding names to invite respectability and acceptability for many kinds of sinful behavior.

Since sin is an imperfection and therefore is in opposition to anything God would have brought forth, how did it arise? Where did sin come from? Could perfection itself produce opposition to its Creator? Would God have brought forth something that opposes all He aspires to do with a determination to destroy his handiwork? Certainly not!

The answers lie in the certainty that something that had been perfect became imperfect. Something broke down, and after the breakdown it no longer performed in accordance with God's Will. When this occurred why did God not isolate or destroy it in its earliest stage? What in God's creation could have broken down so that it resulted in the consequences that have been evident throughout the history of Mankind and yet was allowed to remain to harm and stain humanity?

Such a state of imperfection could have derived from one of *only two possible sources* in the Universe, that is, from one of the two types of intelligent entities. Therefore, imperfection initiated either from angels or from intelligent material beings. Surely, it could not have come from some *material* entity such as a human being because material beings are confined to their own worlds in unbreechable isolation. The imperfection could not spread from that world and God would not have become concerned since a few angels could have resolved the problem. Furthermore, since the imperfection *did* spread between worlds into a significant part of Heaven, and it was considered a malignant threat, God and all Heaven became gravely concerned about its emergence and spread.

What, then, could possibly create this threat, causing such concern among the Heavenly hosts? The answer is obviously centered about an angel as the source of this anxiety. Only an angel would have the abilities and powers to spread the imperfection through Heaven and into other worlds. This required a deceptive influence to induce other angels to accept the imperfection as perfection and join with the perpetrator. An angel is not deceived by a material being, regardless of its intelligence, because such entities are creatures of the angels. Angels consider each other to be messengers of Truth for the Heavenly Father; therefore, an angel is potentially deceived only by another angel.

So we see that the breakdown resulting in imperfection could come only through the failure of an angel. Something within the angel became a flaw and the flaw gave way to a breakdown that resulted in the angel opposing God's Will. Finding itself in opposition to God and not wanting to face him the angel sought comfort in lonely isolation. No angel likes to be alone, separated from the love of God and the companionship of fellow angels. Therefore, this angel desired to surround itself with angels who would appreciate him and applaud his actions and find a way somehow to compensate the loss of God's love and grace. Appropriate companions could be created through causing them to break down and become imperfect as he was. Such deliberate breakdown of angels having loyalty to God can be caused only through deception and seduction skillfully presented to maintain a perception of innocence while shifting their loyalty from God and assuring them that all of it had His blessing.

Power to perpetuate the small coterie of angels could be achieved through increasing the number of such angels and deepening their involvement in imperfect acts or sins. Therefore the deceiver felt compelled to win as many angels as possible to his cause and establish a firm base of power and permanence within a substantial portion of the Heavenly space. This deceiver visualized that he could win an entire galaxy, namely the Milky Way Galaxy, which he could effectively isolate from the rest of Heaven and maintain it as his very own dominion. Under his rule, he and the converted angels could achieve their own forms of grace and bliss derived from proclivities of imperfection.

God saw that He could not tolerate the spread of the imperfection throughout even one of the many galaxies of his Universe; therefore He resolved to oppose it. He forced it to retreat to the place of its origin, the Earthly realm, then isolated the entire realm from the rest of Heaven. He did not destroy it because all the participants were angels whom he had created and loved, including the deceiver himself, and all had corrupted themselves, initially without guile, in imperfection. He decided, instead, to maintain the realm in isolation, giving it no support from Heaven.

The imperfection would eventually be revealed to the angels for what it is. Its futile promises would run their course without fulfillment or providing any hope of their own. Consequently, discontent with imperfection and hope for something better will grow increasingly among the fallen angels and humanity, while they search for that which will restore perfection to their world.

Through his love for these angels, God would offer a way to lift them out of the imperfection and isolation. Then they may return to Heaven with renewed determination to abide in his Will and be restored fully to his Grace. When all who are willing are restored to Heaven, God would destroy the imperfection and all angels who are intractably bound within it. The imperfection would no longer exist and all of Heaven would once more be perfect.

So we see that *imperfection came from a flaw in an angel*, and the angel felt the need to involve other angels in the imperfection and establish a kingdom of self-rule so that they may all survive forever despite being in opposition to God's Will. *This angel was Lucifer*, who desired to be called Satan and be the ruler of this secluded kingdom. *This kingdom is Hades*, which includes the Earthly realm and all the material creatures of Earth and all the angels who allowed themselves to be deceived and seduced into accepting imperfection's desolate promises.

The Garden of Eden and Original Sin

The allegorical story of the creation of the world given in the Book of Genesis in the Holy Bible is based upon great Heavenly truths, but is mistakenly told from the standpoint of humans. In the story, God created a male human whom He named Adam and later a female companion whom Adam named Eve and placed them together in a beautiful pristine area called the "Garden of Eden." With two exceptions, God gave them complete freedom to do as they pleased. The restrictions pertained to the fruit of two distinctive "trees" in the midst of the garden. One of these was the "tree of knowledge of good and evil" which God forbade them to even *touch*. The other was the "tree of life" which He *prevented* them from partaking after they had disobeyed Him and "eaten" of the tree of knowledge.

The meaning of "the tree of life" has remained a mystery that Mankind could never interpret unless God revealed the meaning to one searching in the right way for truth. It does not mean that Mankind will learn the secret of creating life or even of greatly prolonging his life span.

The *meaning of the tree of life* is related to the use of certain creation processes by the fallen angels to focus the physical and mental capacities of Earth's creatures solely upon the causes and effects of greatly increased passions and pleasures for the enjoyment of the angels. Life processes used by creation angels in the Earthly "laboratory of life" would now be manipulated to supplant God's Love with the pursuit of pleasure as the driving force of life. *Satan planned to turn the entire Earth into a gigantic farm in which Earth's creatures would be developed and used solely for pleasurable pursuits by the angels!* Such plans display enormous impudence and disrespect for life. Nevertheless, these were Satan's plans for humanity and most other creatures! Who would serve such a master? Knowing that this was Satan's intention, God forbade and prevented the angels from pursuing this despicable desecration of Earth's creatures by denying them access to the "tree" of life.

The "tree of knowledge of good and evil" has long been regarded as relating to the acts of sexual love. In truth, it is much more than this, because humanity has never been prohibited from performing the functions necessary to propagate his species. These powers are given to all of Earth's creatures as the Will of God. The restriction of "eating" from *the "tree of knowledge" pertains to experiencing all human passions in abnormal ways corrupted through self-indulgence and disobedience of God's laws of righteousness.* This constitutes *perversity,* which is the *abnormal* use or expression of the faculties given to humanity to fulfill the purpose of their creation. Perversity leads to disobedient behavior stemming from self-indulgent and immoral desires, that includes corruption and debauchery, deception and untruthfulness, greed and selfishness, hatred and envy, defiance and licentiousness.

The Biblical story portrays Adam and Eve enjoying a blissful life in the Garden. God had directed them not to eat the fruit of this tree, because He knew they would be tempted to engage in sexual acts and other self-indulging behavior *with abnormal passions.* They did so anyway and thus committed the "original sin", which was disobedience to God's Will in committing an expressly forbidden act. Since Adam and Eve are identified as humans, the guilt of committing the original sin is laid upon humanity, and particularly upon the female for believing the serpent's guile and tempting the male to join her in disobeying God's instructions.

The guilt is not Mankind's. Guilt belongs to the fallen angels. Furthermore, Adam and Eve are *not human beings*, but are two distinct groups of fallen angels, one of whom preceded the other in falling into deception and disobedience. The Original Sin must be attributed to these angels in disobeying God to desecrate and abuse humans and other creatures to satisfy their self indulgent desires.

This story does not represent the fall of Mankind, but of the fallen angels partaking of forbidden "knowledge" which *corrupted the fabric of their beings*. This was the aim of Lucifer's seductive guile. In the account of the tree of knowledge of good and evil, "knowledge" is synonymous with experience. The fallen angels performed acts in which they experienced in unnatural ways the gifts they had given to Earth's creatures. God could never approve such behavior among his angels. They perverted and corrupted the normal processes of creation, not to please God by fulfilling His Will, but to provide pleasures for themselves under the direction of Satan. In so doing, they came to know evil by committing unlawful acts that stemmed from undertakings that had been established for good purposes. Because they disobeyed God and acquired knowledge through forbidden acts, He denied them the use of the powers of life that they intended to use to deepen their sins.

The Garden of Eden symbolizes the Heavenly state of Earth itself and its inhabitants *before* the fall of the angels. Because of their disobedience, God cast them out of the Garden into the "world", an act that symbolizes the isolation of the Earthly realm and the fallen angels from Heaven. Thereafter, they were denied Heaven's Grace and were compelled to accede to the circumstances of the creatures they had desecrated. Not only had they created a cul-de-sac for sin and disobedience, but they had brought about an irresolute separation from Heaven that would afford them the weakest and dimmest of contacts with their Creator and source for Love, Truth and Light.

In their pursuit of pleasurable experience, the angels turned things that were intended only for good into instruments of evil. All things are good when they conform to God's Will, but any good thing can be diverted to evil designs. This is the legacy that the fallen angels left to Mankind. By partaking of the forbidden "tree of knowledge," they created a world in which good without consecrated resolve can deteriorate into evil, evil can masquerade as good, and good must struggle unceasingly with evil. Evil becomes bold and assertive when those who love good become weak and indifferent. This struggle will not be won for good until all souls have repented and returned to doing God's Will.

4

GOD ESTABLISHES
THE AGE OF REDEMPTION

The Time Is Right to Offer Redemption

God was aware of the conditions that had developed in the Earthly realm of Hades bringing confusion and disillusionment to many fallen angels. Of particular interest were the large number of angels who desired to return to Heaven unconditionally and Satan's own vulnerable wavering. But all of the angels had become corrupted by their servility to Satan, had abused themselves and the Earth's creatures, and had acquired the dark passions in opposition to holiness. None had recanted their initial choice to leave Heaven and join Lucifer, but all were trying to attain the greatest share of spoils available from this decadent situation.

These angels couldn't be allowed to simply return to Heaven without going through a process of *remediation, cleansing and reaffirmation* to unconditional obedience to God's Laws and Will. Upon this, God devised a plan of redemption that would be offered to all fallen angels, even to Satan, his princes and the "beasts". Each angel must accept it and submit himself to it willingly to bring about a state wherein any one could be re-admitted to Heaven whole, clean, and without desire to forsake God's Will and His Love and Truth ever again. It must become the unequivocal desire of their heart made through their own free choice.

God called Satan to the barrier enclosing the realm and advised him of the plan in the company of Christ, the two archangels and a large assembly of other angels. The Plan was offered as an all or nothing proposition that Satan could embrace or spurn, but which he could not prevent. The consequences of rejecting the plan would be eternal isolation in the Earthly realm of Hades, with God's presence *totally* removed. Those angels wanting to leave could at that time re-enter Heaven to be transformed through probation or re-creation. Love, mercy and justice would prevail to motivate every angel to come willingly to redemption.

The Father made Christ the Executor of the Plan of Redemption and gave him supreme power and authority to ensure perfect fulfillment of the Father's Will. The time of this event was 121,000 years before the present time. The Plan contained the following provisions and requirements:

- The angels would immediately cease all activities related to the dark passions. God would enforce this if not done willingly.
- The angels must begin a process of remedying the abuse they had heaped upon humanity and their disobedience of God.
- God would allow the Holy Spirit and Heavenly angels into the realm to assist and empower the fallen angels to begin their redemptive tasks.
- The angels will remedy the abuse they heaped upon the animals. They shall teach Mankind to give devotion and care to those which were mistreated the most, such as the horse, dog, cattle, cats, rabbits and others, and allow them to live among them as companions. Those animals that must be free and independent will thrive in their habitats with respect and concern from Mankind. He shall be taught to protect and honor all creatures of God.
- As a concession to the angels, God would permit the angels to continue enjoying animal passions. This would be done in only one animal and God chose this animal to be the human. There would be inviolable rules governing this privilege and these rules include:
  + One angel would infuse into a single human to become its "soul". The angel soul must infuse before birth and remain infused throughout its life, leaving only at death. There would be no willful "coming and going" as before. This would be offered as a privilege to all angels *approved* by God.
  + Satan, his princes, and the most recalcitrant of his "beasts" will not be permitted to become souls. These must await a time when God shall offer a final call for Salvation, unless they decide beforehand to repent and return to God unconditionally. These spirits must all stand before God to be judged for the most atrocious sins committed against Mankind and God. Redemption will come to them at a very high price, because no sacrificial life will be given to redeem *these* angels.

+ As a soul in the human body, the angels will always strive to confer a knowledge of God, His Laws, and an awareness of His Love and Truth into the mental processes of the human.

+ God will communicate rules at the proper time that govern the acceptability of sexual acts between humans and the exercise of other passions. *God* will make the rules.

+ To achieve remediation and compensation for the abuse to which the angels had subjected the human, the soul would consciously help the human to develop mental awareness and capabilities including at least these properties: Love and Concern for others; Intelligence and Consciousness; a sense of Inquiry and Exploration; a capability for Observation and Analysis, Critical Judgement and Discernment; Awareness of Self and Relationships with others; Courage and Persistence; Adoration and Endearment; Graciousness and Respect for self and others; Humility and Dignity; Gratitude and Generosity; Sympathy and Forgiveness; Appreciation of Beauty and Abstractness; and other factors stemming from God's Consciousness, Intellect, and Love. With these gifts humans may become sovereign, benevolent, progressive, peaceful beings in their own world.

+ The soul must develop a mental state within the human that will prepare and enable him to receive, share and apply the foregoing gifts.

+ The soul must impart within the human mind an awareness of divine Spirit and the values it contains.

+ Each angel will successively enter as many humans, beginning at birth and ending at death, as are necessary to redeem the angel's transgressions and impart the gifts of the spirit cited.

+ While infused in the human as its soul, the angel will be empowered with free will, choosing to do as it desires to do good or evil, or simply choose to do nothing. Neither God nor Satan can force the soul to do the will of either or choose one or the other. Any action it takes must be done willingly as a result of its own choices; but the soul will be held fully accountable for the choices it consciously makes with or on behalf of the human. God will presume that a soul who has not voluntarily chosen to do His Will has, instead, elected to serve Satan.

+ The soul will preserve within itself a record or memory of all spiritual, mental and related physical acts of the human host, so that it can be reviewed at anytime by the Father or Christ or an sanctioned angel.
+ The soul will be held responsible for all that it does whether good or evil. All sinful (evil) things done in any life must be accounted for and removed either through God's forgiveness, forgiveness by the soul sinned against, or through remediation (redemption). Some sins are forgivable forthrightly, others are not and must be redeemed.
+ Unforgivable sins committed during a life span must be redeemed at some time, either in that life or in a later life. For sins committed against others, the sinning soul will again meet the soul sinned against to redeem the debt that was incurred. For sins committed against God, the soul must lead the human host into a life of service and holiness that will redeem the sins. Redemption will always involve specific activities and behavior that compensates in kind the sins committed.
+ Each soul will be finally judged to evaluate the degree to which it has done good, in redeeming its abuse to Mankind and Earth's creatures, and in redeeming debts incurred against God and humans.
+ All lost souls will, at some time after being given all possible opportunities for redemption and returning to God, be given a final opportunity to forsake Satan and make an unconditional choice to return to God.
+ God will deal with any soul as He deems fit who rejects His final offer of salvation. Total rejection of God is the only truly unforgivable sin and will be judged at the Final Call.
+ Souls who have redeemed all debts and have unconditionally elected to return to God, shall be reinstated to Heaven to resume doing the Will of God forever as long as Heaven itself endures.
+ When the last soul who will be saved is given salvation, and no more will chose to do so, God will dispense judgement to those who have finally and irrevocably rejected Him. The veil of darkness will be rescinded to end the Earth's isolation from Heaven. Heaven shall flood in to engulf the Earth and its inhabitants, including the angels who were restored to God.

- God will then allow the angels who did not forsake Heaven to escort those who did and were redeemed to their original assignments, rejoicing that all angels have been reunited and are again among the Heavenly hosts of angels. All Heaven shall celebrate with songs of joy and praise.

This is the Plan of Redemption that the Father, in the company of Heavenly hosts, declared before Satan. Satan, knowing that he had little choice to do otherwise, acknowledged the Plan and that it could begin as soon as God is ready. A stunned Satan returned to Earth to decide his course: to passively submit or actively oppose.

Additional Conditions for Redemption

REDEMPTION AND THE HUMAN-SOUL RELATIONSHIP

God's Plan of Redemption required the following: that the angel souls infuse fully into every human for the complete life span to redeem themselves for the defiance of God and the abuse they had heaped upon the human; that the angel would purposely transform the human host by imbuing it with the fruits of God's Intellect and Consciousness, Love and Truth; that multiple life spans for each angel would be required over a sufficiently long period of time to accomplish remediation to God's satisfaction; that the angel as the soul of the human must redeem any further injury it incurs to its human hosts; that God would forgive a repentant soul and provide a means for it to redeem its debts; an unrepentant soul would not be forgiven its debts until it purposely sought forgiveness through repentance; and, finally, all repentant souls who had redeemed all debts to God and Mankind, or had been forgiven those debts, would be returned to Heaven and reinstated as angels.

God will judge only the soul or spirit for its sins of disobedience, desecration and abuse. Mankind did not fall or sin; only the angels fell. Humanity is the innocent victim of the fallen angels. Unrepentant souls shall indeed cause Mankind to sin, which can bring failure, misery and devastation upon humanity. God will give Mankind the opportunity to attain the wisdom to save himself from the terrible consequences into which sin will lead him. God will preserve Mankind and will bless him following the final judgement of souls.

The Plan of Redemption includes God's covenant with the fallen angels that would endure through the Age of Redemption to the time that it should end. It is his Promise of salvation and Life for those angels who turn away from their transgressions of disobedience and self-indulgence to seek God's Love, Mercy and Forgiveness. Then all who willingly do so from the desire of their own heart can return to his eternal Kingdom of Light and Love, where there shall be no further punishment or remembrance of their sins. And Heaven will be whole again because the kingdom of Hades will be no more and there shall be none remaining who defy and corrupt God's Supreme Purpose. Every fallen angel who finds hope in this Promise can participate as a willing soul.

After the soul-sharing phase provides full preparation, every human being will have an infused soul for the full duration of its viable life. The process of infusion of an angel or spirit into the body of a human is a physical process. The angel or spirit must enter the physical realm to accomplish this act. After infusion, the soul and human become inseparable partners, making choices together, sharing the joys and miseries of each and progressing together for good or evil.

The soul will not burden the human. The mind, in fact, will not be consciously aware of the soul's presence. The human, living in a physical world, has material needs that must be attended to for his survival, well being and aspirations. Therefore the mind will have the power to over-ride the urgings and guidance of its soul and may do so as its own will dictates. Indeed, the mind may ignore the soul almost completely. The soul, too, can over-ride the mind to warn of impending danger or the inadvisability of an act or decision, becoming the conscience or "guardian angel" of the mind. God intends for the soul and mind to develop a cooperative and benevolent relationship for the advancement of both to achieve the goals of his Plan of Redemption.

DEVELOPING THE BRAIN-SOUL CONNECTION   To begin re-demption, a deficiency in the human related to direct communication be-tween the soul and the mind of the human had to be removed. This arose from the fact that an angel cannot communicate directly with the human brain. When the Age of Redemption began, mental powers were more advanced in the human than in any other creature on Earth; yet, at that time, the mind was not capable of assisting the brain to interact with an angel soul.

The mental process of all creatures with intelligence includes a brain and a mind. The mind is not a physical entity in the sense that it is material and occupies space. The mind is a power similar to the Holy Spirit that is linked exclusively with the brain and whose purpose is to enable the brain to rationally associate thought with its experiences. The mind is the essence of the brain's ability to *understand* and correlate knowledge.

The brain conforms to physical principles to enable it to think, remember and make associations. It attempts to communicate by transforming impulsive impressions into rational thought forms then into some form of verbal or visual expression that has meaning to others. Human communication requires a language involving meaningful sounds or signs. The angels do not communicate in this way as they have no language and don't use words or sentences. Angels generate the thought or expression within themselves and transmit it directly as pure thought to another angel without transformations of any kind. The human brain is not equipped to accept this type of thought transfer.

The problem of the angels, then, was to develop and prepare the mental capability of the human so that direct communication between the brain and the soul could be achieved. This had to be done before the redemptive requirements could be met. The human could not receive a fully infused soul until this capability was achieved.

THE SOUL-SHARING PHASE OF DEVELOPMENT So about 121,000 years before the present time, the Age of Redemption began with a soul-sharing phase so that humans could be prepared for full infusion, eventually giving each human its own soul. Soul sharing was a preparatory phase in which selected angels infused into *groups* of humans, rather than into a single human. That is, a number of humans, initially six to twelve, would share one angel that was partially infused into each of them. The angel itself was fully infused into the group. These were cohesive groups such as families or collections of families that had common ties and homeland.

A person may wonder how one angel could infuse into a group of human individuals each of whom could meander at will, separating themselves over significant distances. It is not possible for the human to visualize how the angel accomplished this since the angel and the human exists in two distinctly different spaces. Human space is three-dimensional and geometric; *spirit space is six-dimensional* and provides angel spirits with unusual capabilities, one of which is seemingly to be in two or more places at the same time. The human mind has no basis for understanding this phenomenon and its soul cannot impart an understanding of it.

THE FLOOD OF THE SPIRIT God's Spirit fell upon the Earth to initiate the Age of Redemption and empower his chosen ones to accomplish the tasks required in his Plan. The Spirit flooded the Earth to arrest Satan's desecration of its creatures and corruption of the angels in all places, from coastal plains to the highest mountain peaks. God selected those fallen angels who had turned away from Satan's activities and had unequivocally rejected his imperial supremacy, to commission them as a group to manage the accomplishment of the soul-sharing tasks. There were only eleven of these angels in all the realm, and with Christ they were *twelve*. The Spirit filled them with knowledge and understanding of God's plan of salvation, gave them power to restrain Satan, and the power to establish his Will so that the program of redemption could proceed. Though they were ridiculed by other angels, no one on Earth could stop them or stand in their way. Through the Age of Mankind that was to come, these angels would serve as the souls for the holiest prophets and servants of God so that humanity would become enlightened with knowledge of the Creator and his laws of righteousness.

The principal angels influenced other angels who had become disillusioned and weary of following Satan and brought them into the family of select angels. Those who joined with the twelve who had been given irrepressible power numbered in the tens of thousands. Now united in Holy Purpose, they would bring about the preparations required for the soul-sharing phase so that God's Plan of Redemption could be accomplished. All other fallen angels would be prohibited from further desecrating the creatures while the Spirit weakened Satan's ability to dominate their wills. As God's Will grew in strength and scope in the trusteeship of the select angels, He slowly withdrew the Spirit from the Earthly realm so that Satan's powers to corrupt would become vanquished by those whom he had led into disobedience.

While most of the select angels offered themselves to serve as shared souls for humans, others worked to correct the undesirable characteristics which the angels had induced into many creatures through methods of husbandry. Those members of a species, male and female, which did not possess these characteristics were allowed to reproduce freely in their kind; those which had the characteristics were denied the powers of reproduction so that their kind eventually disappeared from the species. In this way, all species would lose the dominance of the corrupt characteristics introduced through Satan's practices and the purified species would replenish the Earth. In a similar manner, the select angels would replenish the multitude of fallen angels seeking a return to Heaven's Grace, requiring their willing commitment to purification before becoming souls in the blameless human hosts during the coming Age of Mankind.

State of Mankind at Start of Soul-Sharing Phase

When the soul-sharing phase began, the human was an intelligent animal who had learned to make and use very simple tools and to use his mind in a rational, cunning manner. He was a vulnerable being in his environment with which he had to contend with rather mild physical attributes. With the average life span for adults at 22-25 years, the human had little time to acquire wisdom, but he had to be mentally sharp to survive.

The human had learned to use spears, clubs and rocks to acquire and prepare food and defend himself. He had not yet invented the bow and arrow. He could use fire to cook food, warm himself or light his dwelling place, provided he discovered the fire after it was caused by lightning or lava. He had not learned to make fire on his own or use it in more advanced ways, such as making torches to light his caves or to melt ores.

Even in his advanced ways, the human did not *think* of himself as being distinctly different from other animals, although he was very much aware of important differences that made him a separate species. He knew that he must compete with them for food and supremacy, to be wary of certain species, to be vigilant and fierce, and always striving to survive in a realm where mercy was shown to no one. The strong, the quick and the resourceful were most likely to survive.

The human had learned the value of observing the behavior of other animals and mimicking elements of their instinctive actions that seemed useful or interesting to him. These activities included climbing trees and rocks, swimming, digging holes, building perches or "nests", and "flocking" to achieve protection in numbers and overcoming quarry or foe. He learned to build simple shelters by piling logs, limbs and brush together or leaning these against trees or rocks. Knowledge learned from his observations helped him to survive and gain some degree of security while inducing a fragile sense of well-being and satisfaction.

He had not developed languages, although each group had invented its own verbalizations that had specific meanings. He could keep track of certain things that required counting by making marks on the ground or rocks or cave walls. He did this by using, as needed, marks in groups of five, usually up to four groups. This coincided, not accidentally, with the five fingers and toes on his hands and feet. His counting system was thus related directly to his own attributes. He used other visual signs to inform or alert others in his group.

Humanity had not developed an appreciation of the beauty that lay all about him and in the sky, did not wonder what may lie beyond the distant mountains or across the wide seas, did not wonder about his origins or destiny. The quest for knowledge and understanding, for familiarity with his broader world and himself hadn't yet become a human pursuit. Interest in abstractions of this nature is engendered by the spirit. The coming of the spirit would begin to illuminate the unlit expanses of the human mind and fill him with curiosity about everything in his world. Until this happened, man could deal only with the abstractions that concerned the practicality of his immediate survival, cravings and well being.

This briefly reflects the state of the human condition about 120,000 years ago. All that you see in the way of human progress and attainment in the world today is a direct result of the contributions of the soul in giving Mankind the fruits of God's Intellect and Consciousness. Can we not now justly say that the angels have, as a whole, redeemed the abuse they heaped upon Humanity before the Age of Redemption?

There is much to say about the accomplishments of the angels during the soul-sharing stage, but that would fill a chapter in itself. Let us leave the discussion of the soul-sharing phase by saying that its purpose was to develop the mental capability for the soul to communicate with the brain by creating inheritable physiological factors and to introduce advancements in human awareness of self and his relationship to others and his world.

These things were accomplished by the dedicated angels in admirable fashion! Now, it was time for the angels to end the preparatory soul-sharing phase and begin the mental and spiritual development of humans so that Mankind could receive the gifts offered through God's Spirit, and each share the blessings of a soul striving to impart the gifts.

So about 86,000 years after the Age of Redemption began, humanity was prepared to enter the Age of Mankind, a period that provided the fallen angels with opportunities to redeem the misdeeds they had directed toward humanity and other creatures of Earth and return to doing the Will of their Heavenly Father.

Angels Become Irretrievably Involved with Humanity and the Material Domain

The fallen angels clothed themselves with the unsuitable circumstances of the material domain through their acceptance of Lucifer's seductive deception and their disobedience to God's entreaties to forswear them. Once the angels became involved in these activities, even those who knew it was against the Father's Will would not abandon them until they had their fill.

On Earth, as on most worlds that contain material life, creatures are interdependent, at least for their livelihood. They can establish both symbiotic and competitive relationships with various other creatures. Some creatures depend upon others as a source of food, but often are both the hunter and the hunted in the food web. Creatures were normally content to fulfill only their immediate cravings.

Humans, versatile and adaptable in a wide range of environments, were always directly dependent upon both animals and plants for sustenance. Humans were endowed with distinctive passions to enable them to feel and express their response to social incitement and to react appropriately to challenges within their environment. Passions were given to humans and all creatures so that they may thrive within their habitats in a manner that satisfies their personal and social needs. Passions are the emotional and external expressions of the inherent response to stimuli associated with self-preservation, aggression, self-regard, social and familial interactions, and sexual attraction and satiation. All of this had been established by the angels for divine purposes and does not in itself involve "sin."

When Lucifer and the angels began to interfere with the natural processes of Earth's creatures, they were interested in the activities that produced the most satisfying passions. To the angels, these became *pleasures*, and they experienced them only to share pleasure with the creatures. Using their creative abilities, the angels began to change response-stimuli factors in the creatures so as to increase the intensity and focus of the passions that pleased them most. In so doing, they deliberately distorted the animal passions and attempted to modify certain physical characteristics in some species to increase their capacity for passionate pleasure. Thus, the angels perverted their creative commissions, corrupted angelic functions and the divine intention of animal response, and diverted both themselves and the animals from God's purposes of creation.

This was clearly intentional waywardness that contravened God's Will and rejected his Love and Grace to seek, instead, pleasure and gratification at the expense of innocent creatures. In this disobedient enterprise, the angels created sin and sinfulness. They not only abused Earth's creatures through unnatural diversions and desecration, but they estranged themselves from God and Heaven.

Once the angels became contaminated with sin and desire and inclinations to continue in them, it was not possible for them to enter the Presence of God without first cleansing themselves. They must unalterably disavow their disobedient ways, rid themselves of sin's contamination, and break the desire and inclination to commit any further sinful act. They must also correct the damaging results of the abuse inflicted upon the hapless creatures, including humanity.

God imposed his Plan of Redemption to help the fallen angels accomplish these goals and seek restoration to Heaven. Many desired to do so, but felt powerless to lift themselves out of it. They had discovered that sin could provide no power or inducement for them to escape its hold and recover their heritage of love and grace. Through his plan, God provided a way for them to overcome the merciless grip of sin and become restored to Heaven's Grace. In so doing, they would be allowed to enjoy the passions of their most valued creature, the human, by becoming infused into live humans for the duration of their lives. They would become the "soul" of the human, but with a Divine purpose.

While enjoying the passions of their human host, the angel soul was also required to impart the gifts of God's Love, Truth and Consciousness into the mind of the human, to develop him intellectually and enlighten him with spirituality. Mankind could eventually reach an exalted intellectual and social state and, through spirituality, would come to know God and his Laws. In this way, the human mind could become a partner with the soul so that human and angel could progress together to achieve holiness and divinity, fulfilling God's Will for both.

5

THE AGE OF MANKIND—
INTELLECTUAL AND SPIRITUAL
DEVELOPMENT

Initial Conditions and Goals of the Early Stages

The Age of Mankind, the second and final part of the Age of Redemption, began about 35,000 years ago. At this point the soul-sharing phase had been successfully completed and each human, whose numbers had increased, would be infused with an angel to serve as its own soul. Now the soul could communicate with the human mind. Humans also had advanced culturally and technically to a remarkable degree as a result of angelic nurture. Human inventions, discoveries, and accomplishments by this time were numerous. It is not our purpose to discuss them here.

There was much to be accomplished by the angels acting as souls. There were two chief goals at this time: to accelerate the development and advancement of Mankind's *mental powers* and to induce into Mankind an *awareness of his spirit* and its values and a desire to seek God. These goals were of preeminent importance to Mankind and the angels and to God's Plan. Once Mankind discovered a spirit within himself and had a mental power to act deliberately and responsibly, he could be a partner with the soul to achieve all its goals of redemption. Through these goals, Mankind would achieve an exalted mental state reflecting the gifts of God's Spirit, and through this the angels would redeem their abuse to humanity and Earth's creatures.

Humans would become the supreme material creature on the Earth, attaining power and dominion through increasing knowledge and understanding, inventiveness and enterprise, and a capacity for discovery and exploitation. To justify his supremacy, Mankind would need to learn to be responsible, just, ethical, compassionate, charitable, and concerned for the consequences of his actions, for he will be capable of leading himself equally into great peril or blessings of mind and soul. He must learn perfection through righteousness, as Heaven is righteous and perfect.

Because the angel soul would be at the mercy of the whims and passionate drives of the human, it was imperative that the soul impart the gifts of God's spirit to moderate him and lead him steadily toward holiness; otherwise, the soul would not progress toward God. The human and the fallen angel souls would stand or fall together, depending upon the soul's resolve and continuous efforts at transforming the human intellectually and endowing him with spiritual awareness.

Mankind is humanity exalted with intellect and spirituality. The human cannot become a spiritual being because he is unalterably of material form. Yet, he can attain spiritual awareness and righteousness. This means that the human can come to know God, learn his Laws, strive to do his Will, and worship Him in love and truth. The human can learn the ways of holiness, and develop a firm resolve to abide in these things in faith and charity. He can become Divine in his personal associations by learning, doing and expressing the things of love and truth in all that he does.

These things come as gifts of God's Spirit through the angel soul. Souls teach Mankind behavior incarnating acts of love and care for everything in his world to restore Earth to Heaven's holiness. The soul also teaches him that he can become noble and divine through accepting the gifts of the spirit, that through holiness he can reach a state "just a little lower than the angels". In teaching the human these things, the soul reaps the benefit of forgiveness and redemption, thereby cleansing its record of some of the accumulated sins. In this manner, the soul can find its way, life-by-life, back to God and Heaven.

Satan's Continued Opposition to God

All of this must be done in a world still ruled by Satan who, with offended pride, feeling powerless and left out, would launch a relentless campaign to disrupt and defeat God's Plan of Redemption. He would sharpen the only tools he had remaining: his talents for seduction and deception. He would make full use of his loyal angels who were not allowed to be souls, as well as those souls that he could keep in his power to lead others astray and entrap them in guilt and shame. He knew that the human would be a weak link and he would exploit the weakness of the relationship of lost angel souls and the unprincipled humans. He challenged God with the warning that the angel soul would not abide the restrictive and depraved relationship of intimacy with the uncivilized irascible human and the hardships and constant challenges that must be endured.

Satan would unleash upon humanity two evil spirits of immense power in a determined effort to interrupt and defeat the Plan of Redemption. One of these spirits is the "beast" of death and destruction whose object is to pit man against man, tribe against tribe, and nation against nation to prevent any progress toward brotherhood and civility. The other spirit is the deceiver, or liar, whose object is to tempt Mankind into sin and disobedience and to confuse his sense of right and wrong in all things with lies and deceit. These spirits, working unceasingly together, would attempt to corrupt all good things produced through repentant angel-souls to turn them into forces of evil and devastation, and turn divinity to depravity.

These realities assured that the Age of Mankind would pose a conflict between God and Satan, between right and wrong, good and evil, and Mankind's passions and the angel's restraint. It would test the ability of Mankind and the angels *to triumph over the things that had caused the angels to fall.*

The Character of Holy Angels

As the Age of Mankind began, the angels in the Earthly realm were about to initiate a new relationship with humanity having profound importance to Mankind and to themselves. All fallen angels were Heavenly angels and, since the Father had created all angels for Divine purpose, each one is holy. God intended for their relationship to become a partnership whereby the angel soul and human host together achieve the goals of redemption, fulfilling His purpose for restoring the angels to Heaven while exalting humanity's intelligence and divinity.

Mankind can benefit from a greater knowledge of the angels whom they host as their souls. To assist in the understanding of angel character, we will summarize the inherent angelic composition and the Divine environment in which they reside.

First of all, every angel was created from the elements of the Father's Intellect and Consciousness, the very composition of the Father himself. In their creation, the Father formed vast arrays of truth structures for incorporation into each of them, so that the angels are small replicas of himself, i.e., they are created in His "image". Secondly, they reside in Heaven, where Love and Truth permeate everything and govern all that is done or made. These powers are the basis of the Laws of God by which Heaven and the Universe are created and ruled. Thirdly, the Holy Spirit, a power comprised of the Father's Love and Intellect, empowers the angels in all activities done in the Father's name. Consequently, the angels' composition, environment and empowerment represent God's own character and inspire the highest degree of aspiration, motivation and fulfillment in the angels.

Therefore, an angel is full of love, sincerity, kindness and charity, knowing that these qualities come from God and are His own characteristics. They love God and all angels; they love humanity and all creatures; they love truth and all things that are good and right. All such things are absolute quantities that come directly from God's nature and are expressed in His Will and Laws. When an angel or person clothes himself in Love, it is difficult for him to harm or wrong anyone or anything that comes from God.

Next to Love, an angel honors Truth most of all. Since angels are created from Truth and Consciousness, dishonoring Truth profanes their own being. They know that Truth comes only from God and that it is necessary for all existence. Why, then does *un*truthfulness exist? It exists because some elements of Intellect used to create angels allow for the knowledge of the opposite of Truth as well as the opposite of Love. This is part of the wisdom given to all angels at their creation so that each may have the knowledge of right and wrong. Some angels were given elements of Consciousness that allow them to have a "weakness" for adopting opposite qualities. Anti-truths can therefore be promoted if the angel comes to desire it. The nature of an angel is to be a fountain and guardian of Truth, despising and avoiding lies, deception, dishonesty, and concealing truth that others need.

An angel desires only to do the things that please their Creator. Love leads them to do good to each other and to all things that are created. They will not deliberately harm any creature, because they know that everything was created from Love out of the Father's substance. In an application of mercy an angel may perform a deed that appears to be contrary to good, but the purpose is Divine and outweighs the harm. They strive to be fully aware of God's Will, and to always do good from it. Good deeds are not done for show, but to truly benefit the recipient whether or not the latter becomes aware of the deed or the doer. Since wisdom comes from experiencing, doing good does not mean doing those things that can or should be done by another for himself; each entity should strive to be sovereign, independent and self-reliant, while sharing Love and Charity with anyone in need.

Angels have the capacity to experience and display anger, but they never harbor resentment or grudges. An angel is not vengeful, hateful or spiteful. They occasionally become angry at events, with the results from some endeavor, with ungodly behavior and even with other angels. But the causes of their anger are always rooted in good. Love will not allow their anger for another to endure for long. Anger runs its course and is forgotten and is replaced with charity and compassion. An angel who is the recipient of anger from another will seek to mollify the angered one through remedying the cause and showing affection; the one who is angered will try to close the anger and show understanding and may seek forgiveness. Their anger is never arrogant or condescending and it serves only to uphold the best of motives in fulfilling the Will of God.

An angel respects all others as much as himself. They know that every entity was created by God and has a purpose in His kingdom, which makes each one equally important and desirable. They do not consider any one to be any less than themselves, for to do so belittles the wisdom and judgement of their Creator.

From Love and Truth come the Virtues, which are the elements of holiness and divinity. From *Love* come many virtues, including charity, affection, tenderness, endearment, devotion, attachment, commitment, loyalty, adoration, worship, concern, generosity, helpfulness, respect, responsibility, and sacrifice. From *Truth* come reality, knowledge, verity, factuality, precision, accuracy, honesty, veracity, sincerity, integrity, candor, faith, righteousness, virtue, fidelity, fairness, and justice. Angels are *virtuous,* just, faithful, loyal, bold, courageous, respectful, self-sufficient, knowledgeable, cognizant, and always display these qualities with a power that comes from their supreme faith in the Righteousness of the Father.

Those who reject or resist God, by definition, oppose his good nature and the things that represent His Will. For Satan and his apostles, Love becomes hate or lust, Truth becomes lies and deception, charity becomes selfishness, kindness becomes seduction, faithfulness and loyalty become treachery, courage becomes brashness and impudence, respect becomes contempt, anger becomes resentment and vengeance. Everything they do is done to confront

God and all things that He loves with contrariness and evil. This comes from their deliberate and continuous efforts to supplant the Virtues with their opposites to defy God because they hate Him.

The anti-virtues are all malicious and destructive and constitute all sin. If they were suddenly to replace the Virtues in the Universe, life would destroy itself because Life cannot exist without Love. All that was created would degenerate, for nothing can exist without Truth. Everything comes from Love and Truth. Is it not possible now to understand why Satan and the sins that he originated are all wrong for this Universe and why *sinfulness should not be practiced or condoned?*

How, Why Angels Infuse into the Human Body

The Age of Mankind is a period in which human mental and physical capabilities would achieve extraordinary advancements. To initiate the Age, humans would be given a spiritual dimension that would awaken his mind to extraordinary powers of perception, dreams and aspirations of achievement far beyond normal human potential alone. This results from the presence of a soul within the human, an infused angel having access to God's omniscient Spirit, the source of all truth and understanding. Angels who become souls in humans retain the qualities that were given them at their creation, a condition that manifests a broad range of personalities and behavior among humanity.

People envision angels or spirits as resembling the human form. This is not so. The angel has hardly any resemblance to the human. An angel is not a human being with wings; yet, such a depiction has deep and wonderful meaning for humans, showing their intimate relationship with the angels who become souls and their potential for attaining angelic divinity through their nurture.

It is not possible for a human to see angels (spirits), but if he could, the angel would appear more like a bird. A witness to this was John the Baptist who was empowered to see the spirit that came down from Heaven to alight upon the shoulder of Jesus Christ after his baptism. It was reported to be like a snow-white dove. And that is the form an angel would resemble. The spirit or soul is invisible to the human eye and cannot be detected by any physical means within or outside the body. A spirit can project its likeness in an assumed human form to other humans, which is a vision communicated through the soul. We remember that the Holy Spirit is not a *spirit*, but is an all-encompassing spiritual *power* formed from God's Love and Intellectual powers.

We previously stated that *infusion is a physical process* that requires the spirit to enter the physical realm. The angel infuses into the body to become its soul, then re-enters the spiritual realm. The angel begins its infusion while the human is still in the mother's womb, at some point that shall never be disclosed to Mankind. The wings of this "dove" are composed of thousands of fine filaments of spiritual form, each of which become imbedded at strategic points within the developing brain and the glands and organs within the head of the human. The "tail" likewise is composed of thousands of filaments that are infused into the brainstem and the system of nerves that lead into the shoulders, down the spine and into the buttocks. Filaments from the tail are imbedded into all the glands and organs of the body, from the thyroid to the ovaries and testicles. No filaments are placed in the arms or legs, since there are no major glands or organs in these members.

When this is accomplished, the angel has become a soul for the duration of life for this person and the human will be its "host". It is not the purpose of the soul to control the human through such intimate connections, although in certain circumstances it could and does. Almost every human has some experience during his lifetime in which the soul assumes partial or total control to help him resolve a critical problem, escape a sudden, mortal danger or to keep him alive after such danger has struck him down. To accomplish such tasks, the soul must convert to the physical state through which it concentrates power in the physical body, enabling the person to accomplish extraordinary feats. Afterwards, the soul returns to the normal spiritual state.

The angel soul provides benefits that are vitally important to the development, capabilities and well being of its human host, as well as directing its spiritual growth. During development of the infant within the womb, it ensures that certain characteristics, talents and abilities are imparted as the Will of God. Beyond birth, the soul monitors all mental, neurological and physical functions and activities; it acts as a guide and conscience; it corrects and heals numerous anomalies; it attempts to direct progress of the human in the most favorable way for it to achieve life's goals; it leaks knowledge and memories from the soul into the brain to prompt recognition or familiarity with an acquaintance, situation or event from past lives; and it attempts to impart all the gifts of God's Intellect and Consciousness that have been given to this spirit to do His Will.

Holiness is directly related to human progress and the angels' redemption. The degree to which the soul strives to help the person can depend upon whether the soul is "saved" or "unsaved" and upon the human's ability and inclination to acknowledge his spiritual nature and receive blessings from it. A saved spirit directs its progress toward God and seeks His Love and Truth and will therefore benefit the human by imparting the blessings of these Divine powers. An unsaved spirit has not chosen God, is influenced by Satan and may not be inclined to help its human host, and may, instead, allow or direct it to serve the will of Satan.

To great extent humans can achieve many of the characteristics possessed and displayed by angels, which were described in a previous section. Persons who do so become angelic in their outlook and behavior. Righteous angel souls are always willing to help the human personality achieve this state. A person must understand, however, that angels do not have the interactive dependency that the human has with the material world and this presents profoundly different circumstances for behavior and attitudes. What may be appropriate for the angel may not be suitable for the human, and vice versa. Find wisdom in these messages that portray the differences between the spiritual and material domains.

Special Benefits and Gifts of Spirituality

SPIRITUALITY LEADS MANKIND TO KNOW GOD AND THE SOUL IS LED TO SALVATION   The development and advancement of Mankind's mental and spiritual powers would be continuous endeavors throughout the Age. Actually, these dissimilar undertakings are very much interrelated and would lead to a blending and marriage of the human intellect and his soul. At the point when Mankind became aware of his spirituality and began to interact with it, many benefits then became possible for both the human and the soul.

With an awareness of spirituality, the human is led through an *inspired* curiosity and desire to know God and to receive the gifts that are available from his Spirit. The human will then begin to grow in mental and spiritual stature. As he learns and applies the substance of Love and Truth he can also become Divine.

God had determined as a requirement of the angel souls, that none would become "saved" until they had endowed Mankind with an awareness of spirituality. Then souls, seeking God, could be saved. Being saved means that the spirit turns away from sin and strives to do the Will of God as directed by its inborn knowledge of the Creator. The saved soul is "anointed" with the Holy Spirit so that it can feel empowered to do good in the name of God the Father and Christ. After departing the body at death, the saved soul is received in a Heavenly state which is not Heaven itself outside the Earthly realm, but is a "half-way house" in which the saved spirit is isolated from Satan's powers and Holy Angels prepare the spirit for future life. The unsaved spirit is not taken into this Heavenly state, but remains among the lost souls in Hades in the power of Satan. The Heavenly *and* hellish states then provide the angel soul with opportunities and motivations to advance toward the goal of unequivocal salvation that restores them to Heaven's Grace.

SPIRITUAL LOVE IN HUMANS RESULTS FROM SPIRITUALITY
One of the consequences of spiritual awareness is the capability of a man and woman attracted to each other in love to know a deeper, more binding and fulfilling love than physical love alone can provide. This is Spiritual Love, given through the Holy Spirit. Spiritual and physical love could now harmonize in the relationship of a man and woman to achieve the highest fulfillment in the sharing of love. The spiritual dimension provides them a vision of their love in a setting that is exalted and eternal rather than the fleeting passions of physical love alone. When united in spiritual love God weds these two in Spiritual Matrimony, and they can enjoy all expressions of sexual love without sinning while sharing the power and beauty of its greater meaning.

Since this love is of the spirit, the mind's physiological boundaries are inadequate to appreciate it fully. Humans understand the powers and passions of physical attraction and love, but spiritual love is distinctive and must be appreciated on a different plane. When two souls are bonded in spiritual love, the human pair feels its beauty and power combined fully with its physical complement, but they have little ability to describe the feelings issuing from their souls to envelop them in the blessings of this love.

At the point when humans attained the aptitude for spiritual love God imposed his laws for sexual love, which He had reserved for this moment. *These rules allow only a man and woman who share spiritual love between them to engage in sexual love without sinning.* Only when they are joined in this bond of Holy Matrimony or through Mankind's matrimonial laws can they perform these acts with God's acceptance. *All else is adultery and perversity.*

God requires this because sexual involvement with Earth's creatures was a cardinal focus of Satan's disobedience and the cause of the angels' fall into sin. The beguiled angels sinned in sexual involvement with humans and animals before the Age of Redemption, debasing and dishonoring a holy endowment, taking it to a level of depraved pleasure without regard to its consequences and Holy purpose. As a result, God decreed that it would never again be so dishonored without sinning against His Laws. Now, when done within spiritual love, sexual love is accepted and blessed by Him and He allows its participants to seek and give the greatest joy and fulfillment from it.

NEW ANGEL SOULS ARE CREATED THROUGH SPIRITUAL LOVE   Spiritual love is also the prerequisite for God to create entirely *new* angelic beings that never existed in Heaven as original angels. Such a new entity then becomes the soul of the baby that is created through the act of sexual love. This new soul infuses into the unborn child with the help of angels, then bonds to its mother and father in order to learn the lessons of life. At its conception the new soul is without prior knowledge of life or God, but God has created it just as the other angels.

A new soul comes with purity and innocence. It is born into the lot of Mankind and the fallen angels, and must from hereon follow the same path to the end of the Age. *The new soul has no responsibility for the sins of the fallen angels and has none of their redemptive requirements for Mankind.* Souls created through spiritual love are responsible only for the debts against others and God that it incurs during life. Yet, they will contribute to Mankind's uplifting and advancement in life after life. After a few lifetimes, there may be very little difference between souls from the two origins.

God instills love and knowledge of his laws into the new soul. Yet, it knows nothing of humanity and life, which must be imparted to it through the bond with its parents and its experiences in life. The new soul cannot bond with the parents if they themselves do not have a spiritual bond of love. This is the reason that spiritual love is required for new souls to be "born".

If the infant is aborted before birth, it is as though the infant soul was cast into a sea of darkness without a compass of awareness or understanding of life or God. The things it encounters in the spirit world confuse it until angels escort it into the care of Heaven, where they prepare it for future life as an angel soul.

There is a *purpose* for God to create new angel souls on Earth and this has to do partly with the multiplying of human populations. There were initially 725 million angels enclosed within the Earthly realm. A certain number of these are not given the privilege of becoming souls. Another proportion is always in the state of death between lifetimes as free spirits.

Hence, the number available for souls at a given time is significantly less than the original number.

New souls have been created from the very dawn of human spirituality. When the human population began to equal the number of original angels available to become souls, God allowed new souls to be created freely whenever the man and woman shared a spiritual bond of love. He did not wish to limit the world population of Mankind to this availability, so that basically his populations can grow without bounds until the Earth's ability to sustain them sets its own limits.

Mankind must become conscious of this reality and his own limitations and act responsibly to restrain his numbers. The human population has already *surpassed by twofold* the numbers that would provide an ideal balance between Earth's resources, environmental preservation and his abilities to attain the highest quality of life in an advanced ideally developed civilization. Continuing growth only takes him further away from this ideal and increases the risks of catastrophic decline.

At some point during the latter Middle Ages, human population increased so that the number of newly created souls equaled, then exceeded, the availability of original angels. By the close of the eighteenth century, the world was becoming progressively influenced by a population whose souls are predominantly without a direct knowledge of Heaven's culture. Only the original angels have had a direct link to Heaven where they incessantly honored the *absolute authority* of God's laws of righteousness. The relative proportion and influence of the Spirituality of the original angels have become greatly diminished by population growth.

Some newly created souls may display aversion to the absolute importance of moral virtue and an ambiguity in choices between right and wrong. Some may more readily embrace what is wrong or evil instead of favoring what they know to be morally right. Without a return to Spirituality that places a priority on the moral laws of love and righteousness over expediency, the world could degenerate toward a Godless condition. During Christ's Millennium of reign God will introduce all righteous souls to the things of Holiness through a baptism of Heavenly Light.

Today the number of newly created souls far outstrips the number of original angels. Whenever the Age of Redemption ends and all saved souls re-enter Heaven, there will consequently be perhaps three to four times the number of angels in the galaxy as when the Age of Mankind began. This increase will pose no problem for God, but will be a joy to all of Heaven. The

Father and Christ will have assignments in Heaven for each and everyone, either in this galaxy or another. Such is the greatness of the power and Love and Grace of God that not a single one will escape His notice, but all will be honored and awarded the gifts of Heaven's grace!

God also has reasons that are important and beneficial to the spirit to create new angel souls. The new souls give inspiration and hope to the fallen angels who can, once again, behold angels of pristine purity unstained by disobedience and sin. For awhile, they can see in a new soul a vision of the character that can be restored within them.

The new soul is without defiance and disobedience to God's laws and, in life, will restrain the desire of the fallen soul to disregard His laws of love and morality, helping them to avoid the sinful pitfalls. For a few lifetimes the new soul may be a beacon of Light to help guide the lost soul along the pathway back to the gates of God's Kingdom. Soon, alas, the new soul will begin yielding more freely to temptations to disobey and to partake of worldly appetites. Like the innocent young sister who soon falls under the sway of the experienced older sister, the new soul learns that it can reap rewards of pleasure and, perhaps, fortune by "loosening up". They then travel this road together, becoming each others watchdog and critic, one restraining the behavior of the other while both compete for the prizes of desire.

The Growth of Spirituality in Mankind

RECOGNIZING THE SPIRIT'S POWER A major impact of the soul was the growth of spirituality in the human which began when the first unborn infants received their own souls. A *solid* awareness of spirituality had taken hold in Mankind by 26,000 years ago. From that point, it began to have extraordinary effects in all that he did. His mind expanded with awareness and appreciation of life. Civilizations began to bloom like the flower at the end of its stem.

Life was unencumbered and Mankind had time and opportunity to commune with that feeling inside of him. He could see God everywhere: in all that grew, in the beauty or whimsical violence of nature, in the heavens with its brilliant Sun and starry skies, and in his expanding ability to create things with and from his surroundings. Spirituality became a powerful and important force in the lives of Mankind everywhere. Many came to worship a god that seemed to be in all the natural things around them; some thought this god lived in the sky and watched them from hiding places above the clouds; some thought he lived in the ground or in the seas; some looked upon their mighty rulers as deities. Some believed the brilliant Sun to be a god.

Satan and his forces were not asleep and they put many obstacles and pitfalls in Mankind's paths, always striving to corrupt his spiritual progress and set human against human, to undo any good that had been done. Satan tries to corrupt and abuse Mankind through his soul. Whether in life or death, unsaved souls are easily influenced by Satan. Such souls communicate with other souls and can tempt even saved souls to do things that Christ would not approve. Some characteristics given by the Creator to humans and other creatures to benefit their survival in an interactive material world are used by Satan as weaknesses through which he can tempt members of Mankind. Through temptation, deception and seduction he feeds self-indulgent appetites which reinforces the souls' inclination to remain in sin.

DEVELOPMENT OF RELIGION   Throughout the period of development of spirituality in Mankind, the angels must abide within the state of their human host, both individually and collectively, whether that involves enlightened civilization or barbarism. The angels endeavor to impart knowledge and understanding of God's Will to the human mind. It is difficult for the mind, whose awareness involves basically material concepts, to perceive that the spirit is also vital to his existence. Spiritual things are perceived as material concerns, and vice versa, which can lead to a pall of myth and irrelevance.

Consequently, many religions sprang up in various places, each of which had some elements of belief and practice that accurately represented aspects of true spirituality and God. These truths were imparted by the angel soul. Basically, all religions postulate a deity from which flow power and mystical truths. Some believe that the deity is a trinity consisting of a father, mother and son. Most believe in the attainment of eternal life, and a hereafter in some sort of enhanced or purified state, or perhaps eternal punishment. Some believe that their deity is capable of extraordinary feats and they can dispense both reward and punishment. Some believe that unlimited blessings can flow from their deity. Above all, the deity is the creator of everything and the giver of life.

All such beliefs result from the soul's attempt to impart knowledge of the true nature of God. Unenlightened humanity combined all sorts of material perceptions, including superstition and symbolic objects, into his spiritual or religious precepts. Even the "pagan" religions, debased as they may seem, were attempts to discover, define and worship God in their skewed perception of

Him in ways that intimately affected all aspects of their lives. Since few achieved holiness, it was easy for Satan to inject his own notions into religious beliefs and practices, resulting in distorted and corrupted worship of the deity. Humans had *externalized* their religion and perceived their religious experiences as emanating and controlled from outside rather from *within* themselves.

It is through the weakness and haze of the mind's connection with the spirit that none of mankind's religions would ever accurately represent God unless He intervened to teach them. This is why God would eventually develop a "chosen people" that He could instruct in His laws and ways, and evolve a righteous relationship with them. With this preparation, the chosen people could become a nation of greatness and righteousness to teach all peoples about the true God. An exemplary nation, such as God attempted to make of Israel, was sorely needed for God to teach all of humanity just who He was, what He was like and what their relationship to Him is, or should be.

For almost thirty millennia God has raised up many spiritual leaders to whom He gave knowledge and insight so that they could instruct the people in His ways. These included patriarchs, priests, preachers and prophets. They organized the people in small groups or families and communities to honor the way of God in all they did. These lived at diverse places over the Earth, not only in the lands of the near-east, thousands of years before the Books of the Bible began to describe the "chosen people."

When the books of the Holy Bible began to be developed, the deeds of the seekers and followers of God were recorded by those who had invented written languages and had learned to express their knowledge and insight. Thus was recorded the diverse experiences of a consecrated people's quest to know and understand the One and True God, for they had been led by Him to do so. In these writings we have been given a vision of God's existence and supreme powers, His Laws for Mankind, His concern for the conditions and moral behavior of all human creatures and those who are placed in charge of nations. We came to know of God's stern laws, His love and demands for obedience and loyalty, and certain justice for those who act against his Will.

God had not yet revealed His best side to Mankind, because He must first mold him into an enlightened being who would care to know God in His fullness. This time was coming and His prophets began to foretell of a glorious Son of God who would come into the world to save and claim his chosen people.

Throughout thousands of years Mankind was being prepared for the approaching end of the Age of Mankind, and the soul for the end of the Age of Redemption. There was still much for them to know and understand so that the soul and mind of every person may unite in common purpose. Together, they can achieve victory over the power of sin, and perfection through the gifts of God's Spirit and a new understanding of their Divine relationship.

The time had come, two thousand years ago, for God to send His firstborn Son to live among Mankind and teach him the true nature of God, to lay claim to the redeemed fallen angels and the newly created souls in the Name of the Father. His mission would include preparing all of Mankind further for the end of the Age. Proclaiming "The Kingdom of God is at hand", he would invite everyone to come into the Heavenly home of God. As their *teacher*, his messages and actions would show them the way.

If God's chosen people accepted him as the Messiah, Jesus could establish his Kingdom of Love, Law and Light through which he could prepare *all* the world for the end of the Age. If they rejected him, God would end his reliance upon Israel and would take his case directly to the world at large. God would redeem Israel through the sacrifice of the Lamb of God, then resurrect him to demonstrate his supreme power over the forces of darkness and death. *Resurrection* would assure the world that Christ is the *living* Messiah whose Presence leads the Church that was established through the apostles and the Holy Spirit. This Earthly mission would prepare humanity for Christ's thousand-year reign of righteousness through which he would complete the development of spirituality in Mankind in all nations, so that the purpose of the Age of Redemption could be fulfilled.

The Ten Commandments

The Ten Commandments are the centerpiece of God's attempt to direct Israel's attention upon Him as the One True God and teach them his Laws of Righteousness. The commandments specify acts of behavior that should not be committed to avoid sinning against God and fellow humans. They are rules of conduct based on love and respect, for they direct behavior expected of people having loving and charitable hearts, desiring peace and good will. A person following these rules will become righteous and just, worshiping God as his Creator and the Giver of all good things. For Israel, the rules would establish their national laws through which they could reject idolatrous, malevolent behavior among themselves and in dealing with their neighbors, while increasing in Divine Wisdom and Love.

Given to Israel through Moses after coming out of Egypt, the command-ments established the crucial framework to mold them into the exemplary chosen nation of righteousness in the "promised land" of their heritage and destiny. After four hundred years of life in a land that had many gods and idols, whose laws were whatever the pharaohs proclaimed them to be, the Israelites found the restrictive commandments difficult to abide and they became rebellious. After serving in slavery to the Egyptians for so long a time, they preferred to celebrate their lives free from all masters. God considered it necessary for them to wander in the wilderness so that the disobedient generation could fade from the scene of life while the new generations under the priesthood of Aaron learned to accept and respect the commandments as their national laws. The obedient Israelites could then settle in the lands that had been promised to Abraham and begin to grow into the exemplary nation of God's purpose.

From the commandments were established the instructions, regulations and codes that formed the social and religious standards of Israel as a nation of righteousness. In time, the commandments also became the moral basis of law and justice for Western civilization. Without obedience to such codes of behavior, order and civility would not emerge and Mankind would not progress toward dignity and morality. Through the commandments, humans manifest love and respect for each other and for laws of righteousness and justice, thereby achieving harmony with the redemptive concerns of his soul.

The Ten Commandments do not establish a *religion*, nor are they restricted to mere religious matters. Rather, the Commandments serve as the foundation for civility and progress in all endeavors of humanity. Without these codes and Mankind's acceptance and advocacy of them, humanity would advance little above the animals of the field and forest. With them, it becomes possible for humanity to attain exalted states of intellectual and spiritual progress. The Commandments have made it possible for God to achieve the purposes of the Ages of Humanity and Redemption. Therefore, they should not be regarded as peculiar maxims of an ethnocentric religion, but as a gift to all Mankind from the Spirit of God for the uplifting of individuals and *all elements of society. Everyone* benefits from them.

Moral and Natural Law

Law, in its most fundamental form, issues from God and He is its sole and ultimate authority. Since the Universe is exclusively and inclusively spiritual and material, Law also has *two forms*. Moral Law pertains to all things spiritual and relates to discretions of the intellect. Natural law pertains to the physical universe alone and cannot be used to assess the nature and dynamics of the spiritual domain. There are bodies of circumstantial law that combine principles of natural and moral law, including some ethical standards. Intelligent entities in both the spiritual and material domains are subject to the moral *and* natural laws of God.

Natural law is the total set of constraints that define all possibilities for actions and reactions, causes and effects, in the material domain. Natural law establishes all *possibilities* and restrains action to abide within the possibilities. Natural law is *not* an option of choice and is not a matter of being right *or* wrong. Nothing in the material domain can escape the restraints of natural law. Like Moral Law, natural law is derived from God's Truth. Everything under natural law is rational because *truth* is rational and nothing that is irrational can take place in the physical worlds.

Natural law is absolute and it remains inviolate for all material creations whether animate (living) or inanimate (inert). These qualities of natural law assure that all physical action is consistent, repeatable and predictable for *everything* in the material domain.

Moral Law is the total set of constraints that define behavior of all that is subject to God's inherent laws of righteousness that are also absolute. Moral Law is germane to all *intelligent life* in the material and spiritual domains. Love and Truth are constraints of Moral Law, and *morality* is this law executed with charitable concern for life and the quest for truth in all things. Within the domain of Moral Law, there is perception of both right and wrong so that both *morality* and *immorality* can exist side by side as options of choice.

Intelligent material and angelic beings are endowed with the *capacity* to be moral or immoral from their knowledge of both right and wrong. Because of their abilities to act as self governing agents in their domains, intelligent beings are given the quality of sovereignty, which requires an ability to discriminate freely between possible options for doing right or wrong. This quality bestows upon them the power and ability to create or destroy, to enhance or desecrate, to honor or disrespect. It was never intended that any entity would choose to do wrong, but this discernment was given *so that* wrongful behavior and its baleful consequences could be avoided.

Immorality is disobedience of God's laws of love and a disregard for truth. Immorality neglects love and seeks to satisfy itself for its own sake, not for the benefit of the one who indulges in it. It inevitably leads to corruption, destruction and the darkness of rejecting God's fellowship. Therefore, immorality carries *within itself* the consequences of separation from God and condemnation for its advocates. It will soon destroy any hopes for exalted fellowship with God and can only be escaped through unmitigated repentance and a search for salvation to return the entity to a state of Morality.

The Supreme Being created the Universe to be moral. All *immorality is forbidden* because it is contrary to the Creator's Supreme Purpose and to the virtues of morality. Therefore, its rewards cannot come from the same Creator who honors Love and Truth above everything. Since immorality disdains such things, its rewards must come from its own corruption, and, since corruption cannot persist in the presence of God, it and all who are unalterably stained by it must be destroyed. For one who strays into immorality, the Grace and Mercy of God will always provide the wisdom and opportunity to turn back into the ways of morality.

The remedy for the destructive and corruptive effects of immorality is repentance, followed by redemption and cleansing. But immorality does not within itself provide the capacity to do this and the entity must somehow find a bridge to Morality wherein does lie the power of love and redemption. That bridge is built when one recognizes that he is sinful or immoral and acknowledges his immorality to himself and to God, then turns away from it with supplications for forgiveness and redemption. Then he reaches the shore of *salvation* from which he can be restored to Morality.

Morality is an expression of one's love for God's laws of righteousness and a rejection of disobedience. Choosing Morality confirms one in fellowship with God, the Creator. Morality is the only choice that can restore and retain one in eternal fellowship with God. Immorality has no connection with anything that issues from God and will invariably lead to darkness and death. Morality makes good enduring relationships possible. Law gives order and constancy to all possibilities.

The Judeo-Christian Concept of God Is Right for the World

The infusion of spirituality into the intellectual concerns of humanity led humans to recognize the presence of some power beyond them that they could not see, hear or feel. Yet, they *knew* that something was there and that they should acknowledge it in some way. This led to the development and practice of rudimentary religions and eventually to elaborate ritual ceremonies that included "priests" or "holy ones" who were thought to have the power to commune with the unseen god. God intervened to teach chosen ones that He was the true God so that they may learn the truth about him and his desires for humanity. This began to direct religion toward Divinity and righteousness.

The foremost religions of the world and their many derivatives result from humanity's search for spiritual knowledge and guidance and comes from the soul's impartation of spiritual awareness. Throughout the Age, God has enlightened receptive human minds around the world with Spiritual truths. Yet, only with few exceptions, they do not represent the true God who must be acknowledged as the Creator of all that is in the Universe, the Source of Love and Truth and the Giver of Life.

Most religions have contributed much to the development of sublime thought and behavior, and have taught many beneficial things such as selflessness, charity, tranquility, meditation and other spiritual values. Some have become corrupted through emphasis on self-promotion and glorification, mysticism, witchcraft, sorcery, hedonism and other such perversions. Such ideas did not come from God. Some have thought that God is vengeful and terrible in his wrath and uses believers as tools of suppression and reprisal; but God does not seek revenge. God *seeks Justice through redemption and shows Mercy to the repentant.* He corrects the unrepentant so that they can experience the results of their own wickedness to soften their hearts and win them to his kingdom.

Abraham, Isaac and Jacob are forefathers of Semitic nations from whom God chose the twelve tribes to establish an exemplary nation of righteousness based on a knowledge and practice of His Laws and Ways. It is on behalf of all the world, for the sake and benefit of all people that God chose and created Israel for this purpose. His supreme purpose was to bring the world to a knowledge, understanding and acceptance of Him as the One True God, for the redemption and salvation of all souls.

Through almost two millennia, God raised leaders, priests and prophets in Israel who were instruments of His Will. As a result, Israel has portrayed to the world the idea of One God and knowledge of His Laws. Then He sent Christ, His Son, to complete the portrayal with Love and Truth and the promise of eternal Life. This assembly of beliefs, teachings and traditions represent a promising unification of the religions of Jew and Christian and the multitudes of both Jew and Arab, whose religion shares the laws and teachings of the Pentateuch, who consider that Abraham, the chosen of God, is the father of their nation. God has given this book to amplify and extend these beliefs to Jews, Christians and Muslims, and to all worshippers of the Divine.

Through these beliefs and the truths given here, all humanity can find what they seek, what their souls strive to impart, what is true and righteous, what will lead them to God's Kingdom. This is the one true religion that should replace all others and result in a Spiritualism that unifies humanity and connects them spiritually and intellectually with the Creator, of whom there is no equivalent.

There must be no intolerance or coercion directed toward anyone who is reluctant to accept these things. *All must accept God's grace and a return to his Kingdom through their own free will and desire to do so.* God's Love, Mercy, and Patience surpass the impatient zeal of Mankind. There shall be a time for all who will to believe.

6

GOD'S GIFT OF CHRIST HIS SON TO MANKIND

Jesus Christ Came to Consummate the Age of Redemption

The Old Testament prophets and priests taught about God and His Laws as given to them through visions and insight through the Holy Spirit. They portrayed God as an all-powerful, all-knowing, stern, sometimes jealous and vengeful, but caring Being who had created everything that exists. They taught that God's Law is supreme, over everything, even Life. And, indeed, it is, for nothing could have been created without Law. Yet, when applied to Life, Law must be applied through Love. To them, the Law was applied for its own sake, requiring submission and unyielding obedience and punishment or death for the disobedient.

The apostle John proclaimed in his Gospel that God sent His Son into the world because He loved the world and wanted to redeem all who would believe in Him. Thus, He sent Christ to be born among Mankind, to become flesh and experience life as a man and, through a Divine ministry, provide a fresh, new message centered on Love and Law. Jesus frequently stated that his messages were of the Heavenly Father and all of his teachings were the things the Father had taught him.

John states in John 1:17 that "the *law* was given by Moses, (but) *grace and truth* came through Jesus Christ". Christ was sent into the world, not just to fulfill the Law and prophesies, but to complete what God had ordained for Mankind in fulfillment of redemption for the fallen angels. As Christ had required that the fallen angels become souls in human beings to achieve redemption, Christ became the soul in a human so that he may *fully experience the human condition of life and death*. He came with a mission to assure all repentant souls that their ordeal will soon end and they can be restored to the Kingdom of Heaven where there *is no spiritual darkness or death.*

Jesus hoped to prepare Mankind to become harmonious partners with God through their spirits, or souls. He taught them the supremacy of love and truth, that Law comes from these, and that Law administered with Love is important to Life. Jesus taught that God is loving, kind, patient, merciful and forgiving and that Mankind should strive to be the same to his fellow man and in his relationships with God.

Yet, his teachings and claims of Divine origin would be received with great difficulty by the strict advocates of Mosaic Law. The Jewish leaders— Pharisees, Sadducees, and teachers of the law—taught and sternly administered law without due regard to Love or Life. Their unyielding zealousness for the law would lead them to the implausible contradiction of extolling their devotion to God's Law while rejecting and executing His Son sent to enlighten and save them.

Sinners such as adulterers and blasphemers should be put to death at the hands of the believers under Jewish laws. Jesus taught that Love is higher than the law of Moses and that such sinners could be forgiven and *redeemed.* To the pious Jews, this was an unaccustomed slant and would be difficult for them to heed since there seemed to be little leeway to accommodate such things in the practice of their law. Mercy, compassion, forgiveness and redemption were hardly mentioned among the restrictive rules for administering justice for the transgressor. Failure to enforce any dictum of the law was unacceptable and advocacy of such could be taken as heresy.

Since the world beyond Judaism would not accept the strict rule of Jewish religion, it could not be used as the means to spread God's kingdom over them. Jesus taught a *new* message that, although rejected by *pious* Jews, would be accepted by *unorthodox* Jews, Gentiles and pagans of the world beyond Israel. Thus, his ministry would be directed from the very start toward the world at large.

The ministry of Jesus Christ was a beginning of his reaching out to all people. Such intentions had been expressed by his prophets centuries earlier. Later, his death would signal the end of God's attempt to make Israel the chosen exemplary nation that God had nurtured from Abraham and his descendants. Rejection and death of Jesus at the hands of the misguided orthodox Jews would resolve the accounts with Israel and begin a new campaign to make all the world his chosen people. Through his message of love and redemption, God would offer salvation and the promise of greatness through righteousness to all nations. God's plan to make Israel the exemplary nation succeeded to the point that the prophets and priests of the Jews gave to the world the idea that God was the One and True god, and gave us his Laws for righteous and just living. Though they rejected his Son, *they led us to know God.*

In his ministry, Jesus walked among the masses of humanity, attending to their needs for hope, love, charity, and relief from burdens of oppression and misery. He tried to show that one is not saved by strict adherence to every factor of the law, but through faith and love and God's grace. Meanwhile, the pious, lofty protectors and administrators of Jewish law isolated themselves behind the marble walls of the temple in Jerusalem. Jesus often taught in the synagogues and in the vicinity of the great temple. He entered the Temple to teach those who would listen and to rebuke the mighty for their arrogance and vehement self-righteousness. Through this, he was trying to teach them the truth that came from the Father, which the authorities summarily rejected.

A primary goal of his teaching was to win the minds and hearts of the priests and teachers and leaders of the Jews. Otherwise he would not be accepted as the Messiah and could not become their "king" to lead them into becoming the pre-eminent nation of righteousness.

An equally great work of the Father lay outside the Temple in the streets, at the city gates, in the villages and on the hillsides. It was anywhere someone was suffering trials of the mind, body or spirit, yearning for Love, Truth and Life. There were many to be healed of hopelessness and infirmities of body and mind and to be *shown* that God loved them and that each one, no matter how lowly and powerless, was important to him.

Christ's purpose was not to save Mankind, for God *will* save Mankind. Christ came to save the angel that is the soul in every person. John 6:63 (NIV) quotes Jesus as saying, "The Spirit gives life; the flesh counts for nothing. The words I have spoken to you are spirit! and they are life." *His messages are of the spirit and were presented to bring the mind into accord with the needs of the angel soul.* Christ also admonished his followers not to fear those who can only kill the body but cannot harm the eternal spirit (soul). The mind must be receptive and obedient to the counsel of the spirit so that both may be led to God. Realizing that this was basic essence of Jesus' teachings, one may find greater clarity and meaning in his words.

All souls must be brought to salvation and righteousness in order to bring humanity to the fullness of intellectual and spiritual maturity. Without this *priority*, humanity could grow intellectually *without* the Divine guidance of the Spirit. Then the world could become a Godless, tumultuous sea of discord, driven only by self-indulgent and uncharitable purposes. A world without God is without Spiritual guidance and Divine purpose and its inhabitants have no hope for anything higher than themselves and the things of the world. Life itself has no meaning or purpose and it is valued only for shallow materialistic concerns. The Spirit of God brings Love, Truth and Beauty and the promise of Heavenly things which can be attained through faith and enterprise.

Insights into the Life Events of Jesus Christ

SOME QUALITIES OF INCARNATION AND BIRTH. Christ was incarnated as a human being, born of a pure and blameless maiden, so that he may experience life and project the authority of Messiah as a member of Mankind. From this came understanding and empathy for the human condition. Divine conception gave him extraordinary powers of perception and sensitivity so that he could fully measure and assess his own feelings as well as those of any person. In this way he was able to experience the misery and pains, the hopes and losses, the faith and despair, the joys and happiness, the love and concerns, the fear and rejection, the anger and hatred, and all passions of any person that he encountered. Through such powers of acute sensitivity, he shared the passions of others from whatever cause. Through these qualities, directed by love and concern for all humans, he acquired an extraordinary empathy and understanding that was crucial to his ministry of love and the Good Shepherd.

Most certainly Jesus Christ was a flesh and blood mortal, like any human being. Yet, unlike any human who ever lived or who ever shall live until he comes again, Jesus was unique due to his soul being the Christ angel. He was born with a Divine mission, a holy purpose that was given to bring the Father's Will once again upon the Earth.

Jesus Christ was born to be Messiah to *all humanity*, not only to the Jews, but to the Jews *first*. His messiahship was dependent upon acceptance by the Hebrew nation, from ruling council to the common person. These are the people that God created and chose to redeem the world, but they must yet approve him by accepting the messages Jesus brought from the Father. If the Jews would not accept him as their Teacher and the promised Messiah, then they must reject him. In this event, he would instead become the unblemished sacrificial lamb to die on an altar for the atonement of their disobedience and sins.

A sacrificial death would not terminate his Divine purpose, but would extend it beyond the Jews because his *resurrection* would recreate him as the *living Messiah.* No power on Earth could abrogate this purpose and deny Christ his commission to become the Messiah to lead all of humanity into the love of God. Jesus' messiahship was accepted by his disciples and the apostles who went forth throughout the Roman world to establish his Church, whose every member also knew and accepted Jesus Christ as the Messiah and Redeemer.

JESUS, THE FATHER'S DIVINE MESSENGER, was born of parents and within a family environment that assured a righteous orientation and familiarity with the Torah and Jewish law. The parents were also dedicated to the fulfillment of the promises given to them by Holy Angels before he was born. Therefore, his training in Jewish religious and social traditions began at an early age.

Throughout youth and manhood, he was intellectually receptive to the voice of his Christ soul and the Divine teachings which it imparted. By the start of his ministry, Jesus was in full possession and understanding of the Father's messages of Love and Truth and their applications to law, life and the needs and aspirations of humanity. This preparation enabled him to perceive and evaluate the motivations and the personal and social inclinations of any person. The whole of society and its congealed bustle were presented to him like a painting in which no detail was lacking. All that was *good,* all that was *stagnant,* and all that was *evil* stood forth in his mind like an all-inclusive tapestry.

In John 3:16, we are told that "…God so loved the world that He gave his only begotten Son, that whosoever believes in him shall not perish, but shall have everlasting life." Indeed, Christ came into the world as a human being *of his own free will* in order to make perfect the Father's Plan of Redemption for the fallen angels. Knowing the options that would face him, Christ came as the Executor of the Father's plan so that he could know fully the effects of living in mortal flesh which he had required of the fallen angels who sought redemption and salvation. Christ could then stand *blameless* with the host of angels before the Father as witnesses on the final day. Satan's accusations were therein rendered baseless and futile and he was left powerless before the judgement of God.

By the time Jesus reached the final months of his ministry, he had seen the multitudes of people who followed him and gathered wherever he stopped to preach and knew that most of them would eagerly accept him. Among the crowds were those who sought to trip him up with attempts to cause him to contradict his own teachings and knowledge of the scriptures. He knew they represented a serious obstacle to his Messiahship because they belonged to the fellowship of priests and teachers who had come to misrepresent the Word of God. These must be convinced of the need to examine their convictions in the light of his messages. Yet, they became increasingly resistive and antagonistic toward him as time passed. Jesus began to realize now that he must confront the priesthood with a major effort to open their minds to the Father's truths by pointing out the errors of their beliefs and practices.

Nearing the end, Jesus placed himself at the center of the struggle and raised the flag of Divine Truth knowing that it would be challenged and attacked by these defenders of the status quo. He presented himself to the high priests in the exact image of the foretold messiah, and contrasted, with argument, that with what *they* had come to represent. He hoped they would see how far they had gone from righteousness and justice to being mere heartless, hypocritical administrators of the law. They had become tyrants without compassion and vision. Jesus knew that if he could not win this victory over their minds that his mission was lost and that death would be his reward. Now, his teachings and arguments would pierce to the very source and core of the problem.

Herein is a puzzle. These members of the priesthood had allowed the inimical Satan to lead them astray due to their penchant for self-indulgences. Christ did not attack Satan directly, but aimed his challenge at the holiest citadel of the Jewish priesthood because they had departed the intent of God. He entered the Great Temple to teach and discuss the Father's love in the domicile of the high priests and teachers of the law. Why? He did so because hypocritical self-righteousness is more abominable and formidable than outright sin. A sinner appears to God as a wolf, while the self-righteous hypocrite is a wolf wearing a cloak of sheep's wool in order to appear righteous before men and God. It is a farce that blinds and impedes the righteous person more so than sin. Sin tweaks the conscience with guilt; self-righteousness and hypocrisy *ease* the conscience with self-satisfaction. The sinner can see his wrongs and repent; the other does not because he thinks he is perfect. Which one is easier to bring to salvation?

Jesus inaugurated his ministry at the age of thirty, signified by baptism by John the Baptist in the River Jordan. His ministry had many purposes: to discover and strengthen the good in the mass of humanity around him and give it Divine purpose; to enliven stagnated and hopeless lives and give them meaning and renewed hope; to turn evil persons to repentance and righteous ways; to give the law a renewed foundation of truth and to administer it with charity and wisdom; to win over the Jewish power centers with messages and arguments from his teachings and lead them into a zeal for *enlightened* righteousness. Through these things he would gather all Jews, both common and powerful, into a unity of purpose that had already been offered to the Chosen Nation.

Jesus did not come to lead a rebellion against Roman authority or the Jewish rulers, but to institute the authority of God's Word and fulfill his promises of Messiahship. Through the power of love and righteousness that would diffuse throughout the nation of Israel, Jesus Christ would lead them into becoming the pre-eminent nation of God's promise to Abraham, to fulfill the Word that assures redemption and salvation to every person and to every nation. The new nation of Israel, enlightened by Jesus' messages of love, truth and law, would become the Light of the world, a source of Divine wisdom through which all nations *would* be led to God.

REJECTION OF JESUS BY THE JEWISH AUTHORITIES   Initially, rejection was not aimed at Jesus personally, but at his messages. The Jewish authorities wished only that he would go away and keep quiet. Since he would not do this but delivered many messages in the synagogues and *the temple*, Jesus became an object of rejection along with his messages. Since he would not be quiet, he must be silenced by whatever means was necessary. Rejection of the Father's messenger was, in effect, a repudiation of God's plans and hopes to make of Israel an exemplary nation of righteousness. It was the antithesis of his intentions, expectations and desires for the life and ministry of Jesus.

Success of God's plan required the acceptance of Jesus as the Messiah by the Jewish centers of power, in particular the Sanhedrin, which was composed of the high priests and teachers of the law. The people of Israel could not rise above these leaders whom they had been taught to respect and obey above all else. These leaders held the destiny of the Jews in their hands through knowledge and the power of the law. These authorities were the interpreters, protectors and administrators of Jewish law and held it to be supreme and inviolate. Their zeal and jealousy for the law became a passion, almost a worship of the law through which they failed to understand that the *law is a servant of love and a companion of truth*. Thereby, they had broken the link with God's Spirit. Rejection of Jesus was a disavowal of God's Promise to Israel and a commitment to law for the sake of law without the consideration of Divine love that redeems and renews all who break the law of God.

THE TRIAL AND DEATH OF JESUS.   Jesus persisted in opposing the religious authority knowing the consequences could lead to the cross. Through this result he would experience the extreme demands of courage and suffering that would also face his apostles in later years. Just moments before his arrest, Jesus committed himself completely to the Father's Will, signifying that *he* would do nothing on his own behalf to change the opinions that would soon determine his fate.

The arrest of Jesus was a spontaneous but premeditated act without proper warrant of charges. The charges brought by the instigators to justify his arrest and trial were baseless and malicious. There was no pretrial hearing to determine the validity of the charges and the extent of guilt. He was not offered the services of an attorney nor was he granted time to draft arguments or gather witnesses that could be used in his defense. His accusers were also not specifically identified, yet he knew from whence they came and understood completely their desires and motives. And his trial did not take place in a court of law.

As Jesus stood accused before either Jewish or Roman authorities, the charges were never formally made and no credible evidence was presented to justify them. The charges that the priests uttered to the *Roman* governors were insufficient to convince them that he was guilty of a punishable offense under Roman law. Yet, fear of the threat of Jewish resistance and uprising that could be instigated by the Jewish leaders held the Romans in a compromising grip. They would comply with the wishes of the instigators to maintain peace and stability in the city and province.

While before the chief priest, Pilate or Herod, Jesus offered no defense of himself because it was Divine Will that the outcome of the trial be determined solely by *human will.* There were those standing nearby in the courts witnessing the trials who could have saved Jesus. Just one witness would suffice for Pilate to release him to the priests, who would not execute him for fear of the crowds. Jesus' silence was an invitation for them to step forward and speak in his defense. No one came forward, and the silence condemned him to the rule of the mob that seized the trial and brought an end to the rule of reason. The failure of Herod and Pilate to find any reason to punish Jesus placed his *condemnation* squarely in the hands of the high priests who required his death.

Pilate washed his own hands of responsibility because he did not acquiesce in the mob's verdict.

The high priests knew exactly what they wanted and would not accept any verdict other than guilty. They could not muff this opportunity to rid themselves of this challenge to their power and influence and were determined to see it accomplished. They used a paid mob as jury to denounce Jesus and demand his execution. Even while the mob was still seething and the hands of Pilate were still damp from his symbolic cleansing, Jesus was being led to the site of his death. His conviction and sentence of death must be carried out before the sleeping city of Jerusalem knew what was going on and certainly before his friends could be marshaled to come to his defense. And most definitely he must be dead and his body put away before the advent of the Passover Sabbath so that his accusers could go into the temple to pray and worship God in penance and piety.

Now that the Jewish power brokers had repudiated God's *final* efforts to consummate his plans to make Israel the pre-eminent chosen nation of righteousness through their rejection of Jesus as the Messiah, death became the appropriate sacrifice for their redemption. There was much to be re-deemed for the Jewish nation.

In the 2100-year long program to raise a nation from one chosen man and establish the descendants in the Promised Land as the Chosen Nation, the tribes of Israel had committed many wrongs against God, their neighbors, and some of their own people. Their sins began at the moment of their treachery and looting in Shechem and later when their jealous rage led them to throw their brother Joseph into the pit and sell him into slavery. Their sins were protracted in rebellions against God, in wars of destruction and rape of neighbors, and in appropriation of lands and wealth without just compensa-tion. Now their sins had come to a focus of self-righteous arrogance and killing of the innocent in the name of God.

They had done these things while God attempted to teach them his laws and mold them into an exemplary nation in the land of his promise, from which would flow the power and righteousness of God's Grace. It was out of their reluctance and stubbornness, their refusal to be led by laws of holiness that they sinned against God and their neighbors. Yet, they did all this in the name of God and under his hand as he attempted to lead them into fulfillment of his promise to Abraham, for the sake of the ultimate salvation of the world.

Therefore, God accepted their sins as his own and claimed responsibility for their transgressions. For this, *He* would pay the price of redemption.

All such sins against God and humanity require redemption through acts of compensation and charity. Redemption follows repentance. God would turn away from helping Israel because they followed their own misguided wilfulness into sin. The signification of repentance for the Jews was the ritual sacrificing of an unblemished lamb and the spilling of its blood upon an altar so that all may see their guilt for which they would seek forgiveness and salvation. In this sign the fact of their sins is symbolized in the spilled blood, an act presented in their behalf and in which all partook for their salvation.

Now, God would give *them* a sign of similar meaning. For the sins of Israel for which God took responsibility and as a symbol of his own repentance and absolution of his promise to the chosen nation, the Father gave his own first-born Christ, the incarnated Son of Man, to be the unblemished lamb of sacrifice. Through the death of Jesus in this sacrificial manner, God paid for the sins of Israel that they had committed on his behalf, but without his approval. Then he extended this act as the sacrifice to redeem the sins of *all Jews and Gentiles* who repent and seek forgiveness for their own sins. Only in repentance can forgiveness be justified.

The wooden cross was the altar upon which the blood of the Lamb of God was spilled. In that blood, God saw the sins of Israel and took responsibility as the sinner. In that blood, the Jewish authorities saw the guilt of their sins, but few repented. In that blood, *all* who sin can see their own guilt from which each can repent and seek forgiveness. God will gladly forgive and save the repentant sinner, for *the cross was an altar of love and atonement* that unifies all who come to him in humility and love.

Jesus' rejection and death ended God's plan to make Israel the exemplary chosen nation. His death also marked a new *beginning*, for it would bring great changes to the Earthly kingdom and to hell itself. The *resurrection* of Jesus' dead body, which reinstated him as the *living Messiah*, initiated God's new plan to bring righteousness to the world. It was the beginning phase of his Church which would come to embody a new "chosen nation" composed of all peoples, Jew and Gentile, and guided by a new message of Love, Truth and Light. All things are become new through the death and resurrection of Jesus Christ.

The rule of law for the sake of law, which can make tyrants of zealous administrators, would rule no more and would be supplanted by the rule of Love. This is the true message of Christ's Church that lives because he was resurrected as the living Messiah: Love and Truth rule all things of God which bring peace and good will to all Mankind, and salvation and eternal life to the soul.

THE DEATH AND RESURRECTION OF CHRIST BRING CHANGES TO HELL   The life, death and resurrection of Jesus Christ represent a benchmark in world history, a critical turning point that changed the direction of human evolvement. His messages based on things of truth and love that emanate from the Heavenly Father gave inspiration and hope to the many searching for something higher than humanity and false gods. This life not only changed humanity, but *his death brought a radical new order to hell* for the sake of departed souls and made it a place of purpose to assist the soul to seek redemption and salvation.

At the start of the Age of Redemption fallen angels began to serve as shared souls in groups of humans to prepare themselves and humanity for the Age of Mankind. This event initiated the development of spirituality in humanity by way of the sovereign soul given thereafter to each human. The human became host to an infused fallen angel that would serve as his soul for the duration of life, departing at death.

Several thousand years passed before the dedicated souls developed a general state of spirituality in humanity. Until this was accomplished, no soul could become "saved". Salvation was a state of a repentant angel obediently sharing in God's Will and Mercy. These angels had committed themselves to doing God's Will and redeeming their sins against humanity and God, who responded with affirmed salvation. Salvation was not granted until the angels demonstrated their commitment. Upon death of the body each soul returned as a free spirit to Hades, the kingdom ruled by Satan. God had imposed rules upon Satan and the fallen angels at the initiation of the Age of Redemption that brought some measure of order and civility to Hades.

All fallen angels, including those who had served as shared souls and sovereign souls shared the same space in Hades without segregation or isolation. While those angels who had not served as souls harbored some resentment toward those who had, there was no strife or turmoil among them. Some angels who had not served yearned to do so, while others resisted.

When humanity began to exhibit spirituality and responded with worship of God, then willing souls could become saved. Whenever a *saved* soul departed its human host at death, it was given special recognition in Hades and accorded some association with the Holy Angels who were imposing God's laws of redemption within the realm. This gave incentive to some angels to seek salvation while increasing resentment and resistance in others. Satan also began to look upon saved souls as traitors and deserters.

As time passed, more and more souls joined the ranks of the saved. Since all souls continued to go to the same "place" following the death of their human host, the departed saved souls began to segregate themselves from the unsaved. Isolation was *not imposed* between the saved and unsaved souls in Hades; just as among humans in life, separation was voluntary and self-imposed. Some angels looked upon this as an expression of superiority and special privilege that heightened the estrangement between saved and un-saved. A gulf of separation and tenseness between the two groups was growing constantly and continued until the death of Jesus Christ.

The birth, life and ministry of Jesus Christ enlivened Satan's opposition to God and Heaven. Satan perceived the Incarnation to be a challenge to his sovereignty in Hades and the Earthly realm. He reacted by greatly intensifying his efforts to weaken and defeat God's Plan of Redemption.

Satan pitched his battle in the minds and souls of those who should have accepted Jesus and his Divine messages. Instead of accepting his messages favorably, these persons considered them to be an affront to their position as religious authorities. They were readily hardened against the would-be Messiah and his unorthodox philosophies. After a short period of curiosity and tolerance they repudiated him and began a campaign to censure and disqualify both Jesus and his philosophy.

Satan pressed hard upon them, and their fight with Jesus grew with increasing jealousy, rage and hatred and growing fears of reprisal from the Roman authorities. When they saw that they could neither defeat his arguments nor repress him, the contest became personal and violent for they were convinced that *he must be silenced.* They soon concluded that only his death could remove this distressing thorn from their flesh. With Jesus removed and silenced, they could calm the growing crowds who eagerly sought him out to hear his messages and talk with him. Respect and authority could then be restored to the center of power and influence in the Sanhedrin. Resolved to be rid of Jesus, they summarily condemned him to death.

With their cooperative minds now firmly in tow, Satan led them into the pursuit and arrest of Jesus, then through a mock trial with Jewish and Roman officials, then to a hasty sentence of death by crucifixion. Jesus was executed in a cruel manner on a wooden cross before scores of witnesses. He died and his body was laid in a temporary tomb owned by a compassionate member of the priestly rulers who had demanded his death.

At death, as God required of all souls, *the angel soul of Christ departed its human host, Jesus, and became a free spirit in the hell of Hades.* Yet, his arrival there was like no other that had ever been. The glory of the Father and the power of his Love and Truth filled all of Hades. The Holy Angels of God came near to receive Christ back into the realm of spirits and to shield him from the taunts of the jubilant Satan.

Satan was ecstatic that the soul of Jesus had arrived in his kingdom as a result of his successful manipulations of human souls and minds. He gloated over his victory while all saved souls in Hades gathered around Christ. The souls of sinners began to withdraw from the presence of Christ in an attempt to hide their sins from the Holy One of God. Many unsaved souls whose worst sin had been that they had not repented and turned to God now turned to Christ to ask for mercy and a chance to share love with him. Many lost souls were saved and recovered from hell on that day of shame and glory.

As a consequence of these events, a great polarization and breach quickly formed in hell, wherein all Holy Angels and saved souls gathered around Christ while Satan and all unsaved souls retreated entirely from the power of the Holy Presence. This caused a conspicuous *segregation* of saved and unsaved souls, that separated hell into a place of Light and a place of darkness.

Christ saw that this separation was *good* because it protected the saved angels from the oppression of evil that they had rejected in life. It was also *just* since it rewarded souls according to their own decisions and behavior. Therefore, he decided then and there that the segregation would become permanent and there should be separate "places" for the saved and unsaved in Hades. From henceforth, all departed saved souls would be isolated from Satan and the unsaved souls.

The place of Light would be a Heavenly state ruled by the spirit of Christ. The saved would be in the company of the Holy Angels who would help them on their pathways back to Heaven's Grace. The unsaved would be confined in the company of the Deceiver and his princes in the place of darkness where they would reap the results of their own sins. Christ and the Angels declared this a victory for Heaven and all saved souls. From henceforth the state of death would provide *purpose* for all departed souls.

In the brilliant radiance of the Father's Love and Grace, Christ returned to Jesus' lifeless body still lying in the sepulchre. He embraced the body while the Angels infused life into it to make him a living being once more. Alive, Jesus arose from the slab, while the glory of the Father's joy filled the cave. To prove to himself that he was alive, Jesus neatly folded the cloths that had lain over his dead body, while his risen body now gathered strength and composure. The sealed door of the sepulchre popped loose and Jesus Christ walked out into the garden clothed in a robe of pure white. He paused near the opening praising and glorifying the Father for his Love and fulfillment of His Promise.

The risen Christ paced through the garden in the early light of the dewy morning, thanking the Father for this miracle and contemplating the tasks to accomplish with his disciples in the short while remaining. Soon, Jesus heard the soprano timbre of familiar voices raised in mourning and sorrow. These voices would soon be proclaiming incredible good news of joy and faith to the disciples. Christ would now go forth to prepare his disciples, numbering in the hundreds, to become the founders and apostles of his Church, an Earthly kingdom of Love, Truth and Light.

Thus, Satan was robbed of the spoils of his empty victory. His elation turned to rage and despair. Once again, he saw *the impotence of his sovereignty and the hopelessness of his cause.* Since that time, hell has been a different and darker place for all lost souls who must abide with a more angry, desperate and defeated Satan. While Christ's Earthly kingdom grows in strength and Divine wisdom, Satan's kingdom of Hades grows ever darker and more malicious. It is the result of the Deceiver's own corruption and pride.

THE ASCENSION OF CHRIST   Following his resurrection, Jesus Christ remained for a short while of several weeks with his disciples and followers until he ascended into Heaven. This brief time was sufficient for him to show himself to all of them in proof that he was alive, even though he had died. His purpose was to administer a baptism of the Holy Spirit upon them to reinforce their belief in his messages and faith in his promises. He commissioned all of them as apostles and instructed them to go into all the world to preach the Gospel and spread his Divine messages to *all people*. This was the great Commission of his Church.

When his mission was complete, he was borne by unseen angels into the sky. The sight of a live human rising effortlessly into the air, moving steadily to higher elevations, was as convincing as any sign that could be given. Their witness to this unprecedented event was proof to them that Jesus was who he claimed to be and that his messages were wholly valid and true. Only a fool could witness this event and not believe.

In this event the body of the *risen* Christ was of mortal flesh, just as it had been before his crucifixion. Therefore, as Jesus rose ever higher into the air, beyond the point at which he could still be viewed from the ground, he began to lose consciousness due to the rarefied oxygen at the high altitude. Painlessly and fearlessly, life faded from his body once again, so unlike the violent, excruciating torture of his death on the cross. Now, all was serenity and contentment as *Jesus the man* slipped into *eternal sleep* in the air.

Christ, the soul, disengaged from the dead body and once more became a *free spirit* and the holiest of all angels. Angels conducted Christ directly out of the Earthly realm into the Realm of Heaven. The Son of God had completed his Earthly mission and now proceeded through celebrations of victory and glory in the presence of the Father and Heavenly hosts without number.

The deceased *human* body of Jesus was disposed by the angels in a *place* of solitude and holiness, where no man will ever walk and no beast will ever lie and the cataclysms of man and nature will never disturb its eternal peace. The body of Jesus engaged the sacred law that joins life to life and unifies and sustains all mortal beings forever upon the Earth. Humanity can rejoice that the Son of Man imposed upon himself the same consequence that is required of all departed flesh to become *one* with the earth, to bless the Earth for the sake of all life to come.

The Purpose and Manner of Jesus' Death

WHY, HOW JESUS SUFFERED DEATH   The death of Jesus Christ had great spiritual meanings and served several purposes. The least of these was to answer a scoff from Satan: "Christ, you may know what it is like to be separated from the love of the Father, but you have never experienced excruciating death in a body of flesh!" Christ became flesh as the baby Jesus, grew to manhood experiencing the things of the flesh as all men do, then he died in the flesh in the most excruciatingly painful and anxiety-laden ways devised by Mankind.

A principal purpose for Christ's death was to show the value that God placed on each soul because of His Love. The value of anything is what someone will give to possess it. The price God paid to purchase our souls was the excruciating death of his "firstborn", the highest in His Kingdom, the creation and fulfillment of the great forlornness of His primal Love: his son, Christ. What more could He have given to show the value to him of our souls and to demonstrate the extent of His love?

Jesus' Death, Resurrection and Ascension constituted a demonstration to show Mankind "the way". It had the spiritual meaning that, though your soul may be in darkness of spiritual death, God can bring you back into the light of the living: "As He has done for me, He can do for you". And just as Christ returned to Heaven, so can any soul because the soul is an angel created by God.

Pure and innocent of wrongdoing, Jesus went to the cross to spill his own blood upon the altar of Love for the ultimate and final sacrifice to redeem our transgressions of God's law. He became the unblemished Lamb offered by God his Father as a sign of redemption for all who repent, to the end of the Age. This was an act that could be understood by all Jews who lived under the law of Moses: because his death was the offer of final blood sacrifice, there would no longer be a need for sacrificial offering of animals for atonement under the law.

In offering himself for this sacrifice, Christ took upon himself all the transgressions of Israel which were incurred in God's name in deeds to establish Israel as a nation in the lands promised to Moses and Abraham. The debts of transgression were, in this way, redeemed for all of Israel and the account was settled. His death signified that Israel and the Jewish nation would no longer be the focus for attainment of a great and righteous nation, but his call for salvation would be extended directly to all of Mankind. The "promised land" would from henceforth be his kingdom of believers distributed over all the Earth. The promised New Covenant was established for all, Jew and Gentile, which extends the old covenant to include everyone as heirs through grace to receive all that is offered from the Kingdom of God.

Jesus' death also redeemed the sins of those who were instrumental in bringing about his death. Because God had led his prophets to foretell that Jesus would suffer, even die, because he was rejected, the Will of God allowed Satan to lead men to desire the end of his life. With fear, jealousy, rage and misunderstanding Satan led those who brought false charges against Jesus; for pay and the lust of blood, Satan led the mob that demanded his crucifixion; then the Father turned his eyes away from those who had power to save Jesus. Jesus would not fold or recant his claims of Divine mission and origin, allowing the Will of his Father to be fulfilled.

While on the cross, Jesus demonstrated that one should forgive those who commit grievous sins against him, and that prayer can free repentant souls from the bondage of sin, even though they are in death. For this cause he cried, "Father, forgive them for they know not what they do!'. And he saved a repentant thief who had died with him.

THE CRUCIFIXION   The suffering that Jesus experienced during crucifixion has never been adequately described. Who best to hear this than from the One who experienced it; but Christ is no complainer and we shall never hear it from his own lips. He had known all his life the fate that would result from rejection by his people because he had helped to establish the plan as his Father's Will while still in Heaven.

There are those who speak of the humaneness of his executioners in that they forced him to carry his own cross to Calvary. They say that this wore him down and desensitized him to the pain that awaited him on the cross. Jesus was already weak, weary, dazed and hungry as a result of the anxiety-laden all-night vigil and interrogation. Then there were the lashes from the scourging whip that inflicted lacerations on his back, given to appease his accusers. The effect of carrying the cross was to agitate these cuts and keep them bleeding as well as to rub his back raw.

Hanging upright on the cross in extreme weariness with the spikes tearing into the flesh and bones of his limbs, his entire torso, legs, shoulders and arms soon became a cauldron of severe, relentless pain. There was no way to find relief from pain or weariness. While vainly trying to relieve the weight on the spikes, he moved his body up and down, back and forth to seek a few seconds of relief, rubbing his bare back against the rough cross. This wore large patches of skin from his back and shoulders, causing most of his back to become a mass of raw, bleeding flesh. His entire body suffered inflamed, agonizing pain.

The two thieves hanging on their own crosses on either side of him knew what he was suffering. Yet, they had no lacerations on their backs from a scourging whip because they had not blasphemed God. They also were not bareback as Jesus was and did not have to carry their own cross. These were only the consequences of proclaiming to be the Son of God.

Some who loved Jesus waited at his feet until death brought peace: his mother, Mary Magdalene, John the beloved of Jesus, Mary mother of James and John. Others who knew him and had followed him openly or discreetly were among the crowds who looked upon the scene from a short distance. These are close witnesses to the agonizing wounds that he endured. They were lifted by his spirit when he raised his voice to ask the Father to forgive those who had done this to him and to promise the repentant thief that he would see him a little later in Paradise.

Satan can no longer scoff about Christ's death experiences or feel triumph in sowing the dark passions that brought about his death. The victory of Jesus' life and resurrection released the power of God's Love and Truth to sweep over the Earth like a swelling tide of pure, living "water". This water shall baptize every repentant soul into God's kingdom and wash from humanity all strongholds and stains of sin.

After knowing what humanity did to Jesus because he went about proclaiming the Father's New Message, can we not now love him more and seek to erase this shame from our souls? He endured rejection, desertion, mock trial, suffering and death for the sake of humanity and their souls. Yet, that was only the beginning of a new period of Light and Love, for he stands *alive* before us all as the embodiment of his Promise of eternal life.

The Miracles of Immaculate Conception, Resurrection, and Ascension

FAITH AND MIRACLES   Since the time of Jesus Christ, Mankind has fretted with the mysteries of his immaculate conception, his death and resurrection and his ascension into Heaven. Believers have accepted these "miracles" on faith, because they are the things that the faithful would expect of Divine beings or sons of God. It doesn't stand in the way of true believers that they cannot understand such things because they do not occur to the sons and daughters of humanity. They believe that God acts in mysterious ways and that all things are possible with Him.

Now, you will be able to see the possibility that such miracles can occur through Divine Will. Death is understandable: since every human will die, the processes of death from whatever reason are well known. The remaining miracles that pertain to Christ have not been understood by humanity, but they are not mysteries to the angels since they involve processes routinely used in the creation of life.

IMMACULATE CONCEPTION, resurrection, and healing of disease and injury all involve similar creative processes. If angels can create life in primal cells, if they can mutate one species into another, why doubt that they can initiate the life of an infant in the womb of its mother. Is sperm necessary to accomplish conception? Sperm is only a vehicle, a carrier of the process of life initiation and representations of the father. Angels only need to start with a single cell in the ovum. Suitable "information strings" such as chromosomic and deoxyribonucleic acid (DNA) replicons are created and inserted, then cell division is forced. It was no great feat for the creative angels to start the process in the Virgin Mary to initiate the life of Jesus. Yet, this was a very special event in the history of humanity; it had never been done before that time or since.

In the BEGINNING, Christ was created in the spirit from the Father's substance *without exogenous conception*, and the virginity of Mary assured that

Jesus the human was created in like manner. The conception of Jesus through Divine creation endowed him with extraordinary abilities not possessed by the normal person. One of these was a perfect coupling between his mind and soul that enabled him to receive messages direct from the Father or the angels Michael and Gabriel, to perceive the thoughts and feelings of other persons, and to project the power of his spirit to heal the infirmities of the afflicted. Another ability was an extraordinary gift of thought and expression through which he could formulate and express complex ideas in simple, beautiful ways that were readily understood by the common person.

Jesus had these abilities from his earliest childhood, and sometimes demonstrated them to his mother and close family members. Otherwise, Jesus matured like a normal man in physical attributes and capability. Yet, he presented regal mannerisms and bearing. He possessed a powerful, attractive personality that engendered confidence and trust. Those who got to know him soon believed his claims and teachings, though they didn't always understand them.

MIRACULOUS OR SPIRITUAL HEALING is possible because an angel has the ability to remove dead or diseased tissue in the body, cell by cell, and discard it into the person's bloodstream as waste to be removed through normal means. The angel brings new cells from good tissue and replaces each cell that has been removed, or perhaps as few as necessary to repair or renew the body part. This proceeds as quickly as the body can discard the waste and withstand the transplantation of cells without intolerable ill effects. Organs such as nerves can be readily repaired or rerouted to restore some capability or sensation, such as sight. Miraculous healing requires a powerful belief within the mind and soul of the person because his soul must bond with the healing angel and the person must offer himself freely to the Will of God.

RAISING THE DEAD Processes used in healing and life creation are used by angels in the restoration of life, which is possible even if the body has lain dead for several days. The power of God can restore a human body to life after as many as five days in temperate zones of the Earth. However, such events do not occur spontaneously without premeditation on the part of the angels. The raising of a dead person is a very special event and is always authorized through the Will of God. It serves a majestic purpose to demonstrate His love for Mankind and His power over life and death. A dead body that is to be restored to life is taken into the care of angels soon after death. They preserve the organs and internal parts from excessive deterioration.

Outwardly, the body may appear to be decaying because it is dehydrated and starved through cessation of blood flow.

Resurrection of the dead serves a Divine purpose to demonstrate God's love for people and His power over life and death. Jesus performed several resurrections to demonstrate to the disciples that God has this power, so that they would believe his own resurrection from death after being crucified.

Restoration of life presents a simple problem for the angels to accomplish; yet, it is no less a miracle. It begins when Christ or the Father, as appropriate, commands the soul to re-enter the body and infuse once again. Then He imparts Consciousness to the brain. An angel primes the heart muscles to restart pumping the blood. The diaphragm is shocked to restore rhythmic breathing. In a few minutes, the body can awaken and regain its sense of orientation. Awed onlookers witness the miracle of a dead body restored to life. The one who was dead feels tired, stiff and weak. Otherwise, he feels as though he has awakened from a deep slumber in which he experienced a strange, vivid dream.

Not all bodies can or should be raised from death. Resurrection does not *renew* the body although the causes of death are healed or removed. There is little merit to restoring life when the body and organs have been ravaged by disease, injury or age, or perhaps life's purpose has been hopelessly evaded. Spiritual renewal and restoration will come through death and *rebirth*. Resurrection requires a Divine reason that transcends human sorrow and compassion.

The ASCENSION of Christ into Heaven was also an easy feat for the angels. We stated previously that angels or spirits can move between the spiritual and physical states. The spiritual state is the normal one. In the physical state, the angel can affect matter and material objects, from the infinitesimal to the large. Indeed, they are able to move material bodies, often with great force, or stop or influence objects moving with high energy.

To transport Jesus Christ into the sky, two unseen angels, one on each side of his body, entered the physical state and lifted him into the air and ascended to an altitude at which another event occurred. Out of view of the incredulous observers on the ground, in the company of Holy Angels of great significance to his mission on Earth, Christ was transformed into the heavenly form, then conveyed out of the Earthly realm to his Heavenly home.

The ascension was witnessed by "about five hundred persons", including disciples and believers and a few who were not yet believers. A broad base of incredulous, but objective onlookers could attest, without any doubt, to this very unusual event.

What more certain proof could be given to these witnesses that Jesus Christ was the Son of God as he claimed? These observers were not foolish. Jesus' disciples and many followers had *demonstrated an insistence upon truth and objectivity* by many recorded instances of their questioning Jesus for understanding and confirmation of his teachings.

His mission in life as a flesh and blood mortal, teaching the Father's message of Love and Truth, dying an agonizing death of redemption for the sins of humanity, being restored to life, and ascending into Heaven had been successfully completed. All unfolded as Christ had planned it with the Father before he was born in Bethlehem. Now, all Heavenly angels celebrated with singing and expressions of love and triumph.

ALL THINGS ARE POSSIBLE WITH GOD because He made all things, possesses all knowledge, understands all things, commands all things, and is the Master of all things. All processes, whether spiritual or physical, are controlled by his Laws. Immaculate conception, raising the dead, ascensions into Heaven are all rational acts within his laws and are easy things for Him and his angels to perform. They involve familiar, routine abilities that all angels possess and are not the impossible things that the human regards them to be.

Have faith! Believe in Him! God rules the Universe and all things in Heaven and upon Earth. Even your life and body are subject to His charge.

Christ and Women

Jesus' ministry took place within the setting of Galilee, Judea and Samaria, among the people of his homeland. He appealed to the full spectrum of society, neglecting no segment of it: men, women, children; old, young, rich, poor; the powerful, the obscure; the educated and common, the healthy and sick; Jew, Arab, Greek and Roman. He welcomed all listeners and hoped all would believe.

Because of the love, compassion, tenderness and hope often expressed in his public and private speech, women found a strength in Jesus that set their spirits free from the repression and impotence that they felt under the law. Not surprisingly, many women came to listen to Jesus and he welcomed them to join his following. They were among the most loyal of his followers, serving in traditionally feminine ways. Through this association he demonstrated that women should be just as acceptable and free as men to walk among the Godly. Likewise, children were temples and storehouses of trust, faith, love and wisdom; so they, too, should not be hindered from fellowship with Jesus and the Father.

Jesus never married. He never loved a woman physically; yet he loved them spiritually. Being the Master of Creation, he was very much acquainted with all aspects of the physical nature of humanity and the shared needs of all life.

Mary, the MOTHER of JESUS, the most exalted of all women, was a woman of purity and the embodiment of all that is physically and spiritually feminine. Her soul was an original angel who had come to the Earthly realm with the fallen angels to help them resist the guile of Lucifer, who became Satan. While in Heaven, she heard the entreaties of Lucifer, but *knew* them to be deceitful and against God's Will. Hence, she rejected them and began to help other angels to understand their true nature and to resist Lucifer. Seeing that many angels followed Lucifer back to Earth, where he hoped to establish the seat of his kingdom, the angel Mary accompanied them. On Earth, she tried to inform the angels, help them see through Lucifer's deceitful, seductive ways. Some returned to Heaven on her account.

When it became evident that God would isolate Satan and the fallen angels in the Earthly realm, she elected to remain to help the fallen angels to resist or turn away from him. So she remained in this Godless realm willingly to spread God's Love and Truth for the benefit of the fallen angels. She had left her beloved complementary angel and close companions in Heaven while she went about her Divine mission on Earth, accepting her lot as a mortal and the deficiencies and suffering associated with life in the material world.

Because of her faithful campaign to uphold the love and truth of Christ before the disobedient angels to counter the influence of Satan, the Father chose her human form of Mary to become the mother of Jesus. For presenting him so faithfully to her fellow angels in Heaven, she now presented him to Mankind as the Son of God who had become the Son of Man through her own body. God preserved Mary's physical virginity before the birth of Jesus to memorialize her *spiritual virginity* in not yielding to Lucifer's seductive guile.

Early in his ministry, Mary had been counseled that Jesus could die at the hands of those who lead Israel, and she accepted and believed these things to be the Will of God. After his death, she became a bright light of encouragement and inspiration to the saddened disciples and followers in Jerusalem and Nazareth, helping to keep their faith alive. She served them like a priest, telling them so many things they could never have known about her son. When Mary died, her soul was taken into Heaven and reunited with her risen Son and beloved fellow angels. She has not returned to the Earthly realm since then and will not return until Christ comes for the final time to receive the redeemed angels into Heaven.

One of Jesus' feminine followers, *Mary Magdalene*, deserves special attention. Mary became one of Jesus' most faithful devotees after Jesus had freed her from personal demons that had entrapped her in the bondage of shameful sins. She redeemed her sins through devoted service to Jesus, including being a financial supporter of his group of disciples. She was able to do this because, like several other women who followed and supported him, she had access to modest wealth from her family. But Mary was special and she became to Jesus the feminine equivalent of John, the beloved disciple.

Throughout Jesus' ministry, Mary attended all the events in the vicinity of her home in Galilee in which Jesus and his disciples were present. She would spread the word of their coming and arrange for support and amenities for the group. During his last days in Jerusalem, she went into the holy city to participate in and witness some of his most glorious triumphs while he still lived as a man. When one of the disciples told her that Jesus had been arrested and was expected to die, she collapsed in shock and despair. Hearing that he was being crucified outside the city walls, she gathered her strength and ran with others to Golgotha to be among the witnesses and sympathizers. Mary was among the few who stood at the foot of the cross while he died, consoling him and refusing to leave the side of Mary his mother.

Then she accompanied Jesus' mother to the tomb of Joseph where his body was laid to rest. Two days later in the early daylight hours of Sunday morning, she was the first to arrive at the garden of burial and peer into the dark tomb, unexpectedly open, and discovered the body was not there. She was the one spoken to by the "grounds-keeper", who turned out to be Jesus risen from the dead. Christ commissioned her as *the first apostle to spread the news of his resurrection* and she ran to tell Peter that he was alive! and that she had seen and spoken to him! She was with Jesus several times following his resurrection and was among those who witnessed his ascension into the sky.

Afterwards, she continued to be a strong apostle of Jesus' messages, never doubting his claims of divinity and holy purpose, always ready to lift the fallen spirit with loving words of comfort and faith. It is fitting that Mary shall be with Christ again while he, *now* once again born into flesh, establishes his Earthly Kingdom that he will rule for a thousand years.

The Church and Bible Preserve Knowledge of Jesus Christ and God

Following the resurrection and ascension of Jesus Christ, His disciples and other close followers became apostles to spread the story to all who would listen. There had been positive witness among disciples and followers that Jesus had died on the cross, and that his body had been placed in a sepulcher for burial, sealed and guarded by Roman soldiers. There was positive witness, despite the precautions, that the seal had been broken, the sepulcher opened and his body removed. Disciples and followers afterwards saw him alive, listened to his heartening messages of promise, spoke with him personally. Then, proof absolute when they witnessed his body rise into the air then disappear beyond clouds in the sky. These feats could not happen to a mortal human and were positive proof to these witnesses that Jesus was the Son of God as he had claimed to be and that he had imparted to them the messages of the Father. These circumstances, along with Jesus' virgin birth and his teachings and certain authorities that he shares with the Father, are the foundations of Christian beliefs and constitute the Gospel.

John, James, Peter, Andrew, Thomas, Bartholomew and the other disciples and followers such as Mary Mother of Jesus, Mary Magdalene, Nicodemus, Joseph of Arimathea, became witnesses to these truths and their faith was inspired by the Holy Spirit. James, the skeptical brother of Jesus, would soon become the head of the infant Church in Jerusalem. All of these witnesses spread out among the towns and villages of their homeland to tell this wonderful news, and their enthusiasm would allow them no rest.

As the final period of Jesus' life became shorter day-by-day, he began to inform his disciples and close followers of his approaching death and gave them his promise that he would return soon to be among them once more. Both statements were incomprehensible to the listeners as they could not grasp an understanding of the events that were soon to unfold. Arrest and death by crucifixion left his close followers in confusion and panic. Understanding began to dawn among them after he died and defeated death. After they watched him depart from them during the ascension, the promise of his return began to burn brightly among them. Faith and hope grew immensely while they watched and waited for their King to materialize once more in their midst. This event never arrived and many must have gone on to their deaths disappointed, but still hopeful.

Yet, *Christ did return*! Not as Jesus, the Son of Man, but as Christ, the Son of God. Christ's spirit returned to Earth to be among the growing swells of disciples, apostles and followers, teaching and leading them while they established the foundations of his church that would eventually encompass the Earth. He was with Peter, John, James, Mary his mother, and the initial set of followers who had seen and heard Jesus while he was alive. He was with Paul, Mark, Luke, Silas and Barnabas, and with the ranks of believers who were in life with him, but had never seen or heard him. His spirit was with those who came afterwards to illuminate with his message and engender faith and hope in a receptive world. Christ had kept his promise. Though not seen by human eyes, Christ's spirit returned faithfully and moved among the apostles. His Presence was joy and power to the believers, yet they saw him not!

James caught the vision of what his brother Jesus had tried to establish among the disciples and believers and, through them, throughout the Roman world. He realized that the future of this vision lay in their hands and that it could fade and die if they did not commit themselves to it fully as a Divine cause. With the inspiration and help of his mother, he organized the believers in Jerusalem to structure their activities. From Jesus' teachings they began to formulate the philosophical messages of the early church and to establish mission goals for it. He then began to lead them into accomplishing these goals and spreading the messages throughout Judea and to lands beyond. He wrote letters of instruction and inspiration to groups of believers in outlying areas. Believers became dedicated apostles in all places.

In the earliest times of this period, the apostles concentrated on converting those of Jewish traditions in Judea and adjoining regions such as Samaria and Gaza. Then, they began to travel far beyond the homeland, to Syria, Asia Minor, Greece, Macedonia and Italy. Far-flung cities such as Antioch, Ephesus, Thessalonica, Philippi, Corinth, Gallatia and Rome became strongholds and centers of the new religion. Followers and apostles were born anew from Jew and Gentile in every city and region where they preached and taught. New converts took up the cause of spreading the Gospel, and went into every part of the Roman Empire, then into lands beyond. The expansion never stopped until it covered the Earth, as Christ had prophesied.

In the process, several very notable personalities were won to the cause. The most dramatic of these was Saul of Tarsus who later began to call himself

Paul. Saul had been intensively trained in Jewish law with aspirations of becoming a Pharisee of the Jewish Sanhedrin. A brilliant, enthusiastic devotee of Mosaic Law, Saul came to regard the followers of Christ as blasphemers and heretics and conducted a campaign of relentless persecution including executions, jailings, trials and suppression. Saul was miraculously converted through an encounter with the Spirit of Christ while en route to Damascus to suppress a growing movement of followers there. God sent Ananias to help him recover and express His purpose to Saul. Saul then spent several years in an undisclosed desert town in Arabia in meditation, reorientation, and enlightenment. Then he returned to Damascus and Jerusalem and joined the apostolic movement along side Peter and other elect apostles. The apostles accepted him as a genuine and devout convert to the cause of Christ and began to instruct him of their first-hand experiences with Jesus.

While John continued to minister to the Jews, Peter and Paul turned their attention to the Gentiles and pagans and the Jewish communities outside Judea. From Antioch in Syria, they began to conduct separate missions of conversion in major cities of Asia Minor, Greece and Macedonia. On these missions, Paul was accompanied by converts such as Barnabas, Mark, Silas, Luke, Philip and Timothy. In bringing Christ's message to thousands of eager listeners, they also reaped the results of Paul's earlier antagonistic treatment of Christ's followers: accusations, trials, persecutions, jailing, scourging, stoning and exile.

About *twenty years* after Jesus' death and resurrection, Paul began writing his letters to the fledgling churches in Asia. Perhaps *fifteen years later* as Paul was completing his *final letter*, Mark wrote the first gospel. Luke and Matthew followed within several years with their Gospels, telling *their* stories of Christ's life and ministry. Luke continued with his account of the Acts of the Apostles in spreading the Good Word. During this period, Peter, John, and Jude continued Paul's tradition of writing letters of explanation and instruction to churches that the apostles had established in the land of Gentiles.

A *half century* after Jesus' Ascension, John and other Christians were exiled on a wretched island in the Aegean Sea by Rome's emperor Domitian because of the official opposition that had been raised against them under Nero. There he received prophetic visions through the Spirit of God. John recorded these as "Revelations" and sent the document to the "seven churches of Asia" to inspire them to hold fast to their beliefs that Christ is supreme over all of the rulers of Earth's empires and kingdoms and that his Kingdom will triumph over all adversaries. This promise was necessary because the Roman emperors considered themselves to be gods and would not tolerate the Christian worship of their God. Rome had crushed Judea and Jerusalem and scattered the Jews and Christ's followers, but God would have the final triumph.

The visions held far more than secular meaning, for they held *spiritual meanings* that are the foundations of faith in repentance, salvation and the eventual triumph over the sins that entrap humanity and the fallen angels. The visions assured John that all those who prevail against sin will join in the Victory of Christ over Satan and the evil that he has brought upon the world. Satan's kingdom shall not stand beyond the rescue of all who will come to Christ to receive his Love and Mercy. The Heavenly Father and Christ, who are called the Ancient of Days and the Unblemished Lamb, are the masters of all of Heaven and Earth. They are Holy and Righteous and those who enter into their Kingdom must become righteous. As only soiled garments are in need of washing, unclean souls who submit to washing in the Blood of the Lamb will be cleansed so that they may be presented before Christ spotless, white as snow, and stand with the Saints before the Throne of God.

These visions revealed to John the need to inform believers of the *true* nature of Christ from the memories and impressions he had received as Jesus' beloved disciple. For this cause he was inspired to write his version of the Gospel to show that God was about Love, Truth and Light and that He would bestow Mercy and Salvation through Grace upon any repentant soul and bestow upon him *eternal life.*

While some followers had been disciples who walked with Jesus and had witnessed his death, resurrection and ascension, most others were unacquainted contemporaries. Eventually, all of these died. Many had been put to death by the Sanhedrin or Jewish zealots or rulers of Rome, charged with being revolutionaries against Rome or heretics and blasphemers of God. Rome's destruction of Jerusalem and other Jewish cities caused Christ's followers to scatter into Asia and countries around the Mediterranean Sea. But the Church had become firmly established and it would serve as an ever-spreading source of His message.

Some of the books and letters written by the apostles became the books of the New Testament. These formed in essence Christ's new covenant given to all peoples of the world. The Holy Bible was developed and organized from these books of the New Covenant combined with the books of the Old Covenant, which had been given to God's "chosen people" of Israel. The Bible became the sacred cornerstone of the Church and was its source of spiritual knowledge and testimony of those who had experienced God and Christ. The Church grew and spread through all villages and cities of every nation of Europe and the Near East, then eventually to all nations of the Earth. It took on such strength in the minds and souls of humanity everywhere that no Earthly power has been able to extinguish it. The Church lives in the minds and souls of believers, not in public buildings or hidden meeting places.

Jesus' Alternative Mission if Accepted as Messiah

All Christians are familiar with the story of Jesus' life from birth to death, from resurrection to ascension. Few may be aware that the Will of God had allowed for an alternative fate from the one of death and resurrection. Two options had been planned in Heaven long before Jesus' birth. Both options were described by the prophets, although only one of them was fulfilled. Sadly, the option that was hoped for in Heaven was hindered by human egocentric arrogance and the power of Satan to distort and camouflage the truth.

God's Plan of Redemption has provided, as a central constraint, for the progressive defeat of evil and emergence of Christ as victor in righteousness and fulfillment of God's Word. *Before the end of the Age*, Christ would reign over humanity as the "king", ruling in love, peace and justice as the Holy One of God to claim all nations and every willing soul for his everlasting Kingdom. This climactic goal of the Plan was revealed in prophesy throughout the Scriptures from the pages of Genesis to Revelations. The alternative *option of acceptance* of Christ as the Messiah was foretold by Isaiah (Is 2:2-3,6:9), Daniel (7:13-14), Jeremiah (Je 23:5-6) and Micah (Mi 5:2) and was reflected in Gabriel's announcement to Mary as told by Luke (Lu 1:32-33). The contrasting *option of rejection* was foretold by Zechariah when he warned of Christ's betrayal for thirty pieces of silver (Zech. 11:12-13) and his rejection and crucifixion (Zech. 13: 3-7 and Isaiah 53). Both options were possible outcomes of the ministry of Jesus Christ, but the options were mutually exclusive and only one of them could unfold.

Jesus was born to be King of the Jews. This was to fulfill the Prophesies as well as to fulfill God's promise to Abraham to make of his descendants a great nation. God intended for Israel to become the preeminent nation of the world with Jerusalem the seat of government and world influence. All nations would look to Israel as their leader and paradigm. Their own leaders would flock to

Jerusalem to seek the blessings of its favor and wisdom. Under Israel's influence and guidance, all nations would become righteous and each would become great among the great. Jesus would have been the titular king of Israel and the spiritual leader of all nations.

This course of events would have followed complete acceptance of Jesus as the Messiah by the center of Jewish authority and the multitudes of its people. The authority of Rome would dissipate in the onrush of power issuing from a *new authority* having a Divine source and purpose. Jesus, King of Israel, would lead Israel to a position of power that would, within a score of years, eclipse and replace the command and influence of Rome. It would project a new culture that would replace that of Greece, Assyria, Babylonia, and Egypt in the Mediterranean realm.

The world would look with awe and admiration to this small nation that had dissolved the great Roman empire while establishing its own empire, replacing the Romans without the use of armed might. It would be like the story of David and Goliath on a national scale. This new empire would be founded and consolidated through the acceptance and promotion of righteousness and things of the mind and spirit. Peace and good will and a culture of intellect, consciousness and beauty would pervade all corners of the world.

Jesus would establish the leadership that has been referred to as the thousand-year reign of Peace and Righteousness. The Church would have been unnecessary and, therefore, would not have been established. His messages of Love, Truth and Light would be extended through the influence and acts of his Kingdom directed from the New Israel and the New Jerusalem.

Jesus would not have been falsely charged and maliciously put to death. He would not have experienced death and resurrection. Jesus *would have* experienced an *ascension,* however. At some point when the human phase of his mission had been completed and his Earthly kingdom firmly consolidated, Christ would have anointed a new "king". Then he would depart upon clouds of glory to await in Heaven a future time when he would return to vanquish the remnants of evil and restore all willing souls to Heaven's Grace. Then would come the *final judgement* and dispensation of justice, then the inauguration of the New Earth to be ruled from the New Jerusalem, all encompassed within the New Heaven.

This was the alternative to the option that historically prevailed. The power center of the Jews *did* reject Jesus and repudiated his Divine messages. This rendered impossible his commission to become King of the Jews and fulfill the Promise of the Messiah because *this must come with their acceptance* and willingness. His death closed the old covenant with Israel, but He has established a New Covenant that will win the minds and souls of all Jews. Christ turned to the world to accomplish the Promise and Purpose of God's Plan.

His rejection and death *delayed* the coming of the New Heaven and Earth, but could not stop it. After his resurrection, Christ and the Holy Spirit set about to establish the Church upon the minds and feet of the apostles. *The Church* would replace Israel as the agent of Divine wisdom and righteousness. It would become a dispersed kingdom among the nations to preserve his messages and convey them to all people of the world and to the seas of humanity that would come in the tides of time.

Now, the time has come once again to prepare the world for the *end of the Age*. This time, no one can stop or delay it. The thousand-year reign of Peace and Righteousness will be given to the world as promised in the Word of God. Christ will initiate and rule it. Afterwards, comes a time of gathering in the final harvest, of cutting and threshing the sheaves of humanity, then the Judgement of those who repudiate and reject the gifts of Life that God had offered to all. The New Earth and New Heaven will come as the fulfillment of God's promise to humanity and the redeemed angels.

The "Second Coming," the Return of Christ

The Second Coming of Christ is the tangible manifestation of the second time Christ comes into the world with a Divine mission to fulfill God's plans for the redemption of the souls of Mankind. There is the question of whether his second coming will be in human flesh as in the first appearance, or in the spirit of God's first born and highest angel. Will he be a material *or* spiritual entity? The apostolic scriptures foretell a second coming of Christ to Earth in the full power and glory of the spirit, but these expectations were built upon optimistic hopes for the Jews accepting him as the Messiah. Such acceptance had within it the fulfillment of the messianic prophesies as well as endorsement of the transforming messages that Jesus conveyed from the Father.

The disciples to whom Jesus personally made his promise of return, as well as the apostles who came after his ascension, thought that he would return very soon with full Heavenly power to vanquish the source and power of evil and claim the saints and the faithful for his Kingdom. He would make his appearance on "clouds" of Glory and Victory accompanied by multitudes of the Heavenly hosts. The disciples understood that he had ascended into Heaven, but thought it for only a brief sojourn before returning to reap the harvest of all who believed on him and were saved. All of these would rise with him in triumph and glory into his eternal kingdom.

It was the primary goal of every apostle to prepare himself and as many others whom they could win with his message for Christ's imminent return. His return in this fashion would have been the culmination of the fact of establishing his kingdom among the Jews and all humankind.

Neither the disciples nor the apostles that came later understood the consequences that rejection and death would have on these prophesies. Perhaps Jesus himself did not have a full revelation of these things; therefore, he did not attempt to convey an alternate scenario to the disciples. The Father is not a *servant* of his own plans, but has the prerogative to establish *and* revise his Will to accomplish his purposes in the best possible way. The prophesies that referred to the Second Coming now properly describe a *Third* Coming. The Second Coming that shall soon begin to unfold will be distinctly different from the Biblical description and will have an altogether different purpose.

Jesus declared that no man knows the day or hour when the Son of Man shall return to Earth to consummate the Word of God. Not even Christ, he said, knew this. The time is known only to the Father. There are two reasons why Jesus Christ *could not know* the time of his return.

The first of these reasons is that, at the time Jesus supposedly spoke these words, there was no certainty in Heaven or on Earth that he would be accepted *or* rejected by the Jews as the promised Messiah. Acceptance implies that Jesus would have been received by all as the new king of the Jews, a necessity for leading Israel into full realization of the Promise for the Chosen Nation.

Jesus would have led that generation into initiation of God's pledge to make of them the great and righteous nation over all nations, to lead the world into his Kingdom. The Kingdom of God would have become manifest in the world at that moment, as reflected in the declarations of John the Baptist and Jesus: "The Kingdom of God *is at hand*!" This would set the stage for the end of the Age of Redemption. He would at some point leave the Earth and return at a future day and hour to consummate the Will of God in the Second Coming.

This, of course, did not happen. The second possibility unfolded as a historical fact and he *was* rejected and crucified. This outcome eliminated the chosen nation of Israel from serving as the basis of his Earthly kingdom. Fulfillment of the purpose of the Age was no longer possible by this approach, and an alternative basis must be established through his apostles. For this purpose they were commissioned to establish his universal Church to carry Jesus' messages throughout the world to prepare all nations for his second coming.

All factors of this second coming were *revised* through the providence of God. Events delayed the *time* of the second coming relative to the time had Jesus been accepted. More importantly, *the purpose and manner* of the second appearance were changed also because the new *conditions* would be profoundly different. The time of the Second Coming as foretold was not known by Christ because of the uncertainty of his acceptance or rejection as the Messiah. He simply did not know which of these possibilities would unfold.

There is *even more* involved in setting the time of the Coming. The fact is, God the Father did not know whether Jesus would be accepted or rejected either. This matter clearly rested upon the free will of human beings. It was a matter of decisions made by human beings who had the power to determine the fate of this one man and the future of Israel as a nation.

For God to know this, or any fact for that matter, would establish the outcome as an absolute certainty that no power in Heaven or Earth, except God, could change. If God *knows* an event is going to take place in a specified way on a given day and hour, this knowledge becomes established as an absolute truth, an unchangeable course that will come to pass exactly as he has thought it. Therefore, God would not allow himself to know beforehand the outcome of the human decisions that would determine the fate of Jesus. This course must be left to the will of humans.

That is true of the matter of his acceptance or rejection and it is equally true of the Second Coming. *God has not set a time for this event.* It is impossible, therefore, for anyone in Heaven or Earth to know it. This book has already stated that God does not use man-made watches and calendars to accomplish his work. He will, instead, use a *cycle*. The cycle will be complete when the *conditions* that define it are all satisfied and the *criteria* have been met, both established by God. Only He knows the conditions and criteria and the present status of their fulfillment.

These factors rest upon the free will of Mankind and the decisions made by humans as partners with their souls in important personal and social matters. Each human will decide whether he will serve God or Satan, whether he will repent or continue in sinful ways, whether he will choose to do good or evil. In this modern age of excessive world population and technological power, the decisions of individuals and nations can be momentous, fraught with possibilities for achieving good on a broad scale or for ravaging civilization. These decisions and their results will affect the conditions in the cycle and the criteria God establishes for bringing the cycle to a close.

The Second Coming of Christ will occur when God has decided that the time is right. When that time comes to pass, there will be no equivocation, nor will there be anything able to hinder or delay it. As this book reveals, that time is "soon" and many alive today will live to see it come. You ask, "If God has *not* set a time, how can anyone, even He, say that *the time is near?*" The answer lies in the truth that God alone knows the *status of the conditions* and how near to satisfaction are his criteria. He also has constant "snapshots" of humanity and the rate at which their decisions and acts fulfill the criteria. Therefore, God can predict that the time will be soon, within a generation or so. He has not set the day or hour with precision because this will depend upon the human decisions that occur as free will.

The end of the cycle will precipitate the Second Coming to fulfill a *new purpose*. But *Christ has come already!* He is a child alive *today* somewhere in the world once again. He is preparing for the day that he will begin his thousand year reign as the "king" of all nations. This will occur after he has become an adult; yet, he does not know the age at which he will anoint the start of his Millennium, but many of the present generation will see it.

Do not say: "Well, the Millennium is a generation or so away and I have plenty of time to change my life and find God." Do not think like a fool. You do not know the day or hour of your own death, or when you will be allowed to return to life, or whether you will be born into conditions that will lead you into good or evil.

Now is the time, *for the Kingdom of God is at hand!*

Following the Millennium, the new apostles of the Lord can begin to look forward to the Third Coming of Christ in the same way as the apostles of the first century looked to the Second Coming.

7

ARTICLES OF SPIRITUALITY AND FAITH

Distinctive Relationship of Human and Soul

Humanity should understand more about the nature of the relationship of the soul and its human host and the distinctions between them. The soul has been identified as an angel infused into the body of its human host for a Divine purpose. They are distinctly separate entities from one another and one does not rule the other. Likewise, one does not "own" the other, despite the use of possessive pronouns when referring to them collectively. Each is sovereign in its realm and responds to its own needs and aspirations. The angel soul is required through the Word of God to serve its role as soul to redeem angelic abuse of humanity and enter the Grace of God for its own salvation. Through this manner, willing souls can bestow enormous blessings, available only from God, upon humanity and they have done so already. So much more is possible!

When Mankind comes to fully understand that the angel souls are trying to lead him to an exalted state of intellect, spiritual awareness and divinity for his own benefit, then Mankind can prepare himself to achieve a state on Earth that is just a little lower than that of the angels. Accepting his soul and its Divine mission, the human host can work in harmony with the soul to pursue worthy goals that achieve God's Will for both. The articles in this chapter will help the reader to understand the distinctions between he and his soul, between the human and spiritual aspects of life, and that *human destiny is critically dependent upon accepting the soul in partnership in all his endeavors and aspirations.*

Spiritual and Human Purposes of the Holy Bible

The Holy Bible was given to Mankind by the Heavenly father working through inspired writers empowered by the Holy Spirit. These obedient and receptive persons were given revelations concerning God and his Will. As the Word of God, these messages are expressly spiritual. People are often mistaken in the results of their attempts to understand many Biblical passages in human or worldly terms. These messages are spiritual, have a spiritual source, and their purpose is spiritual. The *primary goal* of the Bible from start to finish is the salvation of the lost angel soul through which God is freely offering eternal reinstatement to his kingdom of Heaven through repentance, redemption and submission to all that his Grace provides.

Since the fallen angels do not remember their Heavenly regimen before they fell into sin, many Biblical messages are meant to help them understand the truths related to their fall and how they can recover from it. Much that is written in Biblical chronicles of past events and prophesy of the future appears to readers to be centered upon humanity, while the soul understands the messages in a spiritual context. For this reason, many of the Bible's metaphorical stories lack physical logic and historical truth while they accurately portray spiritual affairs in human symbolism.

The *secondary goal* of the Bible is to teach Mankind to be righteous through imparting knowledge, obedience, reverence and love for his Creator. If Mankind becomes righteous he comes into harmony with the angel souls' redemptive goals of exalting humanity with intellect and godliness. *The goal of righteousness for Mankind* is to lead humanity into a state wherein he finds harmony between his Divine character and all of his social and material concerns. This will lead him into a true stewardship wherein he applies his understanding of God's Will to all his acts concerning relationships with fellow humans and all that is in his Earthly home. As his mind grows in love and divinity he will cease to disgrace and destroy himself with misused power and sinful acts and will find unity in the Supreme Purpose for which God created humanity and all things on the Earth. Acting in concert, the soul and human host will abide in God's Will and mature in his Grace.

Prayer and Forgiveness

PRAYER is the most important thing a person can do to establish and maintain a relationship with God. Indeed, prayer is an unavoidable first step.

If one never prays either as a routine activity, or as an unconscious need, it isn't likely that he will find his way to God. Prayer is an outcome of one's belief in the existence of an accessible God and faith that God will accept the prayer and respond to it.

Praying is one of the first things Mankind began doing while spirituality was developed within him. He felt that there was "someone out there" superior to him and often affecting his fortunes or fate. He began to project his thoughts to this unseen benefactor, protector or antagonist. All through the Bible are accounts of prophets, kings and other believers who prayed frequently to the true God that had been revealed to them. Prayer seems to have been a virtue of believers or holy people that was mentioned whether or not any other virtue was displayed, for instance, love.

Talking to God is praying, talking about him is not. We pray to God *through our souls.* The act of praying opens a channel between the mind and soul. The soul already has a channel to God and to angels and other souls, which opens only when the soul desires to use it. The soul can commune with any spiritual entity, except Satan and his princes and beasts. Praying allows the person to direct his concerns through the soul to the Heavenly Father or Christ.

A prayer to God should ALWAYS begin with a salutation such as "Our Father, which art in Heaven..", or "Heavenly Father,...". This will assure that the prayer will go to HIM. This is very important, because thoughts can be directed to other entities, including very undesirable ones. Evil spirits are always near a person and they can know his thoughts if they are not directed specifically, an opening of which they may take advantage to his detriment.

When prayer is directed to the *Heavenly Father,* several things happen. First, a channel is established between the person and the Father because the proper greeting prompts him to authorize the passage of the supplication through the barrier of Hades. Though most people are not aware that this is actually a *two-way channel,* the person can both talk to the Father and receive messages in return from him. This latter use of the channel takes development through much effort and prayer, just as any talent or capability requires training. This is one of the methods used by the Old Testament prophets and others who learn to listen to their soul's "voice".

Secondly, the Father protects this channel while it is opened so that He, Christ and perhaps other entities authorized by him are all who can be aware of your thoughts and concerns. In such protected confidentiality, you can talk to him about anything whatsoever that's on your mind, no matter how personal, painful, shameful or overwhelming. Confidentiality and protection are good reasons why any worthwhile endeavor should begin with a prayer and the prayerful mood maintained throughout the proceedings. Whenever you pray for someone you love or in some way are concerned about, the Father will, most of the time, allow their soul to "hear" at least the portion of the prayer that concerns them. This strengthens their love and affinity for you.

Another thing that happens when you address the Father is that He opens the soul's *account* to reveal to Him your real concerns (since you cannot always understand or articulate the real concern that troubles you). Every soul maintains an "account," which is a record of all thoughts and deeds the soul and mind have done in partnership. This account is extracted and all elements from it are written into a Record that God maintains for your soul in Heaven. All items in the Record are judged as to whether they are acceptable. Unacceptable acts are regarded as "sins."

As you pray, the record of the thoughts and deeds you have experienced since your last prayer can be read from the account. The Father will then know how to strengthen you in the good things you have done as well as to help you overcome your real problems and the "sins" or mistakes you have committed that need forgiveness. All prayers should include a request for mercy and forgiveness even for the slightest things, as this helps to increase your awareness of the things that cause you to sin. The Father then removes the sins from your Spiritual Record and your "chart" is clean.

Love is important and necessary to the success of prayer. Without love, the prayer is insincere, empty, and self-centered. Love opens one to the full power of prayer so the prayer becomes the Power of Love in action. One who doesn't love can't really pray except for forgiveness or to ask for help from God. When one prays for God's gifts of Love, Truth, and Mercy to be bestowed upon himself and others, his prayer becomes a force for good for all for whom he prays.

When you pray for something that is important to you or others, it isn't enough to pray for it *only once.* You should pray everyday until it is accomplished because your prayers contribute to its success. The power from your own concerns and faith are important to its outcome. You should also do whatever you can to help bring it about, for the saying "God helps those who help themselves" has a large measure of truth. God expects you to do your part, which usually involves the *physical or material* aspects of it, along with faith and prayer. God will accomplish the necessary *spiritual* aspects that you cannot perform.

Frequently a person prays for a loved one or friend to be healed of a relentless illness, affliction or addiction, or to be relieved from a great burden.

It is painful to the loving to see someone else suffering, and they feel frustrated and helpless when they cannot remove this burden from them. Such things may be related to fulfilling the purpose that God has given to them. Prayers should be directed for this person not only for healing, but also for strength and courage to survive the suffering, and, above all, that God's Will shall be done to fulfill His purpose.

Frequently, a person will ask God to do something for them, or to give them something, or for a "windfall." When you ask God for something, do not ask for anything that is not His to give. He cannot give you something that does not belong to Him or to you, things that belong to others.

Jesus once replied to his questioners: "Render unto Caesar those things that are Caesar's, and unto God those things that are God's." Basically, the statement means that there is a separation between material and spiritual spheres of jurisdiction or ownership. The reply could be rephrased as, "Do not seek from God those things that are Caesar's, or from Caesar those things that are God's". God has given the material wealth of the Earth unto the jurisdiction of Mankind. Humans are responsible for the adequacy of their material well being. Even the most primitive human being could find ways for he and his family to subsist. Through increasing intelligence and development of skills, the human has found ways to live better and acquire wealth. Therefore, God does not directly intervene in the acquisition or distribution of material wealth. Yet, He is aware of the material needs of every person and has empowered each one to attain through acquisition or sharing those things he basically needs.

God does not own money or material wealth. He cannot give you wealth (money) that should be earned through your own effort and time, because He would have to take it from someone else. He can help you to develop the abilities with which you can earn the wealth, because that involves things that come from you. God gives you gifts of the spirit, not material things; material things come to you through your own strengths or from the generosity of others. Prayers for wealth and material things should be related to the adequacy of one's physical well being and to gratify the needs of his mind and spirit. He may share with others who do not have the ability or opportunities to provide for themselves.

Christ illustrated a very good prayer, called "the Lord's Prayer," that contains all the essentials for which you should pray. Learn the Lord's Prayer and use it regularly, even if you never use any prayer of your own. As Jesus asserted, "The Father knows what you have need for before you pray." He needs to hear from your own lips that you need and desire these things. He doesn't force things upon you that you don't want, except those that are required by laws of redemption. Christ's promise, "Ask and you shall receive, seek and you shall find, knock and it shall be opened unto you", can be realized only through prayer.

Asking God's FORGIVENESS for things done in thought or deed that are unacceptable to him is an act of humility that acknowledges your fallibility and displays willingness to submit to His Will. For those who pray, asking forgiveness has high priority and is one of the major uses of prayer. An unsaved soul does not pray and, hence, doesn't seek forgiveness. The saved person will seek forgiveness at least daily as this cleanses his spiritual Record and provides him always with a clean sheet upon which to write the account of life.

Forgiveness follows repentance and both are essential to the *redemption* of the soul since these cleanse the soul of things that cannot enter into the presence of God. Nothing unclean will be allowed to enter the Kingdom of God; hence, a soul who has not sought forgiveness is defiled with sins and cannot enter the Heavenly state following death. Sins include habitual thoughts and behavior or premeditated deeds that are unacceptable to God because they are contrary to His Laws and Will. Sins are removed from one's Record only through *forgiveness or redemption*.

Each person must accept responsibility for the wrongs he commits. Sins, or wrongs against God or other humans, cannot be forgiven unless they are first acknowledged, that is, admitting that a wrong has been committed and taking responsibility for it. Acknowledgment or confession will not come without a contrite feeling of repentance, a desire to live righteously within God's Will. First, acknowledge them to yourself, then to God. Then correct the wrongs and seek forgiveness. Sins can be deliberate or inadvertent, committed with full knowledge or from ignorance, done openly or secretively. One who desires to live rightly will refrain from sinning to the extent that is possible for him. He will acknowledge any known sins to God in prayer, asking his forgiveness and for the strength and wisdom to overcome those things that have caused him to sin.

One who will not acknowledge his sins, even to himself, is not honest or trustworthy. If he can't be honest with himself, will he be honest with others who cannot know his mind? If a person desires to be righteous, he will desire to be free of wrongdoing. He will be conscious of any such thing that he deliberately does and will confess them to the Father for forgiveness. Acknowledgment of wrongdoing reveals to the confessor his own imperfections so that he may come to understand why he does them and work to overcome these weaknesses.

Not all sins are forgivable. Those things that a saved person does in the normal course of living are usually forgivable since he tries to avoid sinning against others and God, particularly grievous sins. An unsaved person may do all sorts of things that are unacceptable, ranging from contrary attitudes to murder. Some of these are *not forgivable*, in particular those done against another person that inflicts grievous harm to him physically, emotionally or spiritually. Such acts may include: murder, mayhem, and maiming; terrorism; robbery and thievery; abortion; rape; certain destructive acts; adultery and betrayal of love; chronic lying or deceptively influencing others to sin; disregard for the trust, faith and dependency of others; betrayal of oaths made before God; emotional or physical cruelty; traitorous acts against one's country; rejection of God; and many others.

Unforgivable sins cannot be removed through request for forgiveness from the perpetrator, but can only be removed through *redemption*. This is a process through which the sinner cancels the sin from his Record by living a life or performing acts that will compensate for his errors and spiritual debts. This is required by *Justice*, a principle by which God assures that all results of transgression are either replaced with good or are absolved by his Grace in full accordance with the merits of the acts and motivation. *Forgiveness does not eliminate the requirement for justice.* Whether one is forgiven for a light or serious misdeed, he must still accept the responsibility for correcting the harm that was incurred, if only for his own happiness. Only after redemption has been accomplished can the sinner be justified.

No person has been given the authority to forgive sins someone commits against another person or God. Only the ones directly injured by the offense can forgive these sins. This is expressly true for *non*forgiveable transgressions.

Mankind's justice and God's justice are separate and one does not cancel the other. Man's justice aims to arrest unlawful behavior and directs corporeal or pecuniary punishment upon the person or his property. God directs justice toward remediation and salvation of the soul. Mankind's justice is often imperfect and unfair, but God's is not. Paying debts to society, such as serving time in prison as justice for criminal acts, does not remove the acts from his spiritual Record and must be removed through redemption. *It is fitting that both the human and the soul are justly chastised for wrongs deliberately commit-*

ted: therefore, *God respects human justice* that is appropriate and is uniformly dispensed with due regard for the sanctity and redeemability of the person. *Justice without charity is no justice at all.*

If a person asks God for mercy and seeks His forgiveness, God will remove all forgivable sins that he has committed. At the same time, He provides ways for him to compensate those that are unforgivable. God will lead him through experiences that provide the opportunities to repay the spiritual debts made to others or to God. This is Redemption---the paying or restitution of debts made to others. Through love and contrition, the repentant person will welcome a chance to redeem the wrongs done to others and restore goodwill.

Not all such sins are repaid in the lifetime in which they were made. Some may be held over to a future life when circumstances bring the two souls together in associations and circumstances in which the debt can be paid.

A person may die before he prays to seek mercy and forgiveness. In this case, he carries the full list of forgivable and redeemable sins into death with him. He cannot enter a heavenly state with this burden, so he is given over to the control of Satan's kingdom, or Hell. He will carry all of his sins over to future lives in which they may be compounded through continued sinning. His Record grows ever heavier with unredeemed sins, and it gets increasingly difficult for him as he grows further away from God. At some point, he must turn to God and ask for mercy and forgiveness, or his soul will become demonic, satanic, then, possibly, beastic. These are progressive standings of hardened sin in which the sinning soul grows more into a willing stooge of Satan's will.

If the person's conscious mental processes are no longer functional when death overtakes him, no further change in the status of the soul can be made willfully by the person. Therefore, if the body is unconscious before death and the soul is not saved, it is too late for its status to change *through his own* petitions for mercy and forgiveness. Salvation must always be accomplished in partnership with the human host. Yet, if this soul now feels repentant and desires salvation, *the prayers of other living humans who are saved can rescue this soul.* Many are saved before the body dies through the power of the prayers from others. It is never too late, even after death.

Forgiveness was one of the great lessons that Christ demonstrated time and again, even while he was dying on the cross. He taught that you should forgive others for what they do to you. This is extremely important for both you and the one who has sinned against you. You have the power to forgive someone for a sin for which the sinner cannot receive forgiveness through his own prayers.

When sins are committed against you, you can forgive the doer. If you do not forgive him, the Laws of Redemption require that he pay these debts to you. This means that you must meet this soul at a future time, perhaps in a future life, so that he can remove the debts from his Record. Forgiving him, even if he has mortally wounded you, frees you both from the obligation. Then if you should meet this soul in a future life, it can be under more pleasant, positive circumstances. Forgiveness is an act of love, whether giving or accepting it, because it demonstrates your desire to release each of you from spiritual indebtedness and cleanse your records.

The Spiritual Imperative for Forgiveness

There are good reasons for humanity to understand why forgiveness is crucially important and necessary for the soul's salvation. This involves the fundamental nature of the memories of all experiences shared by the soul and human host. Everything that the human and soul do in life is recorded in memory. For the human, memories are imperfect and incomplete since a person rarely observes an event or knows an association with complete fidelity and thoroughness. Mortal human memories are a mix of truth and fantasy pocked with voids and confusion. When the human dies, all of his memories die with him and cease to exist.

The reader already knows that the Heavenly Father created all angels from "truths" which He created from the substance of his own being. Each angel is a unique, boundless selection of truths infused with God's consciousness. Memories are *acquired knowledge* that establishes rudiments of truth. *Additional truths* are created from *memories* of its experiences and *become an intrinsic part of the angel's make-up.* This broadens the angel's distinctive qualities and contributes to defining its Record.

When the soul sins with its human host, the sins are remembered by both. In contrast to the human host, the immortal soul remembers everything with perfect fidelity, thoroughness and understanding. At death, the angel-soul becomes a free spirit and retains the memories potentially forever. Since the spirit is composed of truth, and memories are truths, they remain part of the spirit helping to define its unique constitution. This is not unlike the substances a person takes in as nourishment contributing to the intrinsic composition of his body.

Sinful deeds defy God's Will resulting in corrupt memories for the doer. *Memories of sinful acts constitute knowledge acquired through unlawful behavior and are "stains" that corrupt the truth structure of the soul.* Corruption is "unclean", or impure. God has declared that nothing unclean can enter the Kingdom of Heaven, which is perfect and holy. Therefore, the unclean soul cannot come into the presence of God bearing impure memories. It must repudiate and somehow discharge the memories if is to find salvation and restoration to Heaven's Grace.

Only God can remove the corrupt truths from the spirit's composition. But He does not do this without the spirit's willing cooperation. The principle of Free Will is a powerful, honored gift to all Hosts of Heaven, and God will not compromise it. Therefore, the spirit must ask him to remove this corruption through the power of Forgiveness, which includes Redemption. In this context, Forgiveness is a process in which God excises the impurities from the constitution of the spirit, or the spirit performs deeds of providence that redeem the acts that caused the impure memories. He removes something that has become a manifest part of the spirit's being. It is not a mere attitude as it is with humans. The spirit must truly desire that God do this and submit itself in faith, love and complete willingness. Then God, through grace, cleanses this spirit of the unacceptable truths.

This is why forgiveness is necessary for the spirit's redemption and salvation. The spirit must initiate its own quest for salvation by first repenting of its wrongdoing, then approaching the Father in humility to acknowledge the wrongdoing and his willing desire to be clean. Humility itself is an act that acknowledges that *God alone has the power to cleanse and save the spirit,* requiring submission to this power. When this is done, God always responds in mercy and grace, waiting for the spirit to ask him to forgive the sins. Through the act of forgiveness, corruption is removed from the spirit and its Record is clean and whole once more.

Roles of the Mind and Soul in Becoming Saved

The human cannot physically sense the presence of the soul that resides within him. He is not aware of the seat of influences that lead him to thinking, behaving and accomplishing those things that no other Earthly creature is capable of doing. The human does not know where the powers of the mind leave off and the powers of the soul begin. He cannot discern that fine line that is the demarcation between the two domains.

Both the soul and mind are essential to the physical, intellectual and spiritual *character* of Mankind. They each are sovereign in their own domain, and can act separately or together. Acting together, they can be harmonious or antagonistic. Acting alone, each takes care of its own concerns. The mind is concerned with its well being and survival in the physical world; the angel soul is concerned with its standing with God and its need for renewal through repentance and redemption.

Acting together in harmony, the mind and soul will affect and maintain salvation and receive the gifts that come through God's Spirit to exalt the human with a Divine mind and charitable spirit. Becoming saved is a prerogative of the soul, not of the mind. The decision to become saved is a deliberate act that must be made by the soul in partnership with the mind. The mind cannot make this decision for the soul because only the soul is saved and it must make the choice to become so. The mind cannot save the soul; yet the soul must bring the mind along with it in making the decision. The mind will always act positively with the soul to attain salvation if the soul has properly prepared and directed the mind to do so. The mind will always yield its permission to the soul under these conditions, but cannot affect salvation on its own if the soul itself is unwilling.

Salvation is prompted by the soul and requires deliberate participation of the person to consummate it. It does not happen without conscious effort and desire and full perception of its need and fulfillment by both the angel soul and the human host. No one is truly saved without his awareness and willing cooperation in the process. The soul must prepare the human to desire and willingly pursue the attainment of righteousness. It must act as a conscience to instruct and lead the mind into doing God's Will and chastise it when attitudes and behavior deviate from this goal. *The human must come to recognize the need to avoid behavior, associations and pathways that increase temptation and opportunities to sin, and he should despise sinfulness in himself and others.*

Several stages are involved to affect salvation, and each stage may be distinct or may unfold interactively. First, is a REALIZATION that one is in an unsaved condition of continuous sinning, without repentance and forgiveness. Then, a DESIRE for CHANGE emerges to motivate the person to earnestly pursue change. Then he ACKNOWLEDGES or confesses his sinful habits, weaknesses and desires, that relief must come from without, that Christ is the Master who has the power and capacity to extend mercy, to forgive sins and help you to overcome weaknesses, and that he will do so if truly desired and sought. One does not advance the salvation of their soul by castigating *others* for *their* sins, but by acknowledging the acts proceeding from one's *own* sinful nature and following the steps remaining in this writing.

Following acknowledgment is REPENTANCE, the turning away from sinful desires and behavior, then SUBMISSION to the love and mercy of Christ, of your will to his, opening your mind and soul to the Father through prayer, and letting Christ come in completely to illuminate, change and renew your life.

Finally is COMMITMENT to reject sinful ways, to pray often, to learn God's ways of love and truth, to strive to do his Will and keep His Laws in all that you do, and to live among fellow humans in love and righteousness. Salvation is more than commitment to prepare one's life to face death unafraid. It should include the idea that salvation and righteousness are *eternal,* that they shall bring union with God and His angels in Heaven forever. With this idea we may commit our souls to preserving salvation through future lives.

After achieving salvation and commitment to abide in His Will, one may CONSECRATE his life to the service of God to be an *instrument* of His Will for the sake of leading others into Christ's Kingdom.

Having a *saved soul* doesn't mean that the person is without imperfections, or bad attitudes, or wrong beliefs, or that he is totally righteous. A saved person has turned away from following a sinful life and is *seeking* perfection through righteousness and divinity through accepting and following those things that he knows are pleasing to God. Above all, the saved person strives to know God's laws and his Will and to follow them in all thoughts and actions, in private and in public. He seeks guidance through prayer, meditation and reading the Holy Scriptures to justify his salvation through right living. The psalmist recognized the crucial distinctive roles of both mind and soul when he prayed, "For Thou hast delivered my *soul* from death; wilt not Thou deliver my *feet* from falling, that I may walk before God in the Light of the Living?" (Psalm 56:13)

On the other hand, having an *unsaved soul* doesn't necessarily mean that the *person* is evil, that he is not decent, or has no value to himself or the community, or is not loving and caring, or is not honest and trustworthy. These "unsaved" persons simply have not purposely taken the steps given above and *chosen* to live in ways acceptable in all respects to God. Many of the unsaved are law-abiding, charitable and highly regarded persons who contribute to the well-being and success of their families and communities. Unless the soul *acknowledges, affirms and accepts* the sovereignty of God, the soul is not saved irrespectively of the worthiness of the person. It is the *soul* that is saved or unsaved, and blessed is the person who lives rightly from the strength of his own character and respect for his fellow man.

Therefore, *love* one another. Set an example for your brother or sister or neighbor, and have patience without judgement. One can learn from the other and receive help from him. But do not follow those who are driven by self-centeredness, intolerance, anger and hatred, for those things do lead to evil. Do not follow those who do not respect God's laws as given to Mankind through the Ten Commandments of Moses and the laws of love and neigh-borliness by Jesus, for they will not lead you to good and may condemn you personally and spiritually. Affirm to God your desire to forsake a sinful life and live by his laws of righteousness and love, in all things, forever.

Who Sins, the Soul or the Human?

Before the Spirit became involved in "worldly" matters, the flesh, i.e., humanity, did not sin. Even though flesh pursued and partook of many things that indulge human appetites today, flesh was innocent because it did not know the Law and was not under the Law. (Paul discusses the application of Law *with respect to humanity and the "original sin"* with great eloquence in Romans 6-8.) Flesh did not commit the original sin; rather, it was Spirit embodied in the fallen angels who committed this sin against God and humanity. Through their acts the fallen angels brought sin upon themselves and humanity.

When God initiated the Age of Redemption he gave his Law to the fallen angels. Since the angels were breaking the Law while knowing the Law, they sinned in their disobedient activities. When the angels became souls in humans, through which they brought spiritual awareness to humanity, they also brought knowledge of God's Law to the human hosts. This brought sin to humanity since they continued in their natural acts, knowing that certain acts and behavior were forbidden. However, the humans were like children for they were still being taught right from wrong by their angel souls and they had not yet become responsible. The angel souls were required to continue teaching God's Law to mankind while his intellect and understanding ad-vanced to maturity.

Although the immature human sins, he is not held responsible since he cannot grasp the significance of his acts in respect to the Law. When he becomes mature, he is then responsible since he is able to make his choices based on knowing right from wrong. The soul that strives to lead its human host into righteousness, obeying the Law, does not sin even if the human disregards the Law and disobeys. This soul will chastise its human host through the "conscience," inducing remorse and repentance.

The soul sins when it does not lead the human into the Law. The soul sins grievously if the human tries to live rightly, but the soul causes him to stumble because it is indifferent or contrary to God's Law. This human will exhibit many personal conflicts and often seems to be without conscience. The best of all states attains for them both when the soul and human host live in the Law and are obedient to it. Since it is not clearly apparent to humans whether it is the human or his soul that is sinning, only God can make the judgment.

Whenever a human commits a sin (breaks God's Law) or a crime (break's human laws), God judges the soul for its role in this affair. The soul is innocent if it acted properly as the conscience, trying to teach the human the way of righteousness and dissuading him from performing the act. Otherwise, the soul is not innocent and is held accountable if it was indifferent and did not attempt to lead the human rightly, or, in particular, if it acted as an advocate of seduction and deception to lead the human astray so that both indulged in the sinful act.

The human intellect is now mature. The soul and the spiritual awareness that it imparted have inscribed the Law upon the human mind and within human laws and codes of behavior. Knowledge of right and wrong is his heritage and provides clear signposts to direct his pathways to righteousness. *Mankind is now responsible for obeying the Law, and God will not withhold the consequences of ignoring his inviolable laws.*

Unity of the Human and Soul

Mankind and the angels of the Earthly realm are mutually engaged in a cause that has profound significance and promise for them both. Intimately bound as human and soul, they shall rise or fall together. The ultimate outcome of the fallen angels shall depend upon whether they fully achieve the goals of redemption. The ease and fullness with which they attain salvation will depend upon how well they prepare the mind of Mankind for partnership with the soul and how willingly humans cooperate in consummating the partnership. Since the human is *not compelled* to live rightly, the consequences for the soul shall also depend upon the Providence of God.

Since the Age of Mankind began the fallen angels have pursued God's plan of redemption, which provides opportunities for the faithful to be restored to God's Grace and their former dwelling place in Heaven. Through love, new angel souls have been created to assist and inspire them to fulfill this Divine purpose. To achieve this, the angels, through their own efforts, must compensate humanity and Earth's creatures for the shameful abuse they heaped upon them and induce in Mankind an exalted state of intellectual aspirations and spiritual awareness. Consequently, humans will be inspired to seek and employ all the gifts available through God's Spirit.

Humans have had little knowledge and understanding of their souls, not knowing from whence they came, or their identities, or why they exist at all. Nor has he understood how or why he is rewarded *bodily* with eternal Heavenly life if his soul becomes saved, or suffer eternal torment in the "fires of hell" if it isn't saved. This has been an area of *misunderstanding* resulting from a lack of insight and misstatements issuing from the earliest times because Mankind has not understood the sovereign singularity of the body or soul. Now Mankind has the truths to understand all of these things and to know his exact destiny in God's plan of redemption. He can now be aware of the eventual fate of humanity as well as the fate of his soul. He can understand now the importance of salvation for the soul, and why it has importance for him personally.

The things of which Mankind is not fully aware concern his own present role in fulfilling the angels' redemption and in achieving the full benefits of their association. Consequently, with few exceptions, Mankind does not generally cooperate in fulfilling the souls' objectives. The gentle urgings of the soul, impressed upon the mental functions of the human, are weak and humans seldom know how to deal with them, especially when they conflict with human desires. A fog of confusion still inhibits a full realization of the benefits of mutual aspirations.

Angels can achieve a completely sinless state while involved as souls in their human host only by remaining free from the desire and inclinations to sin and striving unceasingly to lead their host to righteousness. The soul cannot prevent the human host from performing acts that he feels are important to his well being, appetites, ambitions and survival; but it can lead him to desire righteous ways and Divinity.

From Judeo-Christian teachings, the human can be fully knowledgeable of the requirements for righteousness, which is keeping God's laws. From the teachings of Jesus Christ, he knows that holiness or divinity come from righteousness merged with love and truth. The moral teachings of the Bible were given to instruct and inspire humans to live righteously to benefit the soul as well as himself. Unless the human host desires to live righteously and seek and share the gifts of God's Spirit so that he rejects the things of depravity and destruction, the weak souls will continue to sin and fail in achieving their goals of redemption.

With such preparation for his mind, Mankind can know and understand the redemptive goals of the angel souls. Through achieving their goals the angels continually instill into the mental framework of humans an exalted capacity for love, truth, intellect and consciousness from God's Spirit, and the capability to use these powers to attain a world of unprecedented achievement. With these gifts, humans may receive Divine spirituality by which they can pursue for themselves all the gifts available through the spirit.

There is often conflict between the human mind and the soul, so that neither of them achieve the full benefit of their association and both may fail in achieving their life goals. Even if the human had no soul, he would still be a sovereign being capable of directing his activities and destiny through his own desires and decisions. The soul attempts to lead the mind, sometimes quite powerfully, to fulfill the purpose that God has given them together. The human may yield to the soul's almost constant urgings and accomplish many of the goals that fulfill the purpose. Yet, the mind has many things to distract or tempt it in the material world, causing the mind to ignore or resist the soul's urgings. Then the human host follows its own leanings to satisfy its desires and perceived needs.

The soul can become severely frustrated after lengthy, unsuccessful conflict and may cease its urgings. The soul will simply allow the human to go his own way until he realizes he is "missing the boat". Meanwhile, the soul may even hinder or block the central talent or ability that it had been trying to get its human host to apply. In this way the soul hopes to get his attention and build concern. A feeling of loss or aimlessness may then get the human to return, often with greater resolve, to pursuing the aspirations inspired by the soul.

Now that Mankind is aware of the souls' objectives, seeing in them God's holy purpose for redemption and exaltation, each person can commit to cooperating with his soul to affect repentance and salvation. They can become partners together to help each other achieve their purpose while attaining their own goals, each reaping the full benefits of progressing together within God's plan and Grace. In this new association of partnerships they can attain a world in which holiness and God's Providence lead Mankind to achieve the magnificent state promised for the millennium of Christ's reign on Earth.

Baptism, the Way to Achieve Unity with God

How does the human form a partnership with his soul, uniting his intellectual and spiritual natures to accomplish their Divine purposes? First, he must accept the truth of certain cardinal precepts. He must believe in the existence of God and only in Him is the source of those trustworthy and lasting things that can fulfill his aspirations. He must believe that God is holy and that one can find acceptance in Him only through obedience to his laws of righteousness and love. He must accept that God's spirit resides within his own body in the form of an angel, or soul. He must accept that both the body and soul have mutual purposes, given by God, and that through His Will their purposes can be fulfilled. He must accept that only in faith and God's laws of righteousness can he and his soul find unity with his higher purpose for humanity and the fallen angels.

Secondly, he can come to understand that through the full process of baptism the human and soul are joined in acts that unite their purposes. In baptism, both physical and spiritual aspects are combined to achieve salvation and divinity. In true baptism, one acquires and displays a belief in God, acceptance of his Will, submission to purification through repentance, forgiveness and redemption, commitment to attaining righteousness and following God's will in all things, and faith that God's Grace will resurrect the baptized soul into eternal Life with Him and the Heavenly hosts.

The act of baptism must not be taken lightly, for it is not a mere outward sign that one has come of age and has joined the church. Baptism is of such importance that one should enter into it only after much meditation and prayer. One should mentally prepare for baptism to achieve a knowledge and understanding of its full significance, then pursue it gladly.

Baptism was initiated in Judaic beliefs through Mosaic Law as ritual cleansing for those who desired to "come before the Lord", because nothing unclean, including sacrificial offerings, should come into his Presence. Later Jews refined the act as a ritual of initiation and purification for those accepted to take their place among the elite or "chosen" of God, to serve Him in acts of faith. In Jesus' time, John the Baptist extended it further to include repentance, the complete turning away from sinful ways. John preached to masses of believers and followers that they should repent and be baptized, then follow the laws of righteousness.

When Jesus came to John and offered himself to be baptized by him, John knew that here was one who did not need to repent, one who was greater than he. John came to understand, when the "holy spirit" descended upon the baptized Jesus, that baptism had much more than mere corporeal and ritual significance, but was Divinely spiritual as well. Baptism was, for Jesus, an initiation into the start of his ministry, which would lead to the fulfillment of the purpose for which he had been born among humanity. Fortified with commitment and faith, it prepared him to face the decisive trials of temptation of whether to use his great powers to achieve worldly success or to use them for the Heavenly purposes given by the Father, which he knew could lead to rejection and death.

In his ministry, Jesus spoke of baptism in the fullness of its physical *and* spiritual aspects. As given earlier, these include belief and acceptance, submission, repentance, purification, and resurrection into spiritual life. Mark records Jesus as saying, "The one who believes and is baptized will be saved". For those who see baptism as only a physical act, Jesus' formula for salvation seems shallow and inadequate. Indeed, it would be if it were only physical, for it must include the spiritual component as well, and this is what Jesus required. The apostle Paul elucidated the concept and practice of baptism to include all the physical and spiritual considerations extended by Jesus, and having within it the proof that faith alone, not works, *saves* the soul. The apostles James and Peter taught that faith must be proven with works worthy of that faith.

The ritual of baptism as practiced in churches is a physical act that symbolizes all physical and spiritual aspects of baptism. Rituals may offer baptism through complete immersion of the body under water, or by sprinkling or pouring water upon the candidate's head. Since these methods *are only symbolic* and are not the actual baptism itself, either is acceptable and is only a matter of personal belief or preference. John used mostly the immersion method which, it turns out, is more truly symbolic of spiritual meanings.

Whether baptized in a stream, as John performed the act, or in a font, one may regard the water as a symbol of the pure, living water spoken of by Jesus. Of course, a stream is not pure and may, in fact, be quite dirty or polluted. In sprinkling or pouring, purified distilled water may be used; still, this is not the pure, living water of Jesus' promise. In ritual baptism it is not the water that brings purification and salvation (resurrection), but is *submission to and faith in God's power and grace.* The living water of spiritual baptism "washes away" all sins, that is, it purifies the repentant soul through Redemption.

One may also regard the water into which he is immersed as representing the state of death, into which all humans must go. Then he is raised out of the water, symbolizing the resurrection of the soul into everlasting life with God, or of renewal of the soul through rebirth into a new body. This symbolizes resurrection and renewal of the soul to begin a new cycle of life.

True baptism is always integrally related to faith in the power of Christ to save and restore. Through faith and repentance, the soul participates in baptism with the prepared human intellect. Spiritual baptism affects a radical change in the nature of the person's attitudes and behavior and brings him into vital union with God. One may truly regard baptism as a marriage of the soul with the Spirit of God and has no less importance than the vows that unite two souls in spiritual love.

Baptism, then, is an initiation and commitment of the mind and soul into a new and different life. It signals the end of a sinful life and a resurrection into a life of righteousness and faith for the remainder of one's years. Before submitting to baptism, the person begins to purge his mind of unrighteous thinking and directs his desires and behavior accordingly, gives up following the paths that lead one into sin, seeks those things of love, truth and beauty that lead to divinity of mind and spirit. Then, he must learn to submit willingly to the soul's urgings, allowing the soul to be his conscience and guardian angel to always do those things that are right. One can find unity with his soul, both advancing toward achievement of their purpose given before birth by God.

In his ministry, Jesus established a body of disciples and believers whom he had educated in Divine knowledge and wisdom. After his resurrection and ascension, Jesus' spirit returned to lead them and the new apostles into establishing the church among Jews and Gentiles. The church eventually spread around the world, conveying "the word" as it went into all regions. One may rightly view the church as a kingdom of righteous believers, ruled by Christ their king, and interspersed throughout a worldly kingdom of nonbelievers. When a person comes to believe in him and is baptized with the true baptism, he is initiated into Christ's kingdom, his church. Then he becomes a new citizen in this kingdom, a safe, unassailable haven for the righteous established in the very midst of Satan's kingdom of Hades.

When one understands the full concept of baptism as offered by Christ, and enters into it with a repentant and loving spirit, and accepts its full requirements, the Holy Spirit baptizes him, body and soul, into the Kingdom of God. Through these intellectual and spiritual acts, the human and his soul become truly wed in unity of Divine purpose.

Interactions of the Holy Spirit with Humanity

The Bible speaks of the disciples and apostles being 'visited" or led by the Holy Spirit, which Jesus called the Comforter or Helper. Such occurrences are given only to select persons as acts of the Heavenly Father to enable them to perform specific tasks that fulfill the Father's Will. Since the time of Jesus this spiritual power has been generally misunderstood and people have incorrectly acclaimed the presence of the Holy Spirit in routine religious activities. Many believers think that the Holy Spirit leads or instructs them in their daily lives in routine matters, but, in general, this is the influence of their own saved souls imparting the guidance given by the Father.

The Holy Spirit is not commonly available to all humans or souls because God withdrew this power when he isolated the Earthly realm from Heaven. Only the Father directs the coming and going of the Spirit and it cannot be commanded by humans or other spiritual entities. The scriptures inform us that, though John baptized with water, Jesus baptizes with the Holy Spirit in the name of the Father. Jesus spoke of the Spirit before the Holy Spirit had been *given* to him because he had not yet been glorified. Later, he told the disciples that *the Father will send the Holy Spirit* to them in his name, and *the Father will send the Holy Spirit* to those who ask of him.

The Father will send the Holy Spirit to briefly visit each soul that becomes saved to confirm the reality of God and bathe it in the power of His Love. Otherwise, throughout the Age God has given and directed the Holy Spirit to sanctify select persons. This is not done for frivolous reasons. Rather, it is done to accomplish Divine acts of great significance, such as when the disciples were empowered to preach the Gospel in the unfamiliar languages of foreign visitors in Jerusalem at the time of Pentecost, or when they preached the Gospel in new places to enliven the new churches and groups of believers. The Holy Spirit was very active in the establishment of the early churches after Pentecost, in Judea, Samaria, Syria, through Asia Minor, Greece, Macedonia, and Rome. The Spirit led and fortified the apostles, workers and believers to give them powers and gifts of mind and spirit to set up a firm foundation upon which Christ's church would grow.

Believers who undertake special tasks in the name of Christ are visited by the Spirit so that the task may be accomplished in accordance with God's Will to achieve His purpose. A visitation of the Holy Spirit illuminates the soul and mind of the select person with the Father's Consciousness and Intellect. It endows the person with unusual knowledge, understanding and abilities that are then brought to bear upon tasks to accomplish a holy purpose of the

Father. The Spirit brings Truth to the witness and confirms it in unshakable faith.

Belief and Faith

Belief and faith, when combined with knowledge and understanding, are the powers that motivate a person to conceive and achieve dreams of aspiration. Without these powers he is not likely to achieve his goals and may not take even the first steps along the pathway to his dreams or life purpose.

Belief and faith are gifts of the spirit, coming from the infused soul. Before the Age of Redemption, humanity could not display these qualities, but relied upon acquired knowledge and learned response to control his behavior. Belief is not the same as *knowing*, which involves certainty of facts or truths. Belief is the intellectual acceptance of something inferred from fact or reason, unseen factors that go beyond mere knowledge or experience, the possibility of which is assured through faith. Belief can be directed or applied to anything that is important to a person, such as believing in himself, his loved ones, his fellow man, his country, his church, or his God. Faith is the unquestioning conviction and trust in the validity of those beliefs.

Belief and faith can enlarge and extend the powers that come from knowledge and rationality alone. These qualities can bring about miraculous results because they encourage the hopeful person to reach beyond his own capabilities or potential. They connect Mankind with a mental strength that is beyond normal human powers. These positive powers can dispel anxiety, fear and discouragement. Their opposites—rejection, doubt and worry—can cause the "unlucky" to languish in failure and hopelessness.

There is a saying that if belief is strong enough, anything is possible. There is much truth in that saying, but there are many things that are not in a person's capacity to control. What happens when one believes very strongly that something he desires is attainable and, with powerful faith, applies all his physical and spiritual resources to achieve it, yet fails? What happens to faith then? It is possible to continue believing that the thing is attainable, but he has lost faith in himself, or others, or even in God to bring it about.

One often attempts to project the power of his faith to help others who may be caught up helplessly in some personal quandary. Something that is deeply rooted in someone else's mind or soul is not easily changed; it is difficult enough to change something about yourself. Love binds you with the one who suffers and helps to bring a measure of peace.

Some problematic situations seem to be intractable in spite of the faith and effort directed toward them. When everything possible has been done to bring change, you must not blame yourself for failure. It is then up to someone else or to God to change it. When one suffers he is capable of making his own decisions, which may hinder even God from resolving the problem.

Maybe "time" will accomplish what your efforts cannot; but patience and long-suffering are constant companions of time. Faith and patience bring wisdom if you learn that unwanted things that you cannot affect must be left to God; but not to Chance. Therefore, pray often for them, knowing that God hears your prayer, and leave it in His hands. Know also that if there is nothing more that you can do, then the outcome is up to God's Will and He will make the choices. Therefore, believe that God works to bring about the best outcome for all that He must consider. Love, justice, and redemption are often deeply imbedded in such things.

Faith is more than an emotion or a state of mind. It invokes extraordinary mental and spiritual powers. Faith marshals the believer's intellectual strengths and focuses them upon a purpose and the achievement of its goals. Whenever a believer expresses strong faith in his cause and demonstrates his faith through actions, this can have contagious results on others. They become impressed and are inspired to join him or to pursue their own dreams with similar fervor. Pooling their faith in a common cause, such power is projected in their concerted actions that no power on Earth can defeat them.

Faith, fortified with prayer, attracts the participation of angels to assist the believer and assure the success of his dreams. The angels perform sympathetic tasks that cannot possibly or easily be done by human powers, such as in miraculous healing or in the perfection of a talent to express beauty or uncommon skill. Belief and faith lead to remarkable results when one prays frequently about his dreams, allows God's Will to rule his life and opens his mind to His Love and Truth which are accessible through the soul. Wisdom, insight, courage and thoughtfulness then accompany faith to achieve blessings for himself and others, to redeem the misfortunes of life or to achieve the goals of one's aspirations.

Letting God Have His Way

During the final hours before his death, Jesus pled sorrowfully with the Father while at Gethsemane in the garden, adding: "...Nevertheless, not my will, but Thine be done." It was a purpose of Jesus' life to place himself at the apex of human decision to accept or reject him as the Messiah and he was confirming this commitment with the Father just as the critical hours began. This trial, soon to commence, was not for Jesus, but for those who had the power to accept and save him.

There are hardly any words that anyone can speak that are more important to his spiritual and Earthly destiny than these. In so saying, you submit your own will to God so that his Will can be done in your life. The more you are able to do this, the better it is for you. Only in this way can you achieve your God-given purpose in life with certainty and satisfaction.

When the soul is born into life, it comes with a *purpose* given by God. This purpose, if achieved, will assure redemption of certain debts to others and will take one to the pinnacle of his dreams of aspiration and achievement. One who is born with a saved spirit has arrived from a Heavenly state in which he, with the help of angels, has planned and prepared for a life of redemptive associations and expressions of achievement through talents, abilities and learning. In this state, he dreams of the things he wants to do for others through love to redeem mistakes and ill will. He dreams of life's experiences, challenges, occupations, obligations, sacrifices, gifts and blessings he desires to attain and share. He dreams of associations with new and former spirits to share life with them. Together, with God's angels, the prospective soul formulates these elements into a plan that will become his life's purpose. *The life purpose is carried out and fulfilled under the Will of God.*

If one comes into life with an unsaved spirit he arrives from Satan's kingdom with unforgiven sins. In that state, he was not given the opportunity to develop a plan of aspiration and redemption. Yet, he yearns for the same things as the saved spirit, but will not let go of desires that obstruct and destroy his path to redemption. Since life without a purpose is pointless, God gives him a purpose and a plan so that he may become saved, redeem sinful debts and achieve worthwhile things for himself and his life associates.

Pursuing and fulfilling its purpose is the primary mission of every human life. Any person who learns to pray at an early age and turns his will over to God's direction, letting Christ be his master, will be led by Him into experiences that can prepare him to meet all the goals of his purpose. God will lead him into the care of those who will teach him, help him develop his talents and abilities, and strengthen him through diverse experiences. He will lead him into the *pathways* that will take him to those he must meet, to whom he shares redemptive debts and with whom he will share love. Such pathways are constituted by parents, families, communities, schools, churches, organizations, institutions, marriages, friendships, professions, enterprises, travels, and all sorts of activities that provide opportunities for interaction, familiarity and bonding. God will guide him in making the choices and decisions that affect his aspirations, achievements, associations, well being, and journey through life.

Only God knows where you are going and how you must get there. It is a rare person who clearly perceives, from his own insight, his own goals and how best to achieve them. Only by submitting your will to Him can you fully achieve your purpose according to the plan you made or dreamed of before you were born. *Your own willfulness can lead you away from your purpose*, can prevent you from meeting those you will dearly love, can prevent you from redeeming your debts, can keep you from being all that you could become.

People whose lives are intimately interconnected such as families, husband and wife or as institutional associates have their individual and mutual purposes to fulfill. Each of them should understand that all others around them need to fulfill their life's purpose and should help them to have the opportunities and aspirations to do so. Each person must have the personal freedom and personal "space" and time to pursue his goals. No one should be so demanding or exercise such tight control over another or others that these are denied the opportunity, time, energy and inclination for them to respond to the inner drives that can lead them toward their goals. These may involve almost any positive endeavor, such as learning, reading, training, hobbies, exercising talents, associations of friendship or professionalism, working, charitable acts, worshiping, praying, and so many other activities. The concern must be mutual, each doing his part, sharing his portion of the burdens so that all may pursue their goals.

Life's purposes extend beyond any individual to encompass others. Families, groups, institutions, and nations can also have purposes given by God to accomplish his Will on a concerted, broad scale. In fulfilling their own purposes, individuals contribute labor, time, ideas, principles, leadership, energy, and love to accomplish the goals of many joined in common purpose.

You do not need to ask about the meaning of life or what your purpose is. *The meaning of life for each of us is found in the achievement of our purpose.* You are led to achieving your purpose by letting God's Will be your will. Learn to pray, submit to His Will, listen to that quiet voice within you, follow that positive urge that tells you what is right, and overcome the temptations to do those things you know are wrong.

What is "God's Will"?

God's Will encompasses all of his *Laws* that pertain to the spiritual and material domains (Heaven and "Earth") and all of his *desires* that flow from pursuing acts that fulfill his Supreme Purpose. One can know his Will by knowing the Ten Commandments given by Moses and the laws of love and neighborliness as taught by Jesus Christ. Through their souls, humans are also tapped into the Source of Divine knowledge and understanding available from God's Intellect and Consciousness. So each person can always be guided by the voice of his soul, the conscience, and the Holy Scriptures into an awareness of righteousness. Then *through prayer* he can know what God desires of us in all occasions. Doing God's Will is to demonstrate willing obedience in actions, thought, and behavior that reflect God's desires.

It may be easy to think that doing God's Will restricts our actions, behavior and opportunities. Actually, *the opposite is true.* The scope of God's Will is so supremely broad that there are hardly any boundaries once our own willful ways are discarded and His law is written in our heart and mind. It is really our own will that is narrow, shallow, restrictive and obstructive.

Every human has a dichotomous nature because of a unique and temporary situation in which his physical body accommodates a spiritual guest, the soul. This compound entity lives in a worldly realm ruled by Satan, a situation that incurs special rules. Still, *the only real restrictions* are those that are intended to keep the person from falling into the pits of sin which Satan has strewn about to divert the soul from redemption. Doing God's Will, therefore, includes avoidance of those thoughts and actions that can entrap one in Satan's pits of sin. In all of God's Heaven, the Earthly realm is the only place in which such potential for disaster abounds. Elsewhere, sin does not exist and the scope of God's Will appears to be infinite, without restriction.

The dichotomous nature compels each human to live in both the material world and the spiritual world simultaneously. It is desirable that a person learn to balance the needs and aspirations of each world, otherwise he can become too "worldly" or too "spiritual". The worldly character can be detrimental to the soul's progress toward God, particularly if one is too attracted to Satan's temptations. Wealth, power, fame, passions and pleasures of the flesh and other such worldly attractions should not become one's masters or ends in themselves, but rather the amenities and discrete enjoyments in his reach for greater purposes. There is a "worldliness" that opposes God's Divine purposes because it is materialistic and concerned with willful indulgence seeking fulfillment that gives only temporary satisfaction instead of seeking the things of eternal reward.

An overly spiritual character can hinder the material well being and ability or inclination to thrive in a material world, including interactions with fellow humans. The soul must remain spiritual, and the body must remain material; but, for them both to attain the full greatness that is available to them, they must be unified by the powers available from God's Spirit. So united for a common purpose, the gifts of His spirit become available to help them attain their righteous goals in both realms that they inhabit.

Through prayer, earnestly seeking Divine guidance, a person can free himself from temptations and the pits of sin, and from the misguidance of his own will. If he strives to do God's Will, then he begins to grow in mental and spiritual stature. Even the nature of his desires changes to intellectual and spiritual things of higher value. The *harmonious unity of worldly and spiritual forces within* propels him to levels of attainment not achievable through his own willfulness. He will soon realize that there are no real restrictions any longer, and that only the condition and abilities of his mind and body limit him. Nothing can endure outside of God's Will because all such things oppose his Supreme Purpose. There will be nothing in God's Will that obstructs or limits him to achieve his own holy purpose.

Achieving Life's Purpose for a Successful Life

No greater potential for achieving fulfillment, happiness and contentment can come to a man or woman than through realizing the life's purpose that God has given them. *The greatest and highest things available to any person always come to him through his purpose.* All else will fall short and may even bring a strong sense of disappointment or failure. Once a person has submitted his life to the powers of God's Will, then most everything of significance that comes to him, whether good or bad, is related to achieving goals of his purpose.

A man and woman united in marriage, or a family or cohesive group of friends will pursue and fulfill at least some goals of their respective purposes together. Marriage vows include elements of commitment that allow those united in love to achieve the common portion of their purposes, which can bring them joys and sorrows, good health and sickness, fortune and adversity, or perhaps triumph and tragedy. It becomes a greater tragedy when their marriage fails and their purposes face defeat and unfulfillment: more ends than just their marriage.

Only a small percent of humanity achieve all the goals that are given in their individual purposes. Many achieve at least some of their purpose; but most attain little or nothing of it. Some follow their own willful pathways that take them entirely away from the purpose they came into life to achieve.

The surest way to achieve all or most of one's purpose is to find God early in life and learn to follow His lead through major decisions and activities. Pray daily that He will teach you to know and do His Will. Pray that Love and Truth will govern all that you do. Pray that He will strengthen the channels that allow the voice of your soul to speak to your mind. Pray that the power of His presence will guide and mold you. Pray daily for forgiveness of your sins and that He will help you to overcome those things that cause you to sin. Pray that He will help you to redeem all sins that you commit against others. Opening up to God and giving your will over to Him can bring a power, freedom and peace into your life that you cannot achieve on your own.

In human eyes, the measure of success is often the degree of wealth, power and fame that come with one's accomplishments. The greater these factors are, the more successful he is regarded to be. Perhaps this is success, but most probably it does not achieve those things he needs for spiritual progress. For some, one or more of these factors may be needed to fully achieve life's purpose, but for most none of these is necessary. Life's purpose can usually be achieved in the most humble of circumstances and success is measured on a different scale.

Quite often, one finds that attaining all possible material rewards does not satisfy an undefined craving within; something is missing, perhaps terribly wrong. Emptiness, uselessness, restlessness, sadness, despondency, and all sorts of dark miseries may continually sweep over him. His willfulness has brought him great material rewards and humanly fashionable success. Yet, his soul cries out that time is moving and he has not taken heed of the need to consider his purpose. He has avoided all the pathways he should have taken, has made all his decisions for self-indulgent reasons. Frustration, discouragement and anxiety buffet him, and these emotions will begin to mold his character and outlook. Why has this happened? Was this person so strongly attracted to the objects of temptation around him that he never looked inward to hear the guidance of his soul?

It may well be that a person follows the right pathways and achieves his purpose, yet doesn't attain any of the material rewards for which people usually strive. He will achieve something far greater and more satisfying. Once a person has achieved his purpose, he will feel satisfied and contented with life. Then he may begin to feel restless and somewhat empty because life is not over, yet his goals have already been met. He may now be drawn to desire opportunities or develop latent abilities to achieve new heights for himself and those with whom he shares life. This is the time for him to pray for renewed meaning in his life. God can renew or extend his purpose to enable him to attain the goals of his new dreams.

Pray, ask, seek! New directions will come, doors will be opened for you to enter new spaces of mind and spirit. God does not limit you with your purpose that is the minimum He expects of you to progress toward redemption, but He can give you all that you desire and are willing to achieve.

If you achieve your holy purpose, you will by ordination also achieve *salvation*. Be assured that *salvation can be achieved without fulfilling all or any elements of your purpose.* Willfulness does not always mean that one opposes God or acts in contrariness to his Laws. It is more likely to mean that this person has not listened to God through the voice of his soul and has followed his *own* council in making choices that determine the pathways through life. In this sense, he has not acted in accordance with God's Will as it pertains to achieving his purpose in life.

Following this course, you may have conducted your life in a manner that still pleases God. You have accepted the principles and ideals of a righteous life, have set worthy goals for yourself and worked diligently to achieve them, have conducted your affairs with others with justice, charity, truthfulness and honesty, and have worshipped God in prayer, belief and faith.

In following your own course, you may not have attained the highest of your aspirations or of personal and professional goals that were available to you through God's spirit. You may not have met all those with whom you needed to resolve redemptive debts. Since He brought you into life in a time and place and among parents and family that could lead you into your purpose, you have met at least *some* of those with whom you shared spiritual destinies. While not paying spiritual *debts* to any or all of those to whom you were indebted, you may have established *credits* to others through acts of love, good will and sacrifice. Sometimes such credits can resolve unpaid debts owed to others that you will not meet.

God accepts all works of humanity that do not *defy* his Will and constitute sin. God rules his relationships with humans through his Supreme Purpose and renders justice with charity. This assures that full measures of his Grace, Mercy and Patience are extended to all who do not willfully reject them. Do not reject God or whatever He offers you, and He will not reject you.

Experiencing Death

THE EFFECT OF DEATH ON THE BODY AND SOUL   The act of dying for humans involves both physical and spiritual processes. The physical body dies and the processes of nature begin to decompose the flesh into its basic chemical compounds, including fluids, gases and organic materials. These are further transmutable into other compounds and basic elements, but retain their fundamental permanence in the storehouse of the Earth's physical resources. As indestructible resources, these elemental remains of a once-living body will occur again as constituents of living tissues in times to come. All persons and creatures alive today contain residues of life, including humans, from previous times. A body that dies is destined to support life in multitudes of creatures not yet conceived. Thus, life is immortally continuous, and all living things share the resources of life's common substances.

In contrast, the soul does not die or disintegrate but merely changes its status from being a soul to one of being a "free" spirit. After death, the soul is no longer associated with a body of flesh and it resumes its identity as an angel spirit. However, it is not free in the sense that normal Heavenly angels are free: for it must remain in the Earthly realm of Hades, the spiritual kingdom isolated from Heaven and ruled by Satan. In this realm the free spirit is either in a "Heavenly" state or a "hellish" state, depending upon whether the soul was saved or unsaved at the moment of death.

The Heavenly and hellish states exist solely for redeeming the spirit. None who go to either place is yet ready to enter the Heaven where holy angels reside. Those in the Heavenly state have repented and turned to God and will be renewed and prepared for their future lives in isolation from evil. Those in the hellish state have not repented and are punished with the results of their own wickedness to show them through first-hand experience the wages of sin. *God did not create the conditions in Satan's hell;* these were all produced by Satan himself and those who sin, and they precisely reflect his own nature. In death, the saved are isolated from the unsaved because their masters are totally opposite and their respective experiences are as different as noonday brightness and cavern darkness.

THE SOUL DISENGAGES FROM THE BODY AT DEATH   Human death involves termination of the physical processes that give and sustain life and disengagement of the soul from its infused connections within the body. Disengagement, like the initial infusion at the beginning of life, is a physical process. The soul senses that the body is dying and begins to prepare itself and its human host for the final moments of their association.

When the soul senses that death is imminent it begins the preparations, first the mind, then itself for death. This will be followed by disengagement from the body when the body actually dies. Disengagement is commanded through attendant "death angels" and the soul cannot refuse to disengage. In this circumstance, neither can the soul prevent the human host from dying, because if the soul had this power it could hinder the Will of God.

The soul then begins to withdraw the "wing" and "tail" filaments in an orderly process that takes about twenty minutes in the normal process of dying. Withdrawal of the soul doesn't affect the physical functioning of body organs or glands. First is withdrawal from all the glands of the body, including the lymphatic system. Next, comes withdrawal from the organs in the trunk of the body and sensory organs in the head, with the exception of the brain. These organs include the heart, lungs, stomach, gall bladder, liver, kidneys, reproductive system, tongue, voice box, sinuses, ears and eyes. Third in line to be disengaged are the brain stem and the body's central nervous system along the spine, shoulders, back and buttocks.

In some instances, the process of disengagement may be interrupted or even stopped by the time this point is reached. Christ is the final arbiter of death. In some cases, Christ will determine that a person's purpose in life is not complete and that if he lives on for a while, he will complete it; or the person may be granted a new purpose in life which he can and will fulfill if given more time. The prayers of others are helpful in this determination, but are not decisive.

If Christ chooses to prolong life, the soul is instructed to re-engage itself into the parts of the body that it has vacated. The body will then be restored to either full or partial life capability and health is restored accordingly.

If life is not prolonged the soul continues disengagement with the next, or fourth, stage which is disengagement from the brain. This is the most complex and lengthy process. The soul must "read" all pertinent memories in the brain and capture the essential personality of this individual and store these attributes within itself. Other knowledge or "data" monitored and stored during life by the soul concerning the most minute state of the living body are reduced to a "summary". The summary is retained by the soul while the "raw data", no longer needed, is discarded and ceases to exist. These things then become a permanent part of the soul's own personality and helps to define its uniqueness.

The brain is not the last to be disengaged. One last stage remains, but the nature of this cannot be disclosed. Neither the soul nor the death angels have knowledge of or access to this stage. Only Christ is knowledgeable of the final stage and he provides disengagement in it. When this is accomplished death is final.

While the soul swiftly reads the memories, beginning at the present time to the moment of the soul's infusion before birth, the mind senses persons, events, activities, decisions, achievements, hopes, aspirations, sorrows, failures, etc., whether good or bad, that were important to this life. It does this in full cognizance of the attending angels.

Once the death process is completed, the free spirit becomes the real "personality" of the deceased. The human body experiences only one life; the soul has been the infused companion of many humans experiencing life, possibly through many thousands of years. Hence, the soul contains the integrated personalities of all its incarnations and is not likely at all to resemble the person the family and friends were acquainted with in life.

HOW THE SAVED SOUL EXPERIENCES DEATH   If the soul is saved, most sinful things have been forgiven and the debts that it must redeem in future lives are hidden from it. This soul sees the bright light of love and mercy extended through Christ's Presence. The images of others loved by this soul who may have already passed on are often projected into the presence of this soul. These images are not spirits, but only visions or memories of these persons. Only the attendant angels are actually in the presence of the soul. Some images of one or more persons, usually family members, loved by this soul may linger after most others have departed. These images will depart before the soul reaches a terminus of light that signifies that death is final. The soul goes through the point of light and enters a wide region of brilliant light where it sees the death angels who direct the process of disengagement of the soul from the body. Disengagement is now concluded.

When disengagement is complete, the attendant angels conduct the free spirit into the Heavenly place, which is under the direct rule of Christ, the Master of all angels and the savior of all souls. In this place, the soul will be constantly bathed in the light of Christ's Presence whose love and truth will permeate all that is experienced. This soul will begin to meet many spirits it "knew" in this and former lives in reunions of great happiness and joy. It will soon begin preparations for future life, guided and instructed by numerous angels. Assignments will involve it in numerous activities, many of which are concerned with the living and redeeming the soul's debts of sin. It can also visit with loved ones among the living who are still mourning his death.

Most activities in this Heavenly state are concerned with renewing and redeeming the spirit. The spirit is managed by Holy Angels who carry out the will of Christ to cleanse and prepare the spirit and allow it to conceive and pursue dreams for fulfilling its ideals and redeeming debts to other souls. The spirit develops its ideals of whatever it wishes to accomplish or become during its next life. It isn't concerned with power, wealth or fame unless these factors are necessary to achieving the goals, although these may come anyway as a result of its activities. It is presented knowledge in the things that will be important to the goals. The spirit may express or select conditions it desires in that life to help mold the appropriate character and personality and to have the opportunities needed to achieve its goals.

Intrinsic in the plan are things the spirit must do or experience to redeem spiritual debts to one or more souls it will meet again in the next life. In that life, the soul must be available for experiences and associations so that others will have the opportunity to repay debts to it; pathways must be available or provided within the conditions to lead the soul to those it must meet again, at the appropriate times.

At just the right moment, the renewed spirit will be told by Christ to infuse into an unborn infant to become its soul. Angels have chosen the infant and Christ will monitor the process of infusion. Angels will remain with the soul after infusion until birth and will remain with the infant for a few months longer. The parents of the infant live in a time and place and within such life conditions that the soul's goals can be pursued and, perhaps, fulfilled within its lifetime. There is no certainty of anything, for decisions made by this soul and others will be important to its fate. The strength of one's belief and faith and of commitment to doing God's Will can help assure that he follows the pathways to fulfilling his purpose. The soul begins this life with a spotless new page upon which the story of its life will be written anew, and whether old debts are paid or new debts made, or whether other souls have incurred additional debts to it.

HOW THE UNSAVED SOUL EXPERIENCES DEATH   The un-saved soul faces a very different experience during death. During early stages, it experiences very much the same things as the saved soul, except the light of Christ's Presence is missing. The soul knows that it isn't saved and it begins to feel a separation or alienation from the attendant angels and the images of the loved ones who are saved. Because of its unrepentance and the burden of unforgiven sins, this soul begins to experience fear and dread. Before dying, it experiences unpleasant or horrifying images of life associates and deeds.

Many lost souls do not observe the terminus of light as experienced by the saved soul because it is shrouded in the darkness of unredeemed sins. They die and must perform disengagement in darkness. As disengagement commences, the anguished images of loved ones appear briefly then disappear as dark shadows of their evil deeds move in. At the moment disengagement is completed, the attendant angels, which this lost soul cannot see, look upon the soul with compassion and sadness, then turn away and quickly depart.

Light from the Heavenly Kingdom is absent and only a faint glow of God's love remains. Dark forms move in and clasp onto the lost spirit. These are spirits from Satan's kingdom of lost souls who have come to claim another victim. They will conduct the spirit into the presence of others, an experience much like entering an asylum for the criminally insane. Multitudes of lost spirits will demand to know what the arriving spirit did to deserve being among them. The spirit will begin to tell them, starting with the lightest sins. The others think it is holding out on them and mockingly demand to know all. The terrified spirit continues recounting its sins until its memory is exhausted. The multitude continues to mock and belittle the spirit and reflects how easily it could all have been avoided.

Very soon, the spirit will come into the malevolent presence of lesser and greater sinners. Some of them may have felt wronged by this spirit in some previous life. Anger, hatred, bitter cynicism and hopelessness are in all of them. They heap accusations, insults, mockery and threats upon the spirit. It will seek to hide some place; but there are no hiding places in Hell. Woe unto the murderous tyrant whose soul has arrived in hell and begins to meet the spirits that were dispatched there due to his policies and directives: roles become reversed and the tyrant is subjected to the most merciless tyranny from his vengeful victims, and they never forgive or relent. So it is with all murderers, rapists and thieves who have not repented and put themselves in God's mercy.

Soon the spirit will encounter one or more of Satan's beasts that diligently control affairs in this hellish place. The beasts will begin to force the spirit into activities intended to interrupt and interfere with God's plan of redemption, to deceive and entrap the living in sin and shame and to do anything whatsoever to inflict misery and hopelessness, violence and sorrow upon the living, even upon those they loved in life. It is not a privilege of the lost spirit to decline or refuse to do Satan's will, for he has an effective system of punishments for those who attempt to do so.

Being an unsaved soul, Satan will neither reward nor praise you for being a sinner and coming into his kingdom. He is not interested in niceties. Rather, Satan rules in tyranny and his kingdom is one of oppressive fear and loathing, of almost intolerable anxiety and misery, and he gives you no respite. The worse your sins, or the more grievances other spirits have against you, the harder it will be for you. If your sins were light, you don't get noticed so much and may get to do your own thing for a while. Don't get carried away with this, for someone is watching you. They will begin to use you to lead someone astray and entrap them. So don't get too interested in the living, especially those you love.

On the other hand, salvation is possible for you if one or several of those still living remember to pray for you. If they themselves are saved and if you truly desire to be saved to begin serving God rather than Satan, then perhaps some help can come to you.

You will not be able to pray in Hell, only those still living who are saved can do that for you. You have complete freedom to think of almost anything you desire: you can entertain regrets over sinful things you did to others. You can think of those you love and how they showered expressions of love on you. You can wish you could be back in life with them so that you could treat them well and undo the bad things you did. You can wish you could tell them not to make the mistakes you made.

Unfortunately, your thoughts are never private and you will not be able to perform your good wishes. The power to do so is not available for, alas!, there are two things you definitely cannot do in Hell because Satan's ever-watchful forces will not allow it. One of these is to express the name of God or Christ. The second of these is to pray for help and mercy! The instant you attempt to do either of these—and there will be many such attempts—Satan's beasts will be there to crush you. Since salvation requires that you call on the name of the Lord to purposefully ask for His mercy and forgiveness to save you, opportunities to do so are denied.

So, prayers for the salvation of your soul must come from the living. This is a power given to the living who are saved. If those who pray are full of love and forgiveness God's angel will isolate you from the forces of Satan and lead you in repentance into the Presence of Christ. Christ will project his love and mercy upon you while you ask for forgiveness and an opportunity to redeem your debts. Christ will then let the angels conduct you into the Heavenly domain where you will be accepted and treated as any saved soul.

So profoundly great is the difference between the Heavenly and hellish domains!

If you cannot be saved while you are in hell, you will remain there for an indefinite time. Eventually God will cull you from Satan's control to allow you once more to become the soul in an infant human still in its mother's womb. From this point until your new host learns right from wrong, Satan's power cannot touch you. You will be born again as a *new person*, except that you are full of unforgiven sins and unredeemed debts. Be careful that, in this new life, you do not add to these. If your human host should die while it is still *an innocent child*, God will save the soul because death prevented the unfolding of its purpose. This is an act of God's Love and Mercy, to give you another chance with a human partner to find Him, to do His Will and keep His Laws.

Guide and mold the mind of your new host so that it comes to know and love God's ways, so that this person will learn to pray and strive to do what is acceptable to Him. His prayers will get your sins forgiven. Yielding to God's Will can lead you into redemptive associations and activities, if you do not block these with willfulness and lack of heed to His word.

SATAN'S HELL CAN BE AVOIDED   Dying is a doorway for the soul to enter only one of two possible states. One is blessed with good beyond human knowledge and expectations; the other leads to abject misery and darkness. Death of the body is not a finality for the soul. It is not the end of the journey or of opportunities to share love with those you may have wronged or to fulfill life's purpose.

Final judgement of the soul does not follow death. Neither the heavenly nor hellish state that envelops a soul after death is permanent, but is simply a passing phase before new life begins for all but a few. There are some who become so unredeemable, that they may not see life again until God gives the last call before the final judgement. Whether saved or unsaved, death can be the start of a new beginning for the soul, a process of renewal for the spirit and a new opportunity to progress toward God.

Faith and hope in God's Promise of Life hike the bridges that span from life to life like islands in the sea of eternity, along the unbroken journey that leads to the City of Light. All who choose to shall arrive at the city gates on that final day of the journey, to begin a new kind of Life together in a new Heaven that will never end. Accept God, love Him and your fellow person, let His Will become your will, and keep His laws; then you will not fear death because the inhabitants of hell will not greet you.

8

THE AGE OF MANKIND— MATTERS OF CURRENT INTEREST

The Human Perspective

Human behavior and outlook are strongly affected by the interplay between the mind and soul. The soul continuously confronts the human host with evaluations of his thought and deeds. The righteous soul encourages the host to continue in the good things and chastises him when he errs. Yet, the human maintains his sovereignty of decision and action. The soul doesn't *force* the host to follow any course of action, whether good or bad. The host will react to the soul's guidance in a totally voluntary way.

Aside from the soul in every person, humanity has its own *spirit* that is not spiritual but comes from his exalted intellect. This human spirit involves the *mind* and its qualities of *thoughtfulness* as directed toward factors involved in all possible human relationships. Because of the values instilled into the human intellect by the angel souls, it is based on the things of love and truth. The factors include love, loyalty, trustworthiness, faith, commitment to principles and oaths, duty and responsibility, sacrifice for the sake of others, and a regard for the consequences of acts and attitudes. The goal of this spirit is to lead Mankind to divinity and to abandoning those things of adversity, destruction, and ill will. It will teach him that *anything* worth doing should be *justified* in the thoughtfulness that comes through this spirit.

The human spirit is *noble and wonderful*. This spirit leads the human to be concerned for his fellow man and all that has been given to him by his Creator, to respond to the obligations and challenges of life, to give and seek love even when it is not shared, to strive to bring his dreams and aspirations to fulfillment, to seek the knowledge and truth that permits progress, to treasure and seek and create things of love, truth and beauty, and to correct and enhance those things that are disagreeable to his judgement. There are many other wonderful facets to this spirit that help to ennoble humanity. Those that catch this spirit become part of the force that moves humanity toward its highest aspirations and potentials.

His home, the Earth, is full of beauty and marvelous things. Yet, the world is not a perfect place for humanity for many reasons. This is *partly* due to factors which include Mankind's lack of knowledge and understanding in all things, his carelessness for the value of many material and intangible things that define the state of his existence, his preoccupation with self and lack of the discipline that could ennoble him. Many things affect him adversely or disturb his sense of balance and fairness and lead him into short-sighted, self-centered responses. Some factors are beyond his powers to perceive or control.

Many problems arise because of the *limitations* of humanity and to *distortions* that he projects upon his intellectual and industrial pursuits. Adult humans develop from the training grounds of parents, family, community, companions and experiences that mold them during youth and adolescence. There, the constraints are fashioned and learned that will determine the course of his life, manifested in the *attitudes and beliefs* and the *manner in which he will react* to his experiences and all that comes before him. Humans are limited in intellectual and physical observation of any experience and he can take in only a part of it. This will be further affected by his perceptions, attitudes, knowledge, and whether he will be receptive or resistive. *These* are determined by the things that have molded his capacity to face all things with *thoughtfulness* and whether he will share in them freely, justly and charitably.

Humanity still panders to many temptations that serve to diminish the power and growth of his spirit. He allows many things to affect his judgements and actions in unfavorable ways. Preoccupation with personal needs and problems leads him to disrespect the needs of others that *depend upon* him. Feelings of insecurity in a demanding world and the potential for failure prompts him to possess more than he needs while disregarding the security needs of all. Pressures that arise from a growing population cause him to abandon a respect for preserving his resources and environment. The ability to attain and wield power tempts him to overreach the bounds of propriety and responsible use of that power. A lack of congruence between intellectual and spiritual perceptions leads him into irrational beliefs and behavior and sometimes to bizarre, despicable acts.

Humans find it extremely difficult to appreciate some of the Earth's creatures. He can see no good reason for some creatures to exist. These attitudes are understandable. Some of Earths creatures were not created *for* the Earth and they truly serve no purpose for this world. Recall that before the Age of Redemption, the angels used the Earth as a laboratory for life creation *for the galaxy.* Then you will understand that some creatures on the Earth serve purposes only in *other* worlds where life exists. Recall also that when Earth fell to the onslaught of Satan's campaign of disobedience and degeneracy, *all creation activities ceased on this planet.* Creation projects were abandoned without conclusion. This has left humans and many creatures with significant physical problems. These problems particularly affect humans in old age since their life spans have increased greatly during the Age of Mankind *beyond that which the angels had prepared them before the Age.*

God, the Creator of humanity, knows how difficult it is to arise day by day to meet the challenges from obligations and hardships. He knows the difficulty for anyone to lose the ones that are loved and, in particular, *the one* who means more to him or her than one's own life. He knows how difficult it is to have needs and dreams that never seem to be fulfilled. He knows about the pain when someone who is loved falters and destroys all opportunities to fulfill the hopes and expectations others had for him. He knows how brief are the spans of joy and pleasure in a world where hardship and tribulation lie all about.

Yet, through all these things, many remain noble and true to their purpose. Many will not fail or disappoint others who depend upon them, even if they must give all that they have. They will not allow the prospect of failure and loss even to the point of death to stop them or turn them aside. They will sustain and defend the persons and principles they love and treasure even if all else is lost. The noble spirit triumphs through all that may come and it leads mankind ever toward a time when he will have mastered this world and established complete peace and goodwill upon it.

The Earth will truly become the *home* of Mankind: the world will be his *palace* and he will be as a wise and benevolent sovereign. He will love and respect and sustain every natural thing on Earth. He will understand his world and the relationships between all things in it. He will understand *himself* and will be content with his lot as a *mortal.* The thought of death will not distress him. He will be aware that his existence as a sovereign being is limited and will use his abilities, opportunities and resources to achieve the highest of his aspirations, to leave a legacy of contribution to the wealth of all mankind and the Earth. One's achievements will live long beyond his time. Mankind will view himself as an essential and eternal part of all creation and will not abuse any part of it. His aspirations will flow from a perceived purpose that reflects God's own Supreme Purpose and a *spirit* founded in Love, Truth and Beauty will command all that he does.

Mankind, you are still struggling, but consider what you can become. Do not give up the fight to overcome the things that obstruct and tarnish you, for the goal is within sight. You now know what you must do and where you are going. Let your noble spirit continue to grow and lead you to divinity. Join with the power that comes from God's love and intellect. You can be part of it and will receive the blessings in God's promise of a New Earth in which former things have passed away.

Some Expectations for the Present Age

The Church in its many forms throughout the world has preserved the Message of Christ to the present day. In recent decades there was a falling away from religious observance because Mankind's interests have multiplied. His remarkable attainments in knowledge and accomplishments have established a need for a new relevance for religion. Mankind's knowledge and understanding of the world are far greater than when the books of the Holy Bible were written. He justifiably feels that much that was written is difficult to understand from modern perspectives. The social and cultural profiles of today certainly differ from the times and places that molded the biblical writers. Yet, the same elements of righteousness and holiness that are universal and timeless endure like islands of rock in a tumultuous, changing sea, then, now and forever.

Those serving the Church as priests, preachers and teachers have diluted Christ's Message with irrelevant ideas and precepts that Christ would not approve. Many of the messengers and their messages are empty and false. The central core of the Message has remained intact, but so much spiritual pollution and insincerity has been added to it, that the Message seems inadequate to those multitudes desiring to know the Truth. Not everyone desires the truth and some will not welcome it when it arrives upon their doorstep. To those who shun truth, it is a scourge, a despicable lash to be feared and avoided. To those who love truth, it is a brightly shining light that brings peace and freedom and deepens their faith.

The world searches and waits for the arrival of truth that will cleanse the clutter of confusion and corruption from the mind of humanity. They yearn for better knowledge and clear understanding of those things of God that have established their faith in his Promise of salvation and eternal life. For this purpose, the Father has given this book.

The time has come for God to end this period and begin the final times of the Age. This shall begin with the spiritual "war of Armageddon", which shall begin soon and which Christ shall win. *This is not a physical war of destruction between nations, but a decisive resolution of conflicts in moral and spiritual issues that will involve every person, family, social group and nation.* The combatants shall be armed with a new knowledge and understanding of God and his purposes for dealing with Mankind, and the formation of partnerships of Mankind and the angels who are his souls. Christ will not force the victory, for this battle shall proceed so that the truth will emerge from the arguments and strife in a manner to convince all who seek the truth. On the eve of victory when Satan's arguments have been defeated, Christ will establish His Kingdom of Love and Peace on Earth.

To prepare the world for the Millennium, God shall raise up leaders in the New Wisdom who are capable of leading the willing into the New Promised Land. The old cast shall fade from the holds of leadership and influence, and they shall receive whatever honors their labors merit them. Truth will not allow their reputations to emerge as legends larger than life beyond the end of their times, but they shall seem only as they were. Christ will appear as the only Godly one among humanity and the Father shall glorify him. Christ will live in the flesh only for a while during the early part of his Reign, then will be taken, once again, into Heaven.

In His previous incarnation, Jesus Christ was a Jew of the ancestral lineage of King David. In the new incarnation He is not only a Jew, but is of mixed ethnicity. He is now Jewish and Arabic, black African and white European, Indo-European and Oriental. All peoples will be able to see themselves in Him, regardless of their race, and all must accept Him on this basis.

Christ will establish the rule of his Kingdom as a human so that his Divine sovereignty will be agreeable with human nature: his presence in the world will be physical and his leadership will be as an exalted human radiating love and wisdom. His genetic composition from a mixture of races will be a living symbol of his Divine mission to unite all the diverse elements of Mankind in the power of love and acceptance. He will radiate strength and humility, love and firmness, compassion and assurance. His knowledge and understanding of all things and all people will distinguish his capacity for leadership. He will lead with the power and authority of God, His Father, and all shall follow him.

During this second Earthly life, Christ will not be rejected by Mankind and put to death again. He shall be accepted around the world as the Master and Redeemer and the Son of God. Only those blinded and hardened by their determined hold onto sinful ways will be unable to accept and follow him. *Only the Righteous shall live during his reign and the Earth shall be his totally.* In this Kingdom, Mankind shall succeed in all worthwhile endeavors almost as though it is Heaven, attaining accomplishments he has never dreamed were possible.

Following the Millennium, Satan will once again come forth from the pit of Hades to do battle with Christ and the angels. For a short while longer he and Christ shall struggle mightily for the souls who are weak or have not yet chosen God. The times will be terrible for those living, but will soon be over. The Age of Redemption for the fallen angels shall end and the soul-nurtured Age of Mankind will also end. Satan and his irrevocable advocates shall be isolated to stand powerless before the Judgement of God and His holy angels. The failed kingdom of Hades will exist no longer.

The ways of modern Mankind are varied and complex, a mixture of both good and evil. Satan's influence over unsaved or weak souls causes Mankind to sin. The unsaved soul leads its human host into acts of attitude and behavior that can bring abuse to fellow humans. Tempting human weaknesses, Satan leads humans to lie, deceive, cheat, steal, plunder, destroy, maim, kill, hate, betray the beloved, defile love through adultery and perversity, betray trust, deny affection or loyalty, seek self-indulgences, direct hostile acts toward others, bring war upon their neighbors, and many other evil things. The rules of righteousness are changeless and are written in every soul as knowledge of right and wrong to guide human behavior. Anyone can learn to resist temptation and reject inclinations to perform evil deeds, choosing instead to live righteously and responsibly and obey the laws both of Mankind and God.

Humanity is no longer an unaccountable child and must be responsible for his behavior and accept the consequences of his actions. Humans reap the rewards and punishments for their behavior during their lifetimes. They may experience remorse, suffering, despondency, loss, ruin, guilt, shame, imprisonment, violence or perhaps death because of evil acts by themselves or others. The soul receives appropriate reward or punishment following death of the body, directed toward redemption and preparation for future life.

Things of evil are contrary to God's Laws and his Will and defile those things that are good. They will stand only until the last soul willingly rejects sin. Then God shall prevail absolutely: Satan and all who stand with him will fall into eternal oblivion and the power of disobedience and corruption will be gone from the Universe forever.

Behavior That God Abhors

IMMORALITY AND ACTS OF VIOLENCE, HATRED AND BE-TRAYAL   Many in the modern world profess to know God or to be decent, and some are. There are many for whom God abhors the deeds and thoughts they perform, and their souls will pay the price of redemption or die with Satan. He is saddened by those who:

- try to make right seem wrong, and wrong seem right, distorting and turning God's moral truths upside down and treating His Laws as dust on their shoes;
- treat sexual love as though it were free to all for only their pleasure and exploitation and that it should have no consequences or responsibilities; seduce, coerce or force others into immoral acts, violating their chastity or the sanctity of innocence which should be preserved for sharing only within God's laws of love;
- forget the sanctity and necessity of family and that a duly united husband and wife are His requirements for men and women to become fathers and mothers;
- have no regard for the sanctity, the importance, and the preciousness of life, or the homes and property of others;
- destroy the life and body of a growing infant in the womb of its mother, inculpating the mother and those who wield the instruments, for whimsical reasons to avoid the consequences of illicit love;
- give little value to the most solemn and righteous of Mankind's obligations as vows given to wife or husband, or responsibilities to their children, or those who depend on them for life or love, to the needs and duties of the community and nation and to their own soul;
- lead or influence others into activities or modes of life that are demoralizing and destructive of self and others;
- destroy or subvert the character, morals, decency, love, hope and promise of children and youth in unrecoverable ways, through deceit, seduction, coercion, entrapment, indifference or example;
- behave as though God had made them and their kind superior to all others who may differ in some respect, and bestow a tyranny of

indifference and ostracism on them, whom God also loves; yet, God has given each person selective and discriminating minds so that they may make the decisions and choices that guide their spiritual destiny, a quality that must be honored and protected;

- take willfully that which has not been given from others by threat of death, coercion, theft, deception, cajolery, trickery, bribery, greediness, false or undeserved claims and any other such dishonest means; those who take from the poor, the elderly, the disabled, the sick and the trusting. Everything that a person acquires should come from the honest application of his physical and mental powers or from gifts and inheritance freely or lawfully given;

- acts of greed and selfishness that lead one into accumulating wealth or power far in excess of his needs as a means to control or deny the reasonable needs and aspirations of others, or as a symbol of self-pride, ignoring that all good things come from the grace of God to be shared in love. Moderation can provide all that one can truly enjoy or make use of without becoming a slave to greed;

- disdain and distort the truth, rewrite accounts already established as fact, lead susceptible minds and souls astray, undermine the loyalty, hope and faith of the righteous and the institutions they have established, and set themselves against all that is good and right;

- disregard or deny the rights, beliefs, customs, traditions, or legacies of others which were established through time, birthright, sacrifice, travail, or shared love and histories;

- seize the power and authority of a people or nation and bend them to their own self serving purposes, to deny them the privilege and opportunities to govern their own affairs and direct their own national destiny, to act in despotic, tyrannical, brutal and unlawful ways to bring misery and desolation upon the governed, or inflict hostility and violence upon their neighbors;

- refuse to the end, the gifts of love, grace, mercy, and truth that God offers freely to every soul, so that they may ask for forgiveness and redemption to cleanse them and set their souls on the path that leads to God and Heaven.

The consequences of evil thought and behavior should easily be evident to all. These things constitute the causes of failure, sorrow and destruction in human lives, relationships, families, institutions, nations and the Divine purposes given to all. It should be plain to see the difference between Godly and unGodly behavior. Humanity and their souls rush aimlessly through life as if their eyes were closed to all truth, and they see only what they desire to see. Surely, they walk in darkness, for they have not opened their eyes to the Light. Truth is all around in great, clear evidence. The miracles they seek to save and bless them lie within easy reach, if only they will open their eyes.

God has given these statements of sinfulness not so that one can judge the other, rather so that one can evaluate his own standing with Him. Let not the contrite heart be dismayed because of grievous sins that have brought despair and sorrow. God is ready to forgive those who repent and will help them to redeem all debts to others. Affairs can be righted with those you love, against whom you have sinned. God created every soul with His Truth and Laws part of their being. Learn to let its voice be your conscience to guide you in doing His Will. This can bring full restoration to His Kingdom and eternal Life.

SATANIC WORSHIP   Since before the Age of Redemption, many fallen angels came to worship Satan and honored him as an angel of mystery and the champion of pleasure and passion. Becoming souls, these angels began to mold their human hosts in ways of evil to please their master, Satan. They induced into the minds of mankind perverted versions of truth and strange images of reality that led to beliefs and practices which culminated into cults. The cults drafted their beliefs into religious creeds and rituals that could be perpetuated through ceremonial worship directed by and to the angel of darkness. In this manner, Satan had an organized human force through which he could resist and corrupt God's efforts to reclaim the fallen angels through Love and Mercy.

There remain many who worship Satan and the forces that bring evil upon humanity. Satan has infused into the minds of his cult worshipers the idea of sacrificing animals to demonstrate their resistance to God. The mutilation, killing and sacrificing of animals, which sometimes include humans, in ritual worship is a direct act of defiance toward God's Plan of Redemption which is intended to provide the fallen angels with opportunities to redeem the sins of desecration they committed against Earth's creatures.

The use of humans to further violate his fellow creatures is an attempt by Satan to slap God in the face and mock His plan to restore Love to all of Earth's creatures. Persons who allow themselves to be so used, instead, mock their own opportunities to redeem their sins and find salvation in God's Mercy. Used as willing tools of Satan, they compound spiritual debts of sin against God and Earth's creatures that must be redeemed if they are to escape eternal spiritual death.

If they love God, if they love Earth's creatures, if they love their own souls, let them hear this message and forsake these practices. Satan will survive for only a short while longer; but *God will endure forevermore.* All should strive to please God and worship Him only, for He alone is worthy.

Dishonoring God's Gift of Life

ABORTION   Life is precious to God in any stage from the moment of initiation through birth, life and death. Is there anything on Earth more sacred than a womb nurturing an unborn child? It is a sanctuary where life is created in innocence and purity and infused with the Spirit of God. It is not a place where premeditated violence and sudden death should destroy life created through the Love and Will of God. It is not God's Will that a man and woman engage in unlawful sexual love and conceive a child; but once life is initiated, it is taken into His Will because it is HE who gives life. God loves Life and He will not deny life even when it is unlawfully initiated.

Abortion is the *abomination of abominations* in the judgement of God. It is the abomination that devastates. The womb is the one place where life *must* be respected as greatly and reverently as the life of a living child. If reverence for life is not accepted by humanity as one of God's most highly esteemed canons, then death will be regarded as more fitting for you than life whenever that suits the purpose of those who disrespect his laws.

A human life destroyed whimsically and callously while in the womb of the mother is a most heinous sin against God and the one whose vulnerable life is taken. This can be considered to be raping of the womb, an unloving act done to remove and avoid the certain result of illicit sexual love as a charade to characterize this act as having no consequences. The unborn is not to be considered part of the mother's body, for it is indeed a distinct, sovereign human being with its own life, purpose and rights separate from those of its mother.

Those who think they have an inalienable right to love as they please but have no responsibility for the life that may likely follow, must remember God's Law of Love: that sexual love is allowed without sinning only to a man and woman who God has joined in matrimony. Engaging in sexual love and creating a life without the sanctity of marriage or home violates His law that requires this responsibility. If you abort the unborn infant, you certainly end the life for an innocent child as well.

The soul of the unborn child also has its rights. Its soul was given through the love and authority of God with holy purpose. Destroying the body destroys the temple in which the soul has come to occupy as the guiding light of love and truth for that human through life and denies it the possibility of fulfilling the purpose that God gave it.

Whenever the expectant mother knowingly performs practices or behavior that menaces or injures the unborn child, or causes the natural development to go awry, she infringes upon the child's right to wholeness of life. She must protect and nurture her unborn child as the most precious gift she could receive. Someday this child must be presented to the world and to God. A child embodies love and Divine purpose, and presents awesome responsibilities to those to whom it is entrusted.

Unborn babies having newly created souls are the most affected by abortion today. Presently, the world's population has reached six billion humans. Of these, only about one in twelve have souls of original angels, and this ratio decreases as the population grows. This fact shows that new souls are created regularly through spiritual love to support the increase in numbers. Do not use abortion as the means to control this growth and do not destroy the temple of this infant entity that has not come to know life or God.

If men and women follow God's laws of love, there will be no desire to end pregnancy by abortion, and birth of the child will once again be regarded as the blessed Miracle of Life, which endows the parents with God's special love and trust. Society should regard the mother's womb and the children that are created within as its most valued resource, a sacred gift of Life that should then be nurtured in love, honor and grace.

WANTON KILLING   Only God can give Life, and it comes from His Consciousness. All living things are made from His own substance. God has given every person a purpose for living and no one has the authority to destroy that life and annul its purpose. It is only a matter of scale whether the killer acts alone or is a dictator commanding a ruthless army of killers. Even the power of a monarch or dictator does not give one the authority to *capriciously* take away life. Only in the necessity of defending ones life or innocent lives or his homeland from malicious aggression is the taking of life excused: God will forgive killing in these circumstances without requiring redemption if the motive is for protecting the innocent.

Any life taken wantonly and willfully or in revenge by another is a sin against God and the victim, and will create a spiritual debt that must be redeemed. Those who maliciously take the life of another or maim them, for whatever self-given reason, will be like a bug under God's foot. It matters not at all whether the killer is an individual or nation, each will receive the judgement of God and will pay the redemptive price.

You who consider the life of another human to be worthless and subject only to your whimsical judgment as to its fitness to continue, who do not consider life to have any purpose beyond that which suits you, or that you can take that which you do not have the power to give, you will stand defenseless before the wrath and judgement of God. He will give you only the way of redemption to save the life of your own soul. Mercy will be shown only when sincerely asked for and you are ready to dedicate yourself to remediation.

TERRORISTIC ACTS   For those who take the lives of innocent men, women, and children for whatever cause you think you have, as in the bombing of buildings and aircraft, be advised that there is NO CAUSE known to Mankind that can justify such acts. You shall have NO FORGIVE-NESS for them, but must seek remediation of the most demanding magnitude if you are ever to be free from the terrible weight of this heinous act.

For those who commit such acts in the Name of God, believing that you are doing His Will, your requirements for redemption and punishment shall be far greater. God does not condone such killing and does not direct anyone to do them. The taking of life, whether for sacrifice or vengeance, is not justifiable through religious beliefs or practices. God has established no man as his avenger. He alone will avenge all unredeemed transgressions through acts of Justice which none can avoid. God's laws as given to Mankind were never meant to lead him to acts of rage or vengeance, but to lead him to salvation and righteousness and into Good Will toward his fellow human.

There is no escape for you mass murderers whatsoever, not even through death. Death, indeed, is the surest way to come face-to-face with the enormity of your actions and the requirements you must meet to make it right. You will not be free until you have paid for every death, every sorrow, every hardship, every cost, and every penny of loss. If you have done such deeds, first admit to it and let justice be done. Meanwhile, turn unto God and appeal for Mercy and the chance to begin paying your debt, or else you will dwell in Hades with your tormenting crime until God is ready to put you into the fire of eternal death.

Spirituality and Religion

This book is deeply concerned with Spirituality. This is not the spirituality of the popular culture whose high priests are psychics and professionals of healing whose faith is in some strange power that flows from the cosmos. Spiritual power does not come from the material world: not from planets, stars, or galaxies or their conjunctions or relative positions that form apparent constellations. The material world only displays the majesty and mystery of God and inspires the mind and soul to seek Him.

Spirituality comes only from God the Creator of all that is in Heaven and the physical universe. It is the Spirituality displayed by the holy angels, whose high priest is Christ, the first creation of all the Heavenly Hosts. This Spirituality is of the Heavenly Father, Christ, the angels and Heaven. Therefore, we use a capital "s". The awareness of Spirituality induced into humanity by the angel souls is manifested in humans through aspirations of their souls. Humans attempt to express this inspiration through religious ideas and worship.

What is Spirituality's relationship to Religion? *Religion* entails a body of beliefs and practices which aspires to direct the human intellectually and spiritually toward a Divine being. Religion in all forms is a development of Mankind. It is of, by and for humanity. Whereas the angel souls established Spirituality in humanity, humans developed and established religion as expressions of their various perceptions of God and their worship of him. The relationship of Religion is to humanity as Spirituality is to the angels.

Religion restricts belief and behavior to an adopted set of standards and tenets. To some, Religion is adequate and their beliefs are expressed in rituals and dogma, and their faith rests upon miracles and articles of worship. To the religion-oriented, all Divine truth rests upon interpretations of inspired writings; anything, however improbable, is believable if it has been written in the canons of his faith.

Today, Mankind regards and practices his religion as though it were something entirely separate from his personal daily affairs. It is something to be held aside from all else while he works, plays or engages in other activities. It is taken out occasionally, perhaps regularly, to indulge his worship of his god and proclaim its values. Then, he puts it aside once more and resumes his customary routines. The religion is not to be mixed with any other concerns such as family activities, work, education, politics, government, recreation or other secular activity because it may taint his judgement and attitudes with impractical spiritual flavor and may even bias him against certain concerns and rights of others. On the other hand, some of those who do practice their religion "religiously" feel that they have a mandate to persuade unwilling minds to accept their beliefs, or influence public policy to follow the dictates of those beliefs.

One who reads this book cannot help but notice that there is an inseparable association between the human and his soul. The soul constantly infuses the spiritual values that issue from God's Love and Truth into the thought, attitudes and behavior of the host person. His entire intellect, his aspirations and motivations are strongly influenced by the presence of the soul. Furthermore, all that Mankind enjoys today in his intellectual and material world has come because of the nurture of the angel souls. In fact, *Mankind's very destiny will be determined by his acceptance of the spiritual values* which have come to him through the spirit, bestowed through the Grace of God the Heavenly Father and Son.

So, what is God's due in human affairs? Is He to be denied what He has created, can He not be blessed by what He has done, can He not eat from his own garden?

Religion, which is an imperfect practice seeking Divine truth and inspiration, is far more valuable to the individual and society when it becomes a part of one's routine thought and actions. Every soul is fully aware of spiritual values in its need for redemption and salvation. Therefore, *religion should be a personal way of associating one's intellect with the Creator and worshiping him.* It should not be used for coercion of others or channeling everything into the narrow confines of the religion's tenets and standards. Neither should the standards and values of religion be denied a proper place in any affair when it inspires and directs human endeavor toward those goals that improve and exalt Mankind.

Spirituality comes from a higher and purer plane than Religion and is absolute. Religion is imperfect, restrictive and inadequate; Spirituality is complete, infinite and perfect. *The soul and Spirituality abide within the infinite estate of God, while the mind and Religion abide within the limitations of humanity.* Therefore, those who would become holy should seek Spirituality for the soul and mind. Then, he may adopt a religion that is suited to the Divine wisdom directed from his soul, so that he may express and share his worship of the Creator with others. The righteous soul can then find contentment and harmony with the religious connotations of his mind.

If one seeks Spirituality, his consciousness can come into harmony with God's Will and partake freely of his Truth and Love. Spirituality can lead one into the deepness of Truth that is God's gift to the seeker. Then he can enjoy and radiate knowledge and faith fed by Divine, infinite Wisdom. If Spirituality is the body, let Religion be the clothing, which should be tailored to fit the body. The body should not be stuffed into unsuitable garments, but let the raiment express the full splendor of the righteous soul.

Worshiping God

The urge to worship God is a result of spirituality. Angels and Mankind and all intelligent life possess an inborn tendency to worship their Creator because they were made from the substance of His intellect and consciousness. From this, they display love, gratitude, praise, respect and reverence toward this supreme, benevolent deity who bestows gifts of love and beauty, manifests power over life and death, and can award fortune, favor and eternal life.

Through worship, Mankind attempts to express esteem, awe, and love for his Creator and benefactor. This involves praising the Father as the Giver of Love, Truth, Light and Life, respecting Him as being the all-knowing and all-powerful Creator of the Universe, thanking Him for his Goodness and bestowing blessings of love and concern, sharing love with Him and all people, learning about Him and his Ways, and approaching Him in humble reverence because of our weakness for sin and his readiness to forgive and restore a repentant soul. He is worshipped because He is GOD and we are his creatures whom He loves.

Worship comes from within the individual as an interplay of spiritual and intellectual drives and expressions. Worship is displayed collectively through ritual ceremony, creeds, testimonials, songs and chants, icons, garments, objects of art, structures and buildings. It is consolidated by shared belief and faith in the assured constancy of God's love and concern for Mankind, and the hope that each soul will be welcomed into His eternal home despite persistent sinfulness. All this rests on the foundations of knowledge and understanding provided through inspired writers of the Holy Bible, and further illuminated through consecrated preachers, teachers and writers inspired by His Spirit. Worship is a development of humanity inspired and led by the souls attempting to impart love and praise of God.

What does God really desire from worship? It is enough for a person to be repentant, striving to live righteously and virtuously, seeking and sharing things of love and truth, letting God lead through the purposeful pathways of life, and remaining obedient and faithful to His Will. God is thrilled as much by a tiny prayer extolling love and faith as by the mighty voice of a celestial choir. There is as much of God in a plain, wood-frame church on a country lane as in a magnificent, cavernous cathedral lavishly decorated. God is as much pleased by a lonely voice pleading for mercy and forgiveness and offering a life devoted to His Will as by a hundred well-scripted sermons.

Whenever you pray, whenever you *worship*, you enter into a holy sanctuary with the Lord God of Heaven. Do not take *anything unclean* into this sanctuary where his Presence abides. Those things of body, mind and spirit that He has given you *are clean*, and so are your sincere struggles to resolve problems and strive for perfection in respect to any of these matters. Other matters that pertain solely to the body and mind that arise in struggles with worldly things and involve anger, frustration, envy, lust and prejudice that could lead you to sin *are unclean*. Leave them outside the sanctuary, do not take them before the Lord. Do not go before the Lord angry with anyone, or with hatred for any person, or with lust for the one you cannot rightly have. Yet, you may acknowledge these passions and ask that He give you the strength to become the master over them, so that they will not lead you into sin.

God doesn't demand respect, nor does He expect fear and servile submission. If you know and love Him, these things will come in their *proper form* to please him, and the worshiper will feel as a loved child feels for its parents. We are all part of Him, created from the very best portions of His own substance. Aren't all parts of your own body precious and loved by you? How much more so of the Heavenly Father whose Love and Grace are supreme and shared freely with His creatures. Worship God with love, charity, truth, honesty, obedience, gratitude, graciousness, humility and patience, letting his Will be done in all things pertaining to the body and spirit.

Matters of Love and Marriage

GOD'S LAWS FOR SEXUAL LOVE   Among the moral constraints which human societies generally recognize, God's laws pertaining to sexual love are the most difficult for them to understand and embrace. This difficulty arises directly from the dichotomy of the relationship between the human mind and the soul. Human love relationships are often seen as a battleground between two opposing forces, and indeed that is much the situation. Two opposite viewpoints concerning the exercise of sexual love push and shove at each other from strongholds of irreconcilable views.

Now you will be able to understand the true nature of this controversy and why the resolution of this conflict is important to the spiritual destiny of all souls. It is extremely important that Mankind face this with earnest resolve because *it extends to the very cause of the fall of Lucifer and the angels and to their salvation and restoration to Heaven.*

This matter enfolds both the angel soul and the human host within a relationship that is critical to the destiny of both. If souls continue to fall deeper into sin, so will Mankind. If humans do not learn to engage in sexual love with responsibility and Divine respect, civilization can deteriorate into states of disorder and disrespect for life and the moral values that make it worthwhile. If the angel souls don't relinquish their pursuit of sexual passions and seek God's Love instead, they will decrease the likelihood of attaining salvation. In this matter, the angel soul and host exert powerful mutual influences upon each other and it is difficult for the soul to progress if the human is weak and undisciplined.

God's laws of love were made for the fallen angel soul, to help it reject the attraction of seductive passions and to induce into the attitudes of its human host a reverence for love's holy purposes. God imposed his laws upon the angel souls when Mankind began to exhibit spiritual awareness. The souls were aware of their new requirement and knew that it would conflict with the human inclination to freely pursue sexual fulfillment. The soul was put at the mercy of powerful human drives since it cannot prevent the human from acting on his own initiative. This simply made it imperative that the soul teach and lead the human mind into submission to the law, at first through a period of conflict which finally shall yield to cooperation.

Teaching Mankind to give dignity and Divine purpose to the expressions of his strongest urges was one of the primary commissions given to the angel soul to help it uphold God's law. The angels were required to do this without affecting biological changes in humans, as was done in providing a communicable link between the soul and brain. Such changes were to be achieved by elevating his intellectual divinity. Realizing this for sexual love has proven to be one of the most difficult to achieve. Many angel souls were reluctant to restrict their human hosts in an activity that had given the angels great pleasure in previous times and was still a prevalent pursuit.

So that Mankind may learn the divinity of sexual love, God required that the souls endow their human hosts with the idea that sexual love be honored as a privilege only of a man and woman united in the bonds of a genuine, durable love. God required that the union be a spiritual love or one that was secured by open ritual commitment through vows. Children resulting from sexual union would be protected and nurtured in an environment of righteous love.

Souls began to impart consciousness of the laws into the mind of Mankind, and he acquired a growing respect for the love relationship. Permanent union between a man and woman who shared genuine love became preferable to loose bonds. Marriage was conceived and quickly evolved into an important ceremonial and social arrangement in many localities around the world. To adolescents, sexual love became an idol on a pedestal that they were forbidden to touch, and the wedding was an entryway into a mystical preserve wherein love's fantasies were fulfilled. To adults, marriage became a sacrosanct institution where rules prohibited transgression of love's commitments and aspirations. In many places, sexual love became a protected privilege of marriage.

In Mankind's present state of enlightenment, it is imperative for him to reach an understanding of why responsible sexual love has such importance to himself and God. Sexual capacities and desires were given to humans and other creatures of Earth for holy purposes: so that they may be brought together by the attraction of shared love and through this means to regenerate themselves as a continuing species. It is an endowment from God produced by the holy angels to fulfill his Will, to allow humans the powers of procreation and the enjoyment of love's most wonderful blessings.

Humanity and all creatures had conducted their sexual relationships in harmony with this intent until Lucifer began to change and distort their passions. Lucifer diverted the purposes of God into perverted designs of self-indulgence. Prior to this time, the angels had performed creative endeavors completely in a manner to please the Heavenly Father. Lucifer intruded into these activities to corrupt the angels to join him in seeking passionate pleasures instead of the Father's approval.

Such designs of perversion and corruption contain the seeds of willfulness that defy God's Will. If God's Will cannot endure in Heaven, then the Divine laws that unite all spiritual and material life will be subverted so that each entity seeks fulfillment of his own willful desires. This will surely lead to anarchy and chaos in Heaven. *In such a state, the entire Universe can become a hell in its own right, from which there could be no refuge or salvation.* If God cannot rule the Universe in peace and righteousness, then there will be no peace or righteousness or benevolent rule and *no one* to establish it.

Therefore, it was critical that God isolate the Earthly realm and those who had elected to serve Lucifer's willful designs. It also became essential that God prohibit any truant angel from re-entering Heaven as long as he retains the slightest desire for perverted pleasure. God will not permit any vestige of such to enter through the "gates of his Holy City". Each fallen angel must reinstate aspirations to serve God's holy purposes only and affirm this in unequivocal commitment and loyalty to Him.

The desire for fulfillment of sexual passion and pleasure is the one thing above all others that caused the angels to fall into sin. It is the one thing above all passions that the soul indulges that also strongly tempts and defiles the human. Angels are not capable of engaging in sexual love among themselves, but they can sense the passions of humans or other creatures through infused connections, such as the soul. The soul shares all possible human emotions, but passions are the only faculties which the soul shares with its human host to achieve states of sinful indulgence.

The soul is not interested in wealth because the things of wealth give no benefit to the soul. The soul is not interested in fame, because who knows a person by their soul? The soul is already known in Heaven by the Father and Christ and many of the Heavenly hosts. The soul is not interested in attaining power because it knows that power is bestowed through God's grace as He wills. The soul's interest in any of these human ambitions lies in the extent to which they increase the human host's capacity and opportunities to indulge his passions of pleasure or that they may be important to achieving one's Divine purpose.

There is clear evidence before Mankind that there are immense differences in the experiences of those who keep God's laws and those who do not. The love relationship between a man and woman who share a strong, abiding spiritual love in matrimony can be beautiful and fulfilling. As a man and woman who share such love in marriage engage in sexual love, their souls bond to each other to experience the full power of their love as one. It brings mutual respect, affection, and contentment into their lives that diffuse into the home and family. The children are wanted and loved, and they are blessed with shared love and the assurance of enduring concern as they mature. It is honored and treasured by those who see it as God's way.

Behold the contrast with those who disregard his laws and engage in "sexually active" lifestyles. Sexual love becomes cheap and serves only to give pleasure. It is given first to this partner, then to another, with no lasting commitment and little capacity for mutual trust. Betrayal brings pain, jealousy, anger and hatred. It generates rivals seeking the easy indulgence, reaping ill will, rage, violence and death. When the sexually active person finally meets that special "soul mate," they cannot keep the secret that they have already betrayed their love by giving themselves to others. So much potential for sharing genuine love and trust is thereby deprived from their relationship.

Promiscuous love with unaccustomed strangers may visit shameful, debilitating diseases upon their bodies. The unborn baby conceived in unlawful unions may be deprived of life and ripped from its soul through abortion. Children brought forth outside of marriage become unwanted orphans, or are sheltered in make-believe homes, have little promise for their future, and may be marked through life by disease. Those who bring children into life without acts and commitments to establish a home and family for them have committed an unforgivable sin with redemptive indebtedness to God and those innocent children.

When a married man or woman yields to outside temptations to break love's laws, it will rip asunder the fabric of their marriage and family, exposing all of them to the most crushing emotional traumas, the breakup of their home and family, loss of their combined wealth, and the end of hopes and dreams they had shared for their future.

Engaging irresponsibly in unlawful sexual love will surely establish spiritual debts with spouses, children, friends, acquaintances or even strangers. These must be redeemed with each one at some time before salvation is fully bestowed upon the debtor. Active, unbridled behavior can spin a bewildering, complex web of entanglement from which you can never hope to escape without redemption.

All of this and much, much more that could be mentioned is the direct outcome of disregarding God's laws of love. It provides evidence in abundance for an intelligent mind to conclude that there is something terribly wrong in pursuing sexual love in an open, irresponsible manner. There is no responsibility whatsoever in engaging in sexual love outside marriage, regardless of "precautions." Those who do so invite physical, emotional and spiritual disaster of immeasurable proportions.

Therefore, human understanding must respect the soul's need to free itself from desires for gratification experienced through sexual love and other urges of human passion. The soul must relinquish its desire to do so and return its aspirations to a state of holiness wherein it is gratified through God's love, which is pure. The human must cooperate with the soul's aspirations to seek holiness so that it can return to Heaven's Grace through salvation.

Mankind now knows God's laws of love and the reasons God requires obedience. He should mold his behavior to uphold the laws for his own sake as well as his soul's. Mankind should learn to pursue the endeavors that flow from his strongest drives with moderation and discipline and seek the deeper meanings which reside in the Creator's Divine purposes. In his failure to do this, human lives will continue to reap the punishing devastation wrought through unlawful love and their angel souls will continue to be led from the promise of salvation.

ACCEPTABLE STATES OF MARRIAGE   God redeems and ennobles Mankind through His laws of Love. Life and love are His greatest gifts to Mankind. One may feel that he loves everyone, but his love can touch only a few. Love is not some scarce quantity to be hoarded like a miser's wealth, or to display on a shelf like a valuable vase of exquisite design. Love cannot be "given" away, but must be shared! Love is shared through mutual affection, devotion, charity, respect, caring and concern. When given unconditionally to another, shared love is returned, increasing its power and joy manyfold. Love shared between two or more people can bind them in unbreakable bonds of loyalty and devotion and does not demand anything from any of them. Anything may be shared unconditionally among them with no expectation of return.

These gifts of life and love do not come freely, because both bestow solemn responsibilities upon the recipient and those *who share* the gifts with him. These gifts, along with truth, involve all that come to him through the spirit. In receiving life and love, one must accept their responsibilities, else one or both can be lost. The loss of love can render life to seem worthless, then continuance of life seems pointless. If only Mankind followed God's laws for marital and sexual love, he would save himself from much misery and sorrow, waste and cost. Mankind pays dearly for his unprincipled pursuit of passionate pleasures!

Marriage is necessary for a man and woman to make the commitments to life-long love, caring and sharing, to provide a secure place of wholeness for themselves and nurture for those children that shall come through sexual love to bless them. These children have a right protected by God to expect a home of love, nurture, devotion, stability and durability so that they may be prepared to meet the challenges of life and the spirit. It is the responsibility of the father and mother to assure that these standards are kept. *Society* is responsible for expecting them to do so and guarding the sanctity and moral values of the individual and the family so that they may flourish in peace and stability.

Sexual love is permitted without sinning only within marriage, and *God recognizes only two states of marriage in which sexual love is allowed.* These are marriages that come through spiritual bonds of love and through ritual ceremony. The greatest of these is *spiritual matrimony* in which a man and woman are united through the Holy Spirit because of their sincere, spiritual love for each other. God weds them and sanctions the consummation of marital aspirations. They do not sin in expressing and fulfilling the yearnings and needs of their love.

This is not given to all men and women who fall into love, because *both partners must be saved.* God does not unite them in spiritual marriage if either of them is unsaved. Any person knows if he or she has consciously dedicated themselves to salvation and accepted the power of God's Mercy and Grace. Their love leads them into making a life-long commitment to love, honor and faithfully fulfill the expectations and responsibilities each assumes for the other.

The second state of marriage is *the religious or civil marriage* achieved through man-made laws and rituals, usually performed in a church, home, or other honorable place. The man and woman must have a deep, genuine, durable love for each other and must make their marriage vows sincerely before Mankind and God. These vows are sacred rites and are made to God as well as to each other. Then He recognizes their marriage, even if neither of them is saved, and sanctions the consummation of all their marital aspirations, including enjoying sexual love with each other and having children.

ALL marriages should begin with a wedding ceremony in which vows of lifelong commitment and loyalty are exchanged between the man and woman. God then safeguards their marriage as a sacred trust and protects it with inviolable laws. Those who are joined in Spiritual Matrimony should also seek to take their vows socially before God and consummate their love's aspirations only afterwards. Only when they have made their vows openly do people regard them to be married, and the wedding vows verify their commitments to each other. It is important that this be so, because marriage of either type is of sacred importance in itself, for it holds within it the promise of His bond of eternal Love. Mankind is honored and blessed through those things that come to him by God's Spirit, and is known by those things he cherishes.

THE SUPREMACY OF MARITAL LOVE, THE WORTHINESS OF OTHER LOVE RELATIONSHIPS   Like a bouquet of flowers, love displays many patterns and "colors", as well as fragrances. A husband and wife may enjoy a love relationship like none others attainable among humans. This is marital love, which is established upon a spiritual bond. It is both spiritual and Divinely physical, and God opens it to the expression of sexual love. He has given this form of love with a holy purpose: to bind the two spiritually and emotionally with a strength intended to withstand all hardships and suffering that may burden it, and all fortunes and happiness they happen to share together or with others; to draw them together in a bond fitting for the creation of life, and provide a strong, stable, durable family for the protection and nurture of their children.

While enjoying the bond of marital love, both husband and wife may establish and nourish love relationships with others, including the opposite sex. Such relationships may be shared with parents, children, siblings, in-laws, cousins, or friends. Yet, each of these relationships is different from the one shared between husband and wife. Each displays different forms, satisfies different needs, inspires different feelings and strength of loyalty and priority, and involves different kinds of interactions; but none of these forms involves sexual love. All are legitimate, desirable relationships that should be allowed by either partner. And there are those who depend on others for love to make their lives worthwhile and for the basic needs of life so that they may live securely.

God does not forbid or discourage such love relationships between any two people regardless of other associations. As *some of these may have origins in previous lifetimes and may possibly involve redemptive fulfillment*, they are established and protected upon God's laws of love. The persons involved must regard the form of relationship they have and interact in an appropriate manner. Until a man and woman commit themselves to each other in love and marriage, it is their own choice to give importance and expression to any of their relationships as they please within God's laws of love.

The marital relationship is the supreme form and demands the strongest commitment from each other and to the marriage. It demands the strongest ties of faithfulness and is the least tolerant of disloyalty or indifference. It is special and provides the entitlement to create life and the motivation to establish a strong, durable family bond for nurturing and protecting the children. Marriage is given an importance and priority over all relationships which the husband and wife may maintain in common or separately.

Only the love between mother and child is as strongly governed and protected by God's laws of love as are marital love and the marriage. Among the qualities that bind humanity in spiritual purpose, these are some of the most esteemed canons of Heaven.

THE DISSOLUTION OF MARRIAGE   All marriages are formed by bonds made through love and sacred wedding vows. This bond is intended to be unbreakable and those who enter into marriage should consider that death should be the only cause for breaking it. Love is the initiator and strength, the cause and effect, the alpha and omega of this bond. Because marriage is a lifelong commitment intended to withstand all that should come against it, good or bad, the vows are not to be taken lightly.

God does not sanction divorce, the dissolution of marriage. Yet, knowing the imperfections that may abide in any human endeavor, He will allow certain divorces that are entered into with contrite and amicable hearts. Otherwise, divorce is allowable only if one of the marital partners breaks the vows through infidelity.

A husband and wife may recognize that their marriage has become unworkable and intolerable. Each loves the other enough not to hold him or her in unhappy bondage. Not wanting to hurt each other any longer, they agree to set each other free from the bonds of their vows. Each should acknowledge these desires to their betrothed and to the Father in prayer, seeking His forgiveness and grace and the same from each other. They may remain in love as *friends*, helping each other through the trauma of breakup and desiring the best for each other's future.

This marriage can be dissolved in this way only if both partners have similar feelings and have a willingness to end it. If only one of the partners desires the dissolution and the other does not, the marriage bond cannot be broken without redemptive consequences or forgiveness.

If children have come to this marriage, the parents should maintain the marriage if possible until the children become young adults to provide them the material, mental and spiritual nurture of a stable home. The concerns and rights of these innocent children supersede the desires of the estranged parents. Beyond divorce, these parents must assure that the love, nurture and needs of their children are always met. God will *forgive the husband and wife for divorce* made within these conditions, but redemptive debts made against the children and each other *must be redeemed.*

If either husband or wife subjects the other to deliberate pain, anguish, denial, rejection, or suffering, or becomes spiteful, unfaithful and disloyal, because of their failed marriage or as a means to attain a divorce, then God will mark the guilt against them. This becomes spiritual indebtedness to each other and to God that can only be removed through redemption. They will face these trials together again until they are resolved and removed from their spiritual records.

Dealing with Diversity

The status of being a laboratory for the creation of life provides the Earth with an enormous array of animal and plant life. There is so much to interest Mankind and energize his desire for knowledge and understanding of the animate and inanimate phases of creation. When seekers of knowledge come to understand that everything upon the Earth has a Divine purpose, in its own right as well as in its relationships, they will begin to see into the mind of God. All of it is based on Truth and is given through Love.

Mankind himself exhibits a diversity that presents a complex array of racial, cultural and religious factors that he has not learned to assimilate into a unity of brotherhood. Diversity is both a blessing and a challenge and presents issues that must be resolved for Mankind to fully achieve his highest purposes. All divisions of Mankind can advance together to attain a world wherein mind and spirit use the only real powers available to achieve their dreams and aspirations. These powers are Love and Truth, and there are no others that can lead him to higher planes.

The greatest challenges to Mankind collectively are racial and cultural divisions and animosities. Diversity can be a resource for the enrichment and advancement of humanity. Diversity also provides the potential for divisiveness, a weakness that the Deceiver exploits to cause hostility, envy, rejection and hatred between diverse factions of Mankind. Although race and culture categorically divide Mankind, they should not be the cause of hostile divisiveness, but should be seen as resources to complement and enliven all people.

Whereas diversity can be a valuable asset, it is not to be valued over unity. Diversity is not a virtue, but unity is virtuous when it unifies diverse factions with amity. The *willingness* to accept and integrate diversity with impartiality is virtuous. Factors of diversity should be directed toward contributing beneficially to and strengthening the whole. In this manner, the whole body can thrive in peace while progressing toward the highest goals of unified aspirations. Consider the human body and its many diverse members and organs: in their unique functions they all contribute symbiotically to the strengths and good of the body. If any one of these members withdraws into itself and functions for its own sake, then the body will sicken and perhaps die.

Therefore, *the purpose of unity is to join the factors of diversity functionally and advantageously into the whole to attain the highest reaches of its common purpose.* Diversity should not cause enclaves of divisiveness, and unity should not cause enclaves of exclusion.

No person has ever chosen the conditions of his own birth and must therefore accept them as his heritage and birthright. In as much as the conditions of birth could be disadvantageous to any given person, they should never be used against him. Certainly, they should never be the cause of animosity and hostility or the cause of denying rights that are guaranteed to all. Every human should be given the opportunity to prepare for and achieve the goals that have been given by the Heavenly Father. God himself has caused each person to be born into the circumstances that will help his soul achieve the goals of his life purpose. God will hold accountable anyone who purposefully interferes with or denies any person's opportunities to pursue his righteous aspirations.

A nation becomes great because it accepts and pursues those things that unite and strengthen its people. Together, they fashion a framework that allows individuals and groups to freely pursue worthy goals and enjoy the rewards of their achievements. It offers opportunities for all to participate and contribute beneficially and to share in all the fruits of the nation's greatness. Those who are attracted from other nations and cultures to live within its borders can bring their own talents and aspirations to enrich its culture. Yet, they should willingly accept and adopt the culture and social customs of this nation they have chosen to join, and not attempt to establish insular enclaves of their forsaken culture within its borders. If you admire a nation for its greatness and achievements, shouldn't you join with the things that made it great and leave behind those things that keep your own nation in weakness and poverty?

Might alone will not lead a nation to greatness, and certainly not tyranny or any measures that suppress the mind and spirit of its people. Weak, tumultuous nations should see that real, durable strength lies in the advancement of its people, both individually and socially. Do not envy or hate the strong, but learn from them and emulate their methods that suit the needs of your people. The strong nation must learn the limits of its resources and seek personal and national goals with responsibility, discipline, moderation and charity. There can be enough of its rewards for all to share according to their merits; but neither greed, selfishness, indifference, debauchery nor laziness should be allowed to cause disparities that some cannot tolerate.

The purposes for life and God's love unite all humanity with common goals. Regard every person as being a source of love, truth, wisdom and potential gifts of mind and spirit that can be a blessing and joy to all. Love and be loved.

Fairness and Justice

People complain and fret about the lack of fairness in the rewards and treatment that come to them in the experiences of life. Fairness may be seen as equality in treatment and generosity in rewards. However, wealth, economic and social standing, opportunity, education, professional achievement, awards and recognition, and many other such things are unequally, therefore unfairly, granted or available to everyone. The more basic human qualities of health, intelligence, talent, ability and heritage are unequally given as conditions of birth. *One's birthright will not assure fairness or equality with another*, not even within his own family.

Many want equality with the best that is available, or at least their "share of the pie". To have less than others in desirable things is seen to be unfair. No one ever demands his share of misery and misfortune. The desire for fairness is often detached from a sense of worthiness, from the state of deserving or earning something. Yet, some are hindered or prevented from receiving the full share of what they *have* earned or deserve, and this defies God's Grace for humanity. The fact remains that a broad spectrum of qualities separate people from what will be theirs by birthright or through sharing and attainment.

Like beauty, fairness is often "in the eye of the beholder". The thing that may seem fair to one will be taken as unfairness to another. Fairness to some may be achieved by taking what belongs to another so that they may have more. The one from whom it is taken feels that through application of his energies and abilities he has earned and deserves to keep what he has attained. Greed, envy and self-centeredness are often the drivers in the pursuit of fairness and may also be the cause of much inequity. Inequalities that come as a result of applying God-given abilities and aspirations should be neither envied nor despised, as they may be the blessings that come from achieving one's life purpose

Fairness, then, should not be seen as a right to be bestowed upon all with equal blessings. People expect and insist upon fairness in human affairs, as they each perceive fairness to be, but *God does not exact fairness*. Indeed, the laws of redemption and their attendant conditions of life for individuals and nations, will ensure that fairness is not and will not be achieved. Therefore, God does not intend for life to be "fair". No person can know God's redemptive prerequisites for any fellow human, therefore cannot presume to judge the "fairness" that affects another's fortunes. *The best that any human can do is to treat others by the instruction given by Christ when he said: "Do unto others as you would have them do to you!" and the commandment, "Love your neighbor as yourself".*

God does assure that life is *just.* Justice as given by God is fair to every person and comes from Charity and Grace. His justice is dispensed to each as he deserves and no one can escape it. God's Justice is absolute, while fairness can be relative and arbitrary. Only in God's justice is there true fairness. Fairness through justice is a Virtue and Mankind should strive to achieve it in all social relationships.

Justice, in this sense, is a principle of awarding one whatever he deserves on the basis of his behavior and attitudes and may involve either rewards or penalties. It is a form of discipline that assures that nothing increases or persists in the Universe that does not issue from Love or Truth. Anything that is produced opposing these powers *must be reduced to nothingness through compensation*, for such things are contrary to God's nature and cannot abide in his Presence. Justice also assures that every person has inalienable rights as a *being* that cannot be abridged.

Human justice is often unfair, arbitrary and inconsistent in dispensation, and sometimes can be avoided by the one deserving its condemnation. Punishment is its fundamental objective and is often given without concern for equitable compensation; compensation may go to those who have not earned it. Fairness to each and all should be reflected in laws, customs and common aspirations achievable through opportunity and honorable application of ones intelligence, training and abilities. *Fairness should also come with charity*, for those who cannot take care of their own needs are deserving and it is their will to serve and earn their keep. With charity comes forgiveness, even to those who have treated you unfairly; but unforgivable sins require justice to redeem the debt that cannot be forgiven.

Justice without charity is no justice at all. Charity may be accommodated throughout every aspect of law creation and administration to assure *justice.* Fair and reasonable laws are made to guide individuals and all humanity into righteous and orderly behavior so that all may live in a society proffering goodwill, security and peace to every person. In so doing, the law also provides protection, correction and remediation for *lawbreakers* while protecting all others from those who will not keep the law. When one deliberately violates such laws, love for the innocent and the law-abiding whole requires that the lawbreaker remain under its condemnation until repentance and remediation are confirmed so that the lawbreaker may abide in peace and trustworthiness among his neighbors. Charity thusly infused throughout the system of laws provides fairness to all, but charity does not let one escape the justice that his behavior has earned for him. Probation (forgiveness) is earned through repentance and redemption.

Justice and fairness are inseparable, as are justice and charity. Justice rightly dispensed is the only true fairness. Fairness without justice becomes inequity that breeds envy, disrespect, intolerance and contempt. If you seek justice with charity in all things, fairness will follow.

God Does Everything for Love and Truth

God's purpose for all that He does, and for all that he creates, comes from Love and Truth which rules everything and gives it Purpose. The opportunity for Redemption for Satan and the fallen angels of God, and for all souls who sin, is one of the most sublime demonstrations of Love ever shown in His existence.

If not for His Love, He could have destroyed them all and been done with it. He has the power to create new angels, as many as He desires as He wills. But He loves these angels whom He created in the BEGINNING, and He will not wish for any of them to suffer death, unless that proves to be their own wish. All that follows this age, the Second Return of Christ in flesh, Christ's rule of his own Kingdom on Earth through the Millennium, and the terrible times that follow in the world after the Millennium, all result from His Love and His desire to win back every possible soul and reward them with eternal life in Heaven.

Hear this Message, Soul of Mankind! Your misery, your trials and tribulations, your sorrows, and even your triumphs of success and joy, are given to bend and turn you toward His Kingdom and to erase all debts you have to Him and other souls. His Love and Mercy can free you and restore you to Life eternal.

Everything in the Universe that is Divine and Holy springs from love, truth and beauty. All that is worthy of pursuit and attainment comes from these. They are the foundations of God's Will, which embodies his aspirations and intentions for all creations.

Love is not a passing fantasy or shallow attraction; rather it is the *power* that compels all creatures to share things that are good and wonderful, to draw them together in joy and peace, and to give and receive lasting happiness.

Truth is the store of Universal knowledge and wisdom that come from God's immeasurable intellect. Truth is those things that are right in all that you do or think. Truth is the laws that cause the physical and spiritual universes to work to perfection in respect to God's Will. Truth will never change and it will not fail, so it can always be depended upon for all needs.

Beauty comes when love and truth are combined to express God's Grace in which He and all creatures share celebrations of love and praise. Beauty springs from the soul's inner mind to express something beyond the power of speech. Beauty *presents truth* in ways that combine interest with endearment. Beauty provides that which brings joy and fascination to the mind and soul, and entices the observer to share love with it.

All material worlds were made subject to God's Will from the substance of his Being. The Earth, one of these many worlds, displays the grandeur and majesty and infinity of God in radiant and hidden beauty. The natural world provides enjoyment to humankind that is often manifested as worship and praise of God. The creation angels have created the Beauty and things of this world to display their love of the Father, but Mankind has not respected these acts in their wanton use of Earth's resources and landscapes.

The Virtues and all that is worthwhile or good come from love, truth and beauty. Accept these as your counsels and let them rule all that you desire to build, share or attain. If these things fill your mind and soul, there will be no room for ill will, hate, lies, deception, unpleasantness or ugliness. Then you can become like the angels of Heaven.

9

FROM NOW TO THE END OF
THE AGE OF REDEMPTION

A View of Things to Come

The final times remaining in the Age of Redemption have begun. The best of Earthly life and the worst are still yet to come. There will be long seasons of both. There will be a time in which the treasures of Heavenly life shall be given to Mankind and the power and willingness of God to reward the Righteous will be evident to all.

These times of Heavenly blessings will end to begin a final struggle with the forces of evil. Then the times shall begin in which Mankind will witness, in great contrast, the ills that Satan gives humanity in his show of rebellion and hatred toward his Creator. The age in which Satan attempts to turn all things pleasing to Mankind into disgrace and sin will endure *only so long as necessary* to rescue lost souls that still have an inclination to repent.

So that the reader may clearly see the events that are to come, the veil of apocalyptic description has been put aside. This present discernment was not given through visions, which are full of undecipherable symbols, but was given to the messenger through direct thought. The mind must translate visions seen through the eye, but thought is natural and at home with the mind.

There will be no "end of the world" or "end of Time". There shall be ends to worldly kingdoms and world orders. There shall be end of times and ages. Periods of confusion, of Light and of darkness shall come and go; but the *world and Time* shall remain. The Earth is part of Heaven and it shall not be destroyed for it is not within the power of Satan to defeat God's Will.

Time is an invention of Mankind, useful and sensed by every person, in which all material things change. The human is aware of the natural cycles, both regular and irregular, that affect him in his world. He breaks his work into cycles of his own making and frames them in "time" so that he can complete them within a given natural cycle. Time and its importance shall not end for humanity. But time will end for the angel souls, for they shall return to the *timelessness* of Heaven.

The Age of Mankind, initiated by God as a period of spiritual and mental development for humanity, will end! The Age of Redemption, initiated by God as a period of repentance and salvation for the fallen angels, will end! Hades, the state of separation of the Earthly realm from Heaven, will also end! These ages shall end simultaneously when God's Plan of Redemption has been fulfilled. In the sense that all angels will be freed from their obligation to serve as souls in humans, the world will then "end" for them. *The world will not end for humanity*, but a new phase of his importance to the Earth will begin!

A NEW age will begin when all redeemed angels have returned to God's heavenly Kingdom, when all evil is erased in the destruction of unredeemable evil doers, when humanity gives up its souls in exchange for the Holy Spirit, and Mankind becomes truly sovereign in a new world of love, peace and truth. In this new age, Heaven and Earth shall change to fulfill the Promise of God's Word.

Before any of this comes to pass, there must be a short season in which Mankind and his soul shall face the great purpose of why the ages of Mankind and Redemption were given, which were granted to both humanity and the fallen angels. Through a decisive struggle with issues that continue to confuse and mislead humanity, Mankind will come to understand the difference between holiness and evil in all things. Truth will stand before him like a wall of mirrors so that all can see clearly for themselves what is right and good in all that affects Mankind. With this outcome, the mind and souls of Mankind will possess a maturity in which they can responsibly choose, in partnership, whether they will serve God's Will or Satan's. From understanding the Truths now given, every person has the knowledge upon which to base his spiritual decisions and his subsequent behavior. Each one is free to choose in accordance with his conviction, but each shall be fully accountable before the Judgement of God for the consequences of his choice.

This is a time of great promise for Mankind and his soul. The Heavenly Father believes in Mankind enough to allow Christ to be born among humanity once more; but this child is a *mortal* being. These prophesies present only a mutable promise which Mankind has the power to fulfill or reject. It is dependent upon Mankind's commitment to attain righteousness and divinity, and to secure partnership with the lost angel souls that seek redemption and salvation. He who has ears to hear, let him hear!

All of this will determine the future of humanity. Mankind, from individuals to nations, has the knowledge and wisdom and the powers of decision to determine his destiny. His attitudes and decisions have already affected him greatly, for if Mankind had accepted Jesus Christ as Messiah two-thousand years ago, God's objectives for the fallen angels and humanity would have been fulfilled by the present time.

Mankind can ignore this Promise through which he can attain a world of exalted achievement. He may instead use his present powers to mutilate himself and much that is worthwhile on the Earth. He can virtually annihilate his civilizations and leave a terrible legacy of despair and uncertainty for any surviving remnants. Whether those who remain remember this Promise and build a new world of hope and peace resting upon Love and Truth cannot be assured. Let those nations who undertake to establish and maintain a hegemony of self-interest and intolerance for their rivals hear this message and consider the fate they hold in their hands. Will they too give up so much in promise from the Father in exchange for so very little?

The World in Moral Chaos

The present age is one of confusion, transition and indecisiveness. It is also an age of hopefulness and spiritual awakening. Godless behavior is rampant, but is matched by those who do good deeds in a world of turmoil. It is a struggle between the forces of good and evil in which evil defies good, and good attempts to undo the results of evil and champion the love and Will of God.

Moral principles, which in ages past formed the foundation of most people's relationships with each other and life's obligations, have been discarded as unsuitable for this age. Human dignity is often measured in terms of attained wealth and social position. Much of the teachings of modern Christian churches have been changed to accommodate relaxed standards of morality. Most people are searching for spiritual truth and meaning, but many who feel the spiritual call may easily adopt strange religions and their gods.

Mankind lost much of its spirituality when the things of modern times began to usurp too much time, energy and attention. They know of which they search, only they do not know where to look for it. They are told that God is no longer real, if, indeed, He ever was. They are told that it is against basic principles of society to pray in public or exhibit any expression of God where others may see it in places not consecrated to Him. They are taught that nothing is sacred any more, that morals and ethics are old fashioned for this age and are irrelevant. "Get real!", they say. They are told that anything they desire to do is okay if it makes them feel good and there should be no adverse consequences for their choices. The doer is not to be blamed, no one is to feel guilt.

So we see that our streets are filled with children who rape, rob, steal and murder. Youth destroy themselves with drugs, alcohol and suicide. Young girls just out of puberty have one baby after another and no one can be sure who their fathers are. Many young men avoid learning anything of real value to themselves and society, have no concern for responsibility, and do not seek legitimate employment. Many women shun marriage and homemaking; yet they desire babies as their playthings. Some women behave as though they are married to any number of men, but do not want the babies that result from their activities, so they destroy them in their bodies. The men who are their partners share equally in accountability. The values necessary for a secure, nurturing family, where devoted husband and wife are dedicated father and mother, are ignored and denounced.

These are the models we exemplify and impose upon our children because we have neglected the values and morality that give dignity and purpose to human endeavors. We have forsaken the spiritual needs of our children and wonder who is to blame for their waywardness. Life has no direction except to lead one into carnal satisfaction. This is only one of our failures, for similar veins run through all aspects of our social pursuits.

To many of the world's people, life is cheap and disposable. If one has a cause, it can be brought to the attention of all by indiscriminately murdering scores or hundreds of innocent men, women and children. Profits of business seem to have more value than the lives and well-being of the families of faithful workers and careers are turned into a scramble for survival. The birth of a child, once considered a Divinely blessed event, is now to be prevented through abortion. Children are born and discarded like rubbish or may be abandoned to survive as they may. When life, the most precious gift of creation, is regarded so cheaply, all else looses its value as well.

Morality and ethics are essential to a secure and dignified life and to the foundations of civilized nations. This idea, however, is regarded as outmoded and unacceptable nonsense in the "standards" of modern society. Many think that they only need to present an *image* of morality and decency to public view and that their so-called private life can be anything they like. They seem to believe that they are two distinct persons, or that they have two personalities, one to indulge "privately" and the other to present to the world. But they are *one*. Their private and public lives cannot be separate. What they are privately, they will also be publicly, whether or not they are "found out" and chastised for their behavior. You can only be a fool for so long until it traps you in sin and shame, for you have deceived yourself while trying to deceive others. And the Great Deceiver hopes only for those who try to do good, or pretend to, will fall into the pits of shame where their future usefulness is mocked by rejection and failure.

There is also so much that is good among individuals and society. If we would only cleanse it of moral confusion and vacillation and assert the standards of God's Laws that we already know are true and timeless! God's laws of love and righteousness will prevail throughout the world.

Thy Kingdom Come, They Will Be Done on Earth . . .

The "Lord's Prayer" was given by Jesus Christ as an illustration to his disciples of what one should pray about. The phrases "Thy Kingdom come, thy Will be done on Earth as it is in Heaven" have essential meaning to humanity and their angel souls. It is not merely an idealistic request without association with a Divine purpose. These phrases state the entire objective for the Age of Redemption and the Age of Mankind for the angel soul and humanity, respectively.

The objectives for which God granted these ages were to restore the Earth to the Kingdom of Heaven and to bring the Earth and all of its inhabitants once more under the authority of his Will. The Earthly realm is presently under the rule of Satan as the kingdom of Hades. The realm will maintain this status until God brings the Age to a close and resolves the consequences of evil through his final judgment of all souls and fallen angels.

These objectives are the Word of God that was spoken in his promise to the fallen angels that repent and to the hosts of Heavenly angels whose trust is in his Word. The objectives *will* be met, regardless of the scope and severity that shall be required of his Judgment. His Judgment will leave no residue of evil or its consequences in the Earthly realm and all shall become as pure as Heaven itself. The question for Mankind and the angel souls is what shall be the consequences of their choices between good and evil, God and Satan?

Humanity, through its choices, can direct itself toward a future Earthly kingdom of exalted and glorious fulfillment abiding within his Will, or toward a desolation of misery and darkness in which no hope for recovery abides. The angel souls can direct themselves toward salvation and restoration to Heaven's Grace, or toward total rejection and death at the command of God. Evil and those who will not turn away from it can have no place in the coming Kingdom of God: unrepentant souls will die, and incorrigible humanity will return to a state of primitive incivility and hopelessness. The conclusive outcome is dependent upon the choices made freely by human beings and their souls from a desire to be made holy once more, because God will not impose his Will upon the destiny of anyone if it is not their express desire to accept what he offers. Thus, it is up to Mankind to resolve whether they shall be exalted or decline into desolation.

Jesus Christ has shown the Way to eternal life for Mankind and the angel souls through accepting to live in righteousness and brotherhood. They shall achieve this while advancing together, for their mutual destinies shall come *through partnerships* in which both willingly accept the promise of salvation through repentance and redemption. The Father's kingdom will come on Earth through Christ, who shall rule it in peace and goodwill, and fulfilling the Divine promises made to all who will believe. The Father's Kingdom is eternal and his Will shall endure forever.

The False Prophet and the Beast

In the Biblical sense, a *false prophet* is one who bears false testimony against Christ, the Father or the Holy Spirit for the purpose of misleading another person or persons. Such testimony can also be against the Church or its apostles. False testimony constitutes *lying*. Therefore, a false prophet is *a liar, a deceiver.* Such a one is also an *antichrist* (one who believes that Jesus is *not* the Christ, the immaculate Son of God; a gnostic; read 1 John 2:18-23; 1 John 4:1-4 and 2 John 1:7-11).

The false prophet is referred to by Saint John in the New Testament (read Revelations 16:12-16 and Revelations 19:19-21). The false prophet is presented in human guise whose evil lying will manifest itself among humanity more powerfully in the "later days." Yet, the temporal presence of the false prophet is described in terms depicting the past, the present and the future. He *was, is* and *will be.* (To the apostles, the later times was expected to occur *in their lifetimes* and they would see all the apocalyptic predictions come true, including the return of Christ in clouds of glory, and the raising of the dead; then all the saints living and dead would ascend with Christ into Heaven.)

The truth concerning the identity of this "person" who is the false prophet, given by the Father, is that *he is not a human but is a spirit.* This spirit of deception has been in the world since the beginning of the Age of Mankind. He, like the "beast," was sent into the world by the defiant Satan to mislead Mankind and corrupt the efforts of the repentant angel souls to progressively lead humankind to divinity and themselves to salvation. This spirit manifests itself through the willful schemes of human beings who are misled and corrupted by their unrepentant souls.

In unceasing guile, the deceiver attempts to confuse humanity about right and wrong, good and evil, morality and immorality. In this role, he serves Satan's determination to defeat God's Plan of Redemption. If successful, he would prevent the fallen angels from attaining salvation through repentance and redemption and will lead humanity to self-destruction through hatred and irrepressible turmoil.

Through Biblical times, the deceiver tempted the Hebrews into disobedience and stubbornness while God attempted to lead them into the Promised Land and make them into a great and righteous nation. He misled and blinded the Pharisees into opposing, then rejecting and killing Jesus, the Son of God. In centuries that followed, he corrupted the Church and influenced civilized humanity to do all sorts of evil in the name of God.

In current times, the deceiver has lead vast numbers of people, even nations, into accepting the vilest of evil as being preferable to good. He has spawned a great stream of lies that adversely affect and despoil the progress of humankind, generally replacing good with evil. Generally, the strategies of the deceiver include all ideas that pervert love, corrupt and distort truth, falsify and subvert knowledge that should be freely open to all, or cheapen and disrespect life. *Some* of the deceiver's ideas prevalent today are given below:

- God's laws of love and righteousness, as disclosed in the Holy Scriptures, have no place in the secular affairs of the administration of law, justice or government, and the two must be kept entirely separate;
- religion, specifically belief in God and Jesus Christ, is a detriment to social progress and all who express such beliefs are suspect and their

motives are to be examined and questioned closely, and the influence of religion reviled and repressed;

- if only a few are offended by an expression of faith in God, or of the praise of virtue, or the censure of immorality, then it is desirable that these things be silenced in all public places and eliminated in all public pronouncements;
- God's *laws* of righteousness, or laws of morality, are not needed since less inhibiting human laws can be written to replace them without accountability to an authority higher than the state or the individual;
- immorality is to be desired and morality reviled; an immoral person is more preferable than one of honesty and integrity;
- lies are more preferable than truth if that is more helpful; lying can be beneficial to one's strategy or image;
- immoral persons can *appear* to be good by covering themselves with an image spun from deceit;
- one's own self-centered preferences supercede all else, even the importance of life's obligations or shared love;
- the marriage bond and commitment to family is an unnecessary hindrance to doing as one pleases; indeed, personal commitment to any virtuous aspiration should be avoided;
- the freedom to choose to do an immoral act is acceptable, but expectations to behave in a moral fashion are disdainful;
- the child, whether born or unborn, is to be sacrificed to selfish ambitions or shallow purposes;
- an unborn child is not a person, but is an ancillary part of the mother's flesh that can be expunged if she desires;
- an expectant mother is privileged to destroy the human infant developing in her body if she decides that she doesn't want it;
- the family is unimportant as a pillar of society since there are various "acceptable" substitutes for the nurturing care normally provided in the home by the mother and father, and a father is not needed;
- there are also "acceptable" substitutes for the traditional marriage that is founded on love, commitment and sacred vows to join *man and woman* in holy matrimony;
- histories should be rewritten to remove all references to virtue and honor and religious beliefs, which are relative nonsense anyway;
- histories can be rewritten to strip them of "prejudicial" or unwanted facts, replacing them with prevarication and malignity, or to glorify evil men and regimes and vilify those of moral motives;

- God the Creator regards some humans to be fundamentally superior to others, where some are to be favored and others reviled;
- God's "justice" requires an eye for an eye, a tooth for a tooth, evil for evil, and He demands vengeance against the blasphemer or against those who direct evil upon believers;
- God brings both evil and good upon humanity.

There are many more ideas that the deceiver has planted in the modern culture through persons who cannot embrace the supremacy of Divine authority and wisdom. Humanity has not learned that if the intrinsic precepts of morality are ejected, they are replaced with a greater number of more restrictive and arbitrary human laws that soon lead to tyranny and loss of freedom. When God is removed as the authority for moral law and justice, then sanctioned authority rests upon the uncertain vagaries of human power. The alternative possibility is for all society to fall into chaos, without any foundation for order and civility.

These lies are not held only by the few and isolated, but are proclaimed by the masses who make concerted efforts to throw them over the whole of society through force of law, custom and court order. They are proclaimed in the chambers of the noblest institutions and seats of power. In this way, the deceiver hopes to nullify all ideals of morality and integrity that has made the nation into one of greatness and strength, substituting self-indulgent motives of evil and degradation.

The false prophet, the liar, has many followers, ranging from ordinary persons to those in the highest domains of human power. The ideas fashioned from lies that he plants in the minds and ambitions of those who make laws and policy have the power to destroy the mightiest of nations. Widespread adoption of such ideas can cause a nation to decay into a vile morass of corruption, barbarity and hopelessness because they replace the virtues that provide the foundation and structures of strength, unity and durability.

The days of the false prophet, the deceiver, are numbered. The engagement has begun that will bring about his demise and defeat the power of his lies. The righteous are rising in strength to confront the lies of the deceiver and those who serve his cause. This conflict ("Armageddon") will be won by the righteous, and they, led by God the Father, will totally defeat the deceiver and his legions. "The righteous" will win through arguments and expositions based on truth and the virtues of love that shall "destroy" the advocates of deceit by leading them to the altars of Truth and Moral Virtue. Yet, *everyone* must come to this altar. Righteousness will prevail, but love must prevail overall, for without love there is no righteousness.

The deceiver will be bound with the beast and Satan and thrown together into the pit of hell for a thousand years. So also will those who will not turn away from serving him. The Father is preparing the Earth and the righteous for Christ's reign during this period of a thousand years in which there shall be no evil to corrupt or hinder the exalted progress of Mankind.

The *beast, the lawless one,* similarly, is an evil spirit sent out at the dawn of the Age by Satan in his campaign to defeat God's Plan of Redemption. This beast, *the destroyer,* is that lawless spirit from hell that disregards all laws of man and God, and creates his own rule of tyranny. He works to weaken and destroy all great nations, both from without and within, to tear down the fabric and structures that establish the strength, greatness and benevolence of the nation. He manifests himself in men of power who become depraved despots under the influence of the deceiver. Working at the flanks of the deceiver, the beast has incited wars of death and destruction since the dawn of the Age upon peoples and nations as far as his marauding armies could reach.

The beast also leads *individuals* and associations who harbor hatred and ill-will for others, for various reasons, into despicable acts of depravity and death. He instills motives of disdain, avarice and revenge into one or many to do his evil work.

Like an ill wind, he sweeps over the Earth and manifests himself in overly ambitious men of power whose ambitions are only to destroy and ravage all around him. Tyrants raise mighty armies and cast covetous and vengeful eyes on the cities and nations who are neighbors, then surge forth to destroy their cities and villages, kill the men, rape and enslave the women and children and take the wealth of their labors as their own. He is responsible for causing an endless string of rapacious wars and movements in the times before and since the Son of Man lived among humanity. The deceiver proclaims the work of the beast to be for the good of humanity.

In the time of Jesus Christ, the beast was personified by the Roman emperors, each of whom considered themselves to be a god. All citizens and visitors were required to fall prostrate in worship of the person of the emperor. Those who worshipped the One and True God and professed belief in Jesus Christ were in mortal danger from the forces of the emperor because they would not worship him or his image. His image was seen as statues in the courts and in the coinage stamped with his likeness. His mark was seen in the banners of his legions and the attire of the centurions.

During the present period, the beast has emerged in many places and times, to expand and intensify his evil war against the righteous, for his time is drawing short. He has manifest himself in a procession of rulers, both great and small, in Asia, Europe, Africa and elsewhere. He incited the tyranny that overtook socialism and fascism in the twentieth century, then inspired the spawning of puppet tyrants and scions who then performed genocidal atrocities in the name of the beast.

The most notorious of these sons of the beast was "der feuhrer" of the Third Reich. His evil deeds of destruction and death are well documented, so also his ideology of propaganda guided by the deceiver. Today, the *image* of this tyrant is recognized instantly by all around the world. There are many today who worship his image. The *mark* of this beast is the Swastika that is also recognized instantly anywhere in the world. The mark is borne on banners and emblems by those who worship the image and is frequently plastered on doors, walls and buildings as an icon of hate and intolerance. The beast is manifest in the evil inspired to the present day through *der feuhrer's* image and his mark.

The beast continues to work in a frenzy of irreconcilable hate and intolerance in many areas of the world, gaining foot holds where morality is weak, religious animosity is strong, appetites for power and wealth are corruptible, and the peoples' hope is in unsuitable ideals and false gods. But, the righteous are rising with new resolve directed from the King above all rulers to defeat the deceiver and subdue the beast. These spirits will go down together, powerless and broken, to wail with their prince in the darkness and misery they have created (read Revelations 20: 1-6).

The Spiritual Battle of "Armageddon"

The age has come when all shall face the issues of right and wrong, of good and evil. The stand on issues will become a fight and it shall reach every person. Everyone shall be drafted into the battle, on one side or the other. The issues will affect all levels of society from the individual to nations. The combatants will rage against each other and the contention shall split families, friendships, organizations, nations and alliances of nations. Some wars may be fought, violent demonstrations organized, outbreaks of violence and mayhem, divorces, name-calling and all manner of attempts made to neutralize the unwanted arguments.

This conflict shall be a spiritual "Armageddon" between the Angels of God and Satan's angels, between the saved and the unsaved, and among Jew, Gentile, Muslim and non-believers. The battle will be waged within the Earthly realm of Hades, in its heavens and on the Earth. It shall bring the issues of good and evil before all Mankind and resolve each as to whether it is right or wrong and for which side you shall make your stand. There shall be no neutrality. It shall divide the righteous from the unrighteous, for at the end, Christ shall live and dine with the righteous, while the unrighteous will descend into darkness with Satan and his cadre of beasts.

This conflict is God's "Holy War" against human wickedness and the deceptive and destructive forces of darkness. Unlike other "holy" wars, it is not a war of hatred and vengeance fought to destroy the nonbeliever or the "blasphemer." It shall not be a war of destruction and devastation fought between nations. Indeed, Armageddon shall be a process of personal and social introspection and renewal whose purpose is to enlighten and save the nonbeliever, to bring him to repentance and holiness, and to defeat the lies of the deceiver. God's Holy War shall be waged because He loves the nonbeliever and the believer, and it is the exercise of His power of Love and Justice to save all souls while time remains.

In this great conflict, God will be the Commander of the forces of Righteousness. God will not set one human faction against another, or one nation against another, but each side shall include those of all nations, all races, all creeds, all religions and all factions. Empowered through the command of God, humanity and the angel souls will confront and defeat the power of evil that comes to Mankind through "the beast" of oppression and the deceit of "the liar." The clash shall be between beliefs and ideas that set wrong against right, evil against good. Human passions shall be inflamed and displayed, but hatred among humans must fall, and the stand made only for God or for Satan. The rebellious and stubborn and the intolerant of God's Supremacy shall finally withdraw from the presence of the righteous, and those who do so will find no peace of mind or power to stand before Him. The victory shall be for Christ, the true Prophet and the Master of all souls, and he shall reign in his Kingdom of Righteousness.

Armageddon Ends on the Eve of Christ's Millennium of Reign

This spiritual and social turmoil will not last but for a season, perhaps the span of a generation, so that all souls shall experience it. Then comes the victory for Christ when right and good prevails throughout the Earth. The losers will rage defiantly in lost pride and frustration, but their power has been taken away.

A new voice begins to speak with great authority, proclaiming wonderful things soon to come. The voice had already been added to the arguments and gave strength and hope to the victorious. The voice proclaims the arrival of an unfamiliar man, coming in the Spirit of Christ, who shall claim victory for the Righteous and the hosts of Heaven in the Holy Name of the Father.

This man of whom the voice speaks IS the CHRIST, who has come into the Earth once more to establish His Kingdom and rule it in Love, Truth and Peace. He has come to establish a kingdom of righteous souls in the very midst of Satan's kingdom. A millennium of Love and Peace shall begin now for the Righteous, and Satan is powerless to have the least effect.

God has decreed that no *un*righteous person, no unsaved soul, shall live on Earth during Christ's Reign, for this Kingdom will demonstrate the power and possibilities of a world without evil and that He can establish it as he wills. Starting in the first generation of the Millennium, no unsaved spirit shall become the soul of any new human. Those alive who are unsaved shall not be able to reproduce their kind because God shall make their bodies as children who are unable to conceive and give birth. Only the saved soul, the righteous person, will be able to bring forth children and they shall all have saved souls.

Satan is Bound for a Thousand Years, Rules Hell in Terror

When Christ's Millennium begins, the unrighteous souls shall vanish from the Earth for a thousand years. These souls shall be confined in Hell with Satan and his princes of destruction and lies. God will totally limit Satan's power to harm only those constrained with him in Hell. All traces of God's Presence and the Holy Spirit will be removed from Satan's kingdom of lost souls and they will experience total spiritual darkness.

Unprecedented sorrow, misery and tribulations will afflict these lost souls! What is the WORST thing that could ever happen? Satan will discover that he is bound, has not the slightest contact with God, has no power to mislead any of the living through seduction and deception, and is completely powerless to do his own will in his own kingdom. In ensuing rage and absolute frustration, Satan will become INSANE. The elements of Intellect that God used to create Lucifer as a Holy Angel shall become confused and disorganized, and Satan will lose all awareness of truth and reality. He will be MAD.

In his madness, Satan will storm about Hades in terrible rage, terrorizing the beasts and lost souls confined with him. He will suppress all with him in terror and tyranny. They will seek places in which to hide, windows of escape. There will be no way out. So terrible shall Hell become for the lost that many of *them* will be driven to insanity. Woe to those lost souls, for Hell has finally become the very antithesis of Heaven. Christ will comfort those who have loved ones among the lost and they shall forget their sorrow for those in Hell.

Christ Rules the Earth

With no evil in the world to mislead and corrupt and destroy the living, Mankind shall achieve a world of unimagined success and beauty during the Millennium of Christ's reign. Christ will not rule his kingdom from a base of politics, or culture, or even religion. His rule will be based upon the gifts of God's Spirit, enlightening Mankind and his soul in the things of Love and Truth, inspiring a new philosophy of life's meanings and purposes, and teaching Mankind to value those things of eternal importance. Christ will not remain throughout the Millennium as a man of flesh, but shall be taken up into Heaven after a brief period. His Spirit will endure to inspire humanity to live righteously and benevolently.

Every person alive during the Millennium will achieve a partnership of cooperation with his soul, helping it to achieve its goals of redemption while making full use of the gifts of God's Spirit. Mankind will succeed magnificently in all of his endeavors and nothing evil or contrary to God's Will shall be undertaken.

ALL fields of human labor and endeavor shall be blessed with God's Grace. This will include Government and Administration, Health and Medicine, Economics and Finance Industry and Manufacturing, Science and Engineering, Architecture, Agriculture and Archeology, History of Nations and Mankind, Education of Mind and Body, Social Arts, Music, Literature, Visual and Dramatic arts, Communications, Psychology and Psychiatry, Crafts and Skills of all kinds, Exploration of Earth and the Planets, Religion, and many others that encompass all of Mankind's interests and aspirations. Entirely new fields of endeavor will be discovered or developed. Mankind shall be faced with many new challenges and he will conquer them with skill and knowledge.

Mankind shall learn the truth about all things. Those things that are false or useless shall be abandoned and pass into oblivion, never to be remembered. True knowledge of God and communion with Him shall replace such things as astrology and psychics, witchcraft and false religions. Every religion will give way to a singular Spirituality and all of Mankind shall be bathed in it constantly in all their affairs. God will be looked upon as the constant source of truth, knowledge, understanding and wisdom.

It is not to say from this that Mankind will not have problems, either of his own making or imposed externally. Confronting problems and seeking solutions through analysis and creative thinking is one of the things that interests and enlivens human beings. Each person will still be counseled by his own mind, personality, preferences and discriminatory behavior and generally will have his own way. People may still have differences of opinion, debates, fatigue, frustration, and disappointment that come from pursuing goals and enterprise with positive motives.

With diminishing significance, disease, illness, afflictions and pain will continue to beset people. Sexually transmitted diseases, including AIDS, shall vanish. People will learn to deal with the problems that cause personal and social misfortunes with new perspectives and faith. There will be no deep and lasting sorrow or despair, no soul-rending disappointments, no poverty, no crime, no murders, no killing of unborn children, no illicit love, no births without spiritual or secular wedlock. There will be none of those things that degrade and destroy persons, families, communities and even nations. All shall have whatever they desire, but desire will not arise from greed or selfishness, but from sharing things of good-will and the spirit. The social, cultural and political causes of poverty will be confronted and resolved in all nations around the world.

New resources for foods that do not depend upon animal resources will be developed to promote better nutrition and health by providing all that the body needs without leading to obesity and other health problems. Livestock farming as practiced today will change as the slaughtering of animals for human nutrition will be greatly curtailed. *Products* of living animals will continue to be useful. A variety of delicious new foods will diminish malnutrition around the world. The customs of dining itself will change greatly.

Peace shall reign over all the Earth. There will be no tyrants, despots, dictators or iron-man rule; no anarchy, wars, rebellions, violent demonstrations, uprisings against authority, or terroristic activities. Problems between persons, states, institutions and nations shall be worked out in negotiation and compromise so that all sides will achieve the best that is possible. In public affairs self-interest will give way to common-interest and common goals. Each nation will have its own form of benevolent and efficient government to suit its own culture and needs. No system of government or rule will be imposed upon one nation from another or others. Everyone will be committed to peace, security, brotherhood, sharing, achievement and advancement for all. Such shall be the effect and the fruits of a world living in righteousness, ruled by the Spirit of Christ, without unlawfulness and evil.

New angel souls will not be created during the Millennium. All souls will have lived previously in humans who were led to God. God shall reward those now who served Him and those who desired to do so but were prevented or hindered through ignorance, repression or adverse circumstances that denied them this association with Him.

The Millennium Ends; Fate of the Righteous

The Millennium will be the most splendid, peaceful, and success-filled periods Mankind has ever enjoyed on the Earth. Yet, it is not Heaven and was not meant to last forever. Lost souls are being tormented in Hades by a mad Satan, and many of these can be saved for God. His love will not let them remain lost if they will only choose Him and come willingly and without condition to seek forgiveness and redemption. There will be Time remaining in the Age of Redemption for all who will to come. There are also some among the saved who must be strengthened through adversity and confrontation with evil, for they are not steadfast in their faith or righteousness.

For the sake of these, the Millennium will end and a period of difficulties, tribulations and despair will commence to remove the wheat from the chaff. This is the final time of Harvest for lost souls.

Many of the souls of the righteous who lived during the Millennium shall not return to life during these final times, because they have won the victory over Satan's deceptive seduction and their desires to taste of it. They have reconciled all debts of redemption between themselves and other souls. There is no need for them to rejoin this struggle. These shall remain in a Heavenly state within the Earthly realm to serve as angels for Christ, to help those saved and unsaved who remain in the struggle so that they may come resolutely to God. Other souls among the righteous must redeem or offer themselves for redemption for debts existing between themselves and lost souls returning to life.

There are many souls who are *very strong* in their faith and their affection for God. These shall return to life in these difficult times to be among the living as fathers, mothers, brothers, sisters, children, friends and acquaintances of the saved and the unsaved. These will be called as God's instruments to help the lost and weak to find and know God.

Return of the Unsaved to Life; Satan Is Unleashed

When the Millennium is over, unsaved souls will once more be born into life. The Archangel Gabriel will unleash Satan. When Satan discovers that he is no longer confined and lost souls that he controlled in terror are being infused again into humans, over whom he has little control, he will remember his fight with God.

Satan will come forth, raging insanely, beguiling with irrational fervor those who are weak and already lost. There will be no limits to what he leads them to do in an attempt to destroy God's redemptive efforts. These times will become the worst Mankind has ever experienced. From now to the end of the Age of Redemption, good will struggle with evil, back and forth, up and down, now winning, now losing, in a dreadful fight to the death. Satan shall seek revenge against God for locking him away during the Millennium, ruining his personality and taking away his opportunities for mischief.

Those living who come under Satan's sway will do terrible things. Satan will give them no rest in leading and compelling them to do his bidding. The beast and the deceiver, freed once more from bondage, will assault humanity with angry revenge. Those under their sway will murder who they want, when they want and for whatever reason under the sun. They will break in and take whatever they want, and destroy all the rest. They will have no respect for any person, their safety or well being. Destruction, rape and death will be their style of life.

Satan will try to deceive and lead the lost to destroy all the good things that were built up during the Millennium. All the fruits of righteous souls shall be his targets. He will burn, pillage, rape, destroy, undermine, subvert, desecrate, denigrate, and mock all that he suspects as having the favor of God. Governments, nations, institutions, communities and families will be torn asunder with disloyalty, hatred, disobedience, mischief, adversity, unlawfulness, and tortuous, despicable actions.

The SAVED will find it very hard to remain so, as they will be drawn into the whirlpool to defend and avenge. They will turn totally to God for Hope and Salvation. They will establish havens of retreat for Godly living and prayer to strengthen their faith and shield themselves from life's evil travails. Many angels shall come to help them so that they may win their struggles with the lawless and wicked.

The UNSAVED will find it very difficult to find God because Satan rides them unceasingly with hateful motives and vengeful resolve. Many of these will become so sickened of their own wickedness and depravity that they will cry out for deliverance and forgiveness. They will turn to the strong in faith and love to seek hope and refuge. Many shall be won to God.

Hope, faith and prayer will sustain the righteous during these difficult times. This period will not last as long as the Millennium, for God will end it with a final call. Just as God, through His Love, gave these times to save the hard-hearted and reluctant, so will His Love bring them to a close. It is, and has always been, within the power of God to begin and end periods given to prepare Mankind for the fulfillment of His purposes.

God Ends the Age of Redemption

God's purpose for the terrible period of times following the Millennium is to strengthen the weak souls and save all who willingly choose salvation from wickedness. At last, God shall issue a final call for salvation to all lost souls. This will involve a final generation in which humans will host angels as souls. *Prior to infusion as a soul, each lost angel will be informed by Christ that this life is the final chance and no more will be given.* Many saved souls strong in love and obedience to God shall also be born in this last generation to help persuade the lost to find the pathways to God, leading them to refuge and restoration to Heaven's Grace.

Finally, during this crucial generation, the last soul who will accept God shall do so. When there are no other souls among the living or dead who will repent, God will do nothing else to persuade others to come. He has done all he can do short of forcing them to come. *THIS* He will not do. He will not force anyone to accept Him and return to Heaven against his will. If they prefer not to be there, then they will elect to die. He will not fight against them any longer. Nor will he keep Earth in isolation, separated from Heaven and maintained as an eternal jailhouse of punishment for Satan and his hardened converts. Neither will God allow any unclean soul to enter Heaven, so that none can return to Heaven with conditions or demands, or without complete forgiveness, redemption and cleansing.

Therefore, God shall welcome the final soul to accept Him. Then through His angel Michael He will issue a final call to Satan, his beasts and all those corrupted souls who refuse to repent. He will give them one last chance, for most can still be saved if they will. At this point, Satan cannot be saved for he has irreparably destroyed his own intellect through terrible anger and hatred. God cannot repair him and he must be destroyed completely. Satan could have been saved if he had taken this step when the Millennium began; but now it is too late. This is also true of those souls who were driven to insanity by Satan. All others can be saved if they repent.

When these reject Him, the Age of Redemption will end!

A Summary of God's Acts of Redemption: He Has Done All That He Can Do...

From the beginning of Lucifer's defiant waywardness and throughout the fallen state of the holy angels, the Heavenly Father has displayed his supreme love for the angels and the creatures of Earth that they abused. The Father initiated a series of actions on behalf of the angels who did not succumb to Lucifer's guile to reclaim these angels. These actions, described in the manuscript, are reviewed in this summary section.

THE FATHER'S EARLY ATTEMPTS TO CORRECT LUCIFER'S DEVIANT BEHAVIOR   From the moment the Father realized there was a problem with Lucifer, He began an investigation which confirmed the facts of Lucifer's deviant behavior. He sent the angel Michael and Christ to persuade Lucifer with charity and kindness to cease his unlawful activities and to extend to him offers of help. Several such attempts were unsuccessful, even with the promise of rewards from the Father. Then the Father tried explanations, persuasion and an offer to elevate his standing and power among the Heavenly Hosts. These attempts at reconciliation also failed. The Father still refused to consider destroying Lucifer and, instead, desired to transform him through gifts of love and grace to correct certain traits that were emerging as flaws in his character.

The Father was willing to transform Lucifer into the most perfect angel in Heaven with power equal to the power given to Christ; but, Lucifer had dreams of his own, born of willfulness and pride. Was Lucifer willing to give up the promise of the greatest power, the highest glory, the most intimate association with the Creator given to any of His creatures, to attain, instead, his own limited small world of self-indulgence? Regrettably so!

THE FATHER SHOWS FORBEARANCE WHILE LUCIFER AS-SAULTS THE HEAVENLY SANCTUARY OF THE ANGELS   In contrariness, Lucifer intensified his efforts to deceive the Earth's holy angels and seduce them into joining his acts of perversion. The desire and determination to establish his own kingdom based on forbidden activities involving the Earth and possibly the entire galaxy became firmly fixed in Lucifer's mind. Resolved to accomplish this through acts of defiance and pride, he launched a vigorous campaign to win all of Earth's angels and establish Earth as his base. He succeeded in alluring most of these to his cause, but about a third of the Earth's host of angels remained firmly loyal to God. These loyal angels remained on or near Earth to help the deluded angels to understand Lucifer's intentions and turn them away from supporting his activities before any real damage was done and they ventured too far into disobedience and defiance.

THE FATHER COMMISSIONS ARCHANGEL MICHAEL TO OP-POSE LUCIFER'S ASSAULT   The Earth had fallen to the power of Lucifer's influence. Lucifer turned his attention toward winning the entire galaxy in like manner. Lucifer took many of his most inspired angels into the galaxy to proselyte and help win new converts. The Father then commissioned the angel Michael to confront Satan with a host of loyal angels to interfere with his activities and impede his progress. As Lucifer's growing legions advanced toward the heart of the galaxy, Michael's angels began to instruct the angels ahead of the advance about Lucifer's deception, disobedience, and defiance of God, disclosing the unlawfulness and dangers of yielding to his persuasion. Angels now knew how to counter Lucifer's arguments and guile, and it became ever more difficult for him to win converts.

By the time Lucifer's legions reached nearly half-way into the galaxy, it had become exceedingly difficult for him to proceed further and he began to withdraw to within more secure bounds. Michael continued to press him and Lucifer withdrew toward his Earthly stronghold, taking the very large company of angels who had succumbed. Michael succeeded in pressuring Lucifer's legions into the confines of the Earth and the Solar system. Michael was saddened to know that Lucifer had taken about a third of the galaxy's angels under his deceitful influence.

THE FATHER COUNTS THE COST AND CONSIDERS A CAMPAIGN TO RESCUE THE FALLEN ANGELS   The Father realized the enormity of the loss and the problem that now faced Heaven. These angels were no longer part of God's Kingdom and they presented a seriously pernicious threat to the galaxy and possibly to all of Heaven. Yet, they must not remain lost in this entanglement of deception and corruption forever. They must be won back as loyal citizens of Heaven.

Thereupon, the Father decided upon courses of action that were intended to let the angels learn for themselves the folly of their decision to join Lucifer and to adopt a desire and willingness to forsake Lucifer's ways and return to Heaven's Grace. The Father would provide means for them to repent and redeem the abuse they would inflict upon Earth's creatures, and accept back into Heaven those who unequivocally repent and redeem all debts to God and the Earth and cleanse themselves of all sinful desires and inclinations. All remains of evil and its results, including angels who refuse to the end all offers of the Father's Love and Mercy, would be finally redressed in accordance with the Father's judgement.

THE FATHER RELINQUISHES THE EARTHLY REALM TO LUCIFER TO RULE AS HIS OWN KINGDOM   Lucifer, now calling himself "Satan", and his legions of fallen angels were now confined to a small locality, the Earthly realm, which God would yield to Lucifer as "his kingdom." Yielding the Earth was the first step to convince the angels of the futility and shame of yielding to Lucifer's guile, for the Father knew that Lucifer would be powerless to create the kind of kingdom he wanted. The angels would become disillusioned and disaffected over their choice of masters and would begin to desire a return to Heaven.

The Father then withdrew his angels, the Holy Spirit and his own presence from the Earthly realm and yielded it completely to Satan. God enclosed the realm in an imperceptible barrier that the angels could not penetrate. The angels could neither leave the realm nor communicate with any Heavenly host outside the barrier unless God authorized and permitted it.

The Earthly realm was now completely isolated from Heaven and would, at least for a while, not be regarded as part of Heaven. It was a separate place, ruled by Satan, which would now be called Hades. Lucifer's stubborn pursuit of his willful dreams to rule a kingdom wherein his corrupt desires could provide creations contrary to the Father's Will at last had brought God's capitulation. However, Satan would have only his own powers to make his dreams succeed. So much offered in promise from the Father had been rejected for so little!

Compared to the galaxy and certainly to the supremely vast expanse of Heaven, Hades is a very tiny place. In this respect, it seems inconsequential and not worthy of God's concern. Certainly He shouldn't become obsessed with the problem of Hades, since He must direct his attention to *all* of Heaven.

THE FATHER ASSIGNS CHRIST TO THE TASK OF REDEEM-ING AND RESTORING THE FALLEN ANGELS TO HEAVEN   What great loss would Heaven suffer if Hades were to remain in isolation *forever*, or if God simply destroyed all that was in it? The answer lies in the fact that Love and Truth are the foundations of Heaven and the purposes for all that God does. God loves the fallen angels, each of them, including Satan, for they are all his very own children. He wants every one of them to return to Heaven where He can share love with them and they can pursue things of truth and beauty and all the wonderful dreams of his intellect. He would not want anyone of them to remain lost or to perish. Therefore, God will do everything possible to win them back. Yet, He is wise and just, and his fight with them will not last forever.

The Father, knowing the love and concern that Christ has for his fellow angels, assigned the task of reclaiming the fallen angels to his Firstborn Son. Christ is the Master of all angels and they are his charges. He is their "shepherd" and he is concerned with each one of the Heavenly "flock". The task is the love and concern of his heart and he will pursue it until the Father's Will is completely satisfied.

The planet Earth and her Solar house environs is one of the beautiful gardens of the Milky Way galaxy, the literal Garden of Eden. The planet is full of life and magnificent things of Creation that must be preserved. The Earth and all that is upon it will be restored to honored prominence in Heaven, whole and clean, gratifying the Father's love for the creations of his angels. The yearnings of his heart are that not a single angel shall decline to return with the Earth into his Kingdom.

THE FATHER ALLOWS HADES A LONG PERIOD TO FESTER IN CHAOS AND FAILURE Allowing Hades to fester in the shameful pursuits of Satan, where confusion, frustration and malevolence ruled in lieu of any imperial order, most angels did indeed become disillusioned and dissatisfied and wanted to return to their former Heavenly tasks. Satan saw that he had lost their loyalty and that his kingdom could only be controlled through the harsh force of tyranny, which would drive them further away from him. Neither love, nor trust, nor truth would be useful in his kingdom any longer. The angels had begun to realize the extent of their loss and the folly of abandoning the constancy of Heaven's love and grace. In this place devoid of the Father's Love and Truth, the sorrowing angels continued to dine at Satan's feast of perverted passions since there seemed little else they could do to satisfy their quest for fulfillment. Satan himself had assured their receptivity for repentance and salvation because they realized that all of their misfortunes, disappointments and miseries came directly from their lot with Satan.

THE FATHER PREPARES A PLAN OF REDEMPTION FOR THE ANGELS AND GIVES IT TO CHRIST TO EXECUTE Conditions in Hades were ripe for God to begin the next step of his plan to recover the fallen angels. He would now announce and begin his Plan of Redemption. Taking Christ, Michael, the new archangel Gabriel and a host of Earth's loyal angels, the Father called Satan out to the barrier and announced the Plan to him. The Father informed Satan that the Plan would proceed with or without his cooperation. Christ was appointed the executor of the Plan and he would be fully empowered to make it succeed. Satan perceived that his kingdom of chaos would be slowly taken from him through this plan, but knew that he could not stop it. He must decide whether to allow the plan to *proceed* without his help, or to actively oppose it. Satan returned to Earth and, in arrogant, stubborn pride, proclaimed that he would oppose God's attempt to reclaim the Earth and the angels which he had deceptively won.

CHRIST, BY THE AUTHORITY OF GOD, BEGINS THE "AGE OF REDEMPTION" Thus, the Age of Redemption was begun so that willing angels could repent and start redeeming the desecration and abuse they had inflicted upon humanity and Earth's creatures, and to atone to God for their sins of disobedience and self-indulgence. In this new age, angels would be required to become souls residing within the physical human, enjoying his passions while imparting to the human the gifts of God's Spirit and qualities of spirituality.

To begin the new age, the angels would need to prepare the human mentally and socially to accept the soul as a partner. This was accomplished through a soul-sharing period in which select angels infused into coherent *groups* of humans, usually families or small tight-knit groups of individuals. The angels serving as shared souls would develop the mental and social qualities within these individuals that would lead them to a state wherein each of them could receive and interact with a soul of his own.

CHRIST ASSIGNS FALLEN ANGELS AS HUMAN SOULS TO BEGIN THE "AGE OF MANKIND"   Following the successful soul-sharing period, God began to infuse an angel into individual humans while they were developing within the womb of the mother, until every newly-born human had his own soul. Thus would begin the intellectual and spiritual developments of humanity. This period was called the Age of Mankind. Its purpose was to provide the fallen angels with opportunities to develop intellectual and spiritual qualities within humans so that they could interact with the soul in a partnership beneficial to the goals and purposes of both. Satan's counters with a spirit of deception and destruction to disrupt God's plan.

MANKIND ADVANCES IN INTELLECTUAL AND SPIRITUAL POWERS BECAUSE OF THE SOULS' NURTURING   At some point, humans began to accomplish extraordinary things of mind and spirit due to the increasing intellectual aptitude imparted by the angel souls. At the same time, they became aware of their spiritual nature and began to seek God and worship him from whatever standpoint they could perceive of him. To assist Mankind to seek the true God, the Father consecrated select individuals and enlightened them with knowledge that could be imparted to fellow humans.

THE FATHER RAISES A NATION OF RIGHTEOUSNESS FROM A "CHOSEN PEOPLE"   The time came for God to begin preparing Mankind for the end of the Age of Mankind, culminating in achievement of the purposes of the Age of Redemption for the angels. Consequently, God selected a worthy man and his family and created a nation from their offspring, to be his chosen people. These would be a nation of righteousness who learned God's laws and his expectations for behavior and worship and which would then inspire all other nations and peoples to seek the One and True God and learn his ways. To these people who became the nation of Israel, He gave prophets and priests who were empowered to receive inspired messages from the Father for leading and instructing the people. These messages, along with allegories and histories, were codified into written documents and books that have since been made available to all the world. In this manner, all the world's people have been given an awareness of God.

CHRIST BECOMES FLESH TO INSTRUCT MANKIND ABOUT LAW, LOVE, AND TRUTH AND ESTABLISH HIS CHURCH   At this point, Israel's knowledge was incomplete for they only knew the Laws for righteous living that had been given by the One God. They must yet understand how the law should be applied in love and compassion and that the purpose for all of this was to achieve or reinstate eternal life in Heaven for the souls of all Mankind.

To instruct them in these matters and resurrect them from their own sins of disobedience and self-indulgence, God sent his Son Christ to live in the flesh among them. As Jesus, the Son of God, he delivered the Father's messages of love and truth to all who would listen. He gathered about him those who would follow him as disciples to learn these messages and commission these as apostles to spread the messages to Jew and Gentile. He taught the messages among all groups in the homeland of the chosen nation and attempted to win the minds of the leaders of the Jews so that they would recognize and accept him as their promised Messiah.

Because the Jewish leadership rejected and vilified him, Christ died at the hands of misguided pious Jews whom he tried to edify with understanding and grace. His death had been preordained by the Will of God as the response to rejection for the Divine purpose of redeeming the sins of Israel and demonstrating the supreme love He had for humanity and the fallen angels. In life and in dying, Christ taught Mankind the Divine arts of mercy and forgiveness.

The Father resurrected Christ to establish him as the Living Messiah to all of humanity. Upon the faithful apostles, he established a movement that he called "his church" which would become established in the minds and souls of all people, first, throughout the Roman world, then throughout the whole world. The church was founded upon the inseparable elements of Law, Love and Truth, with the purpose of enlightening Mankind in God's ways and affecting salvation to eternal life for the soul through repentance, redemption and Grace.

THE FATHER INSPIRES WRITERS TO DEVELOP THE HOLY SCRIPTURES.   Christ's teachings were the foundation of the church. Its supporting pillars were provided through another purposeful gift from the Father: the Holy Scriptures. For almost two thousand years, the Father had given messages to consecrated persons to whom he had conferred the ability to receive such messages in visions and meditation. These were recorded in traditions of oral memory and writings, and eventually gathered together to form the Old Testament and Covenants with his "chosen people," the Jews. After the time of Jesus Christ, other writers produced accounts of Jesus' ministry and messages and written testimony from inspired apostles. Some of these became the New Covenant between Christ, the Father and all of Mankind. Together, these writings became the combined Bible, the set of basic knowledge and instruction for all who desire to know and follow God. The Bible teaches Mankind about God, what He expects of righteous persons, and about the gifts of Love, Truth and Light that are available through the spirit. The Scriptures have been a light unto the feet of humanity that has sailed like an ark through the ages, to keep his Name and a knowledge of his laws of love and righteousness alive forevermore.

GOD INSPIRES MANY THROUGH THE AGES TO HELP PRE-PARE MANKIND FOR THE EARTHLY KINGDOM OF CHRIST   In the centuries since Christ departed the Earthly life, he has inspired many men and women to serve him in innumerable ways, to demonstrate to fellow humans the power of God's love and grace and that He can impart to each the power over temptation and sin. Now, in this present time, He has provided additional truths to extend knowledge and understanding of his relationship to Mankind, the angels, the Earth and the Universe. This will prepare Mankind for a battle between good and evil that shall culminate in the dawning of a period of a thousand years in which Christ will rule the minds and souls of Mankind in love, truth, peace and consciousness, in which evil shall be totally absent and only good shall result from human desires and endeavors.

THE FATHER ESTABLISHES AN EARTHLY KINGDOM OF RIGHTEOUSNESS WHICH CHRIST SHALL RULE FOR A MILLEN-NIUM   The Father will establish the Millennium of Christ's reign to demonstrate the possibilities of achievement in all human endeavors when evil is not present to pervert, corrupt and destroy the good that can come from the aspirations and labors of humanity. The Millennium will also demonstrate the power of God to establish a kingdom of righteousness in the very heart of Satan's kingdom of Hades, accomplishing his Will in the

Earthly realm as and when He pleases. Only righteous souls will be in life during the period of Christ's reign, while all souls who have not rejected the ways of evil will be confined in Hell, where Satan is bound with the beast and the false prophet. This should prove to all souls that Satan has no power to impede God's Will in the world. Satan can only divert individual souls from doing God's Will and keeping his Laws. Satan has power only over the soul who yields to him!

THE FATHER GIVES A FINAL PERIOD IN WHICH SATAN RULES IN TURMOIL TO TURN THE UNDECIDED LOST SOULS TO GOD FOR SALVATION   Lastly, God will give the lost souls a final period in which to repent and redeem all sins of desecration and disobedience. Lost angels will return to life and will be given opportunities once more as souls in humans living in a world of evil turmoil to meet requirements for redemption and salvation by leading their human hosts into the folds of righteousness.

These times will be difficult for the living, because the spiritual nature of Mankind will be influenced by the most recalcitrant and malevolent of lost souls, those who have rejected all previous opportunities given through the Love and Grace of God to save them. The times will vacillate between short periods dramatically affected by good or evil as Christ and Satan struggle to win the unredeemed souls. It will be desperate times for Satan who will hope to restore his pride and perverted aspirations to respectability and credibility. Knowing that he has lost his war with God, Satan will pitch a final battle in a futile gamble to keep his kingdom of Hades. He will not succeed. For his refusal to repent and seek redemption for all the evil that he has done upon the Earth and to God's angels he shall reap only the reward of eternal death and shame. The "seven plagues" of prophecy will be poured out upon the Earth during these times. These plagues should not be viewed in a physical sense, but they shall be manifested through physical consequences.

Even when the Age of Redemption is declared to be concluded, the Father will once again extend the opportunity for lost angels to repent and seek salvation through redemption. If any should accept, He will save them from the flames of eternal death and help them to be restored to the status of holy angels and reinstated in their Heavenly home. Then, God shall judge those who continue to refuse his final offer of salvation, and they shall be con-demned to eternal death. Satan and Hades will be gone forever. The Age of Redemption will end now. The Plan of Redemption has been executed to fulfill the Word of God; Christ is once again the Master of ALL angels.

THESE ARE THE ACTIONS GOD HAS TAKEN TO RECLAIM AND RESTORE HIS LOST ANGELS TO HEAVEN'S GRACE   Such a long program of opportunities and actions God has given to bring all the fallen angels back to his fold, to help them see the corrupt nature of Satan and his activities, to turn away from him and return to the Father and their Master, to let God's love and mercy cleanse them of sinful desires and free them from the evil effects of their sins through forgiveness and redemption, to give them the means to redeem their abuse to humanity and Earth's creatures, to prove their love for the Father and all that He has created in the Universe, and to return to Heaven restored to righteousness and holiness wherein they can share in doing God's Will forevermore.

These things are all that He can do short of forcing the unrepentant angels back into Heaven against their will. This He will not do.

The FINAL JUDGEMENT:
God Brings an End to Satan and Hades

When no other soul answers God's call for salvation, that shall signal the end of Satan and the kingdom of permanently lost souls. God will now bring upon the Earthly realm his FINAL JUDGEMENT that shall be directed at the Great Deceiver, his angels, and the souls who refused God's unceasing offers of Love, Mercy and Grace.

Since the time Lucifer began to fall, and throughout the Age of Redemption, the angel Michael has witnessed on behalf of all angels all that Satan has done to corrupt God's Love, distort His Truth, and subvert His Will and Laws, and all he has done to harm humanity and Earth's creatures. The record will be open for all the Heavenly hosts to see the deeds that Lucifer, who preferred to be Satan, performed to defile the Heavenly home.

Now the Heavenly Father, Christ, the archangels Michael and Gabriel, and a countless host of holy angels will gather in the spaces about the Earthly realm for the final judgement and dispensation of justice. Michael shall present the records for Lucifer and all unredeemed angels and restate their unyielding rejection of God's Mercy and Grace; then he will sound the mournful song of God's sorrow.

The Father will bring an end to these angels and souls who refused His Love and Truth to remain, instead, in defiance and disobedience to honor perversion and corruption of the Liar and Destroyer. Consciousness shall be removed from each of them. The elements of intellect that had formed God's Truths within them will be disassembled in the "fire of the second death" described by John. Satan will be the last to die so that he can witness the sorrowful end of those he led to eternal death; he will hear the angels' songs of love and sorrow as each of his victims is taken away.

Finally, they shall all be DEAD and know neither Life nor God any more. The indestructible residue of these angels will return to the Father's substance to become once more part of Him, a hidden scar upon his heart.

Without Satan and these permanently lost souls, there is no more sin or hell! Hades, Satan's kingdom of wickedness and failure, has vanished into nothingness. All corruptive, destructive things of Hades are gone forever. Now the Earth and humanity and all creatures can begin to heal.

The Father will remove the veil of darkness that had isolated Earth from Heaven. The Father's Presence and the Holy Spirit will rush in to engulf Earth and embrace all of humanity and the souls who had endeavored to know God and do his Will. Once again the redeemed angels can see the Lights of Heaven, and they see Christ and His hosts of angels coming toward Earth in the glory of Victory and Love. Christ will come before all the saved souls and enfold them in his love. Since no soul could achieve complete sinlessness while involved in the human condition, Christ will extend the power of mercy and grace to complete the cleansing of each soul. Then all angel souls may enter Heaven whole and perfect to fulfill the Word of God.

The Word of God is his Truth, it is his Law, which comes from his own substance. The Word was there from the BEGINNING, imprinted in his Being before He was ever aware of it, and it flowed into everything that He has ever done and those things which He ordains. His Truth is unfailing and his Law is inviolable because his Supreme Purpose governs everything in Heaven.

After the end of the Age, no separations from Heaven will remain. There will only be Heaven, and Earth will once more be part of it. The reinstated angels will once more have free access to the "tree of life" and the powers of the Holy Spirit. Earth shall again be a laboratory for life and the angels will resume tasks to support creations on worlds throughout the galaxy. No trace of opposition to God will remain among the restored angels. All angels shall be of one accord: to do God's Will, keep His Laws and endure in love and truth to sustain a Universe of sublime progression. The Archangel Gabriel will be the governor of the region of Heaven that contains Earth.

The deeds and death of Lucifer and his angels will be remembered in Heaven only as a memento to the folly of abandoning Heaven and disobeying

God's Will and transgressing His inviolable Laws. There shall never be another angel like Lucifer because this experience has increased the wisdom of the Father and all the Heavenly Hosts. Never again in Heaven will there be an angel with the desire to sow the seeds of disobedience, discord or destruction among others. Never again will there be one who desires to disgrace his own being with the stains of deception and corruption. The Beauty of Truth and Love will glorify all beings and all things of matter and spirit, forevermore.

What Will Become of Earth's Angels and Mankind?

The souls that were redeemed who shall not remain as Earth's creative workforce shall return with Christ into the galaxy and Heaven. Christ, their Master, shall lead each of them to their new assignments. All of them shall be received by angels who did not desert God, showing their welcoming love in joy and singing. Their music will ring through all of Heaven. Those original angels who left their assignments to join Lucifer will be received by their former companions like the best of old friends who were lost and have returned home.

Angels who were created in spiritual love on Earth and who have never seen Heaven or Heavenly angels will be in awe of the incredulous views of beauty and wonder and the multitudes of the Heavenly Hosts. Christ will tour them through the galaxy for magnificent views of Heaven, then bring them before the archangels and the Father's heart. Their joy will know no bounds. The angels and archangels will usher them to their assignments of creation in Heaven and they will be trained to do the Father's work.

On Earth, humanity has changed. Humans no longer have souls, as these have all been called forth to their Heavenly charges. The souls departed the bodies and left the humans standing or sleeping, working or playing, loving or eating, at whatever they were doing at God's call. Now, the humans on Earth will be like the creatures in other worlds who have advanced intelligence, but are without souls.

What is it like not to have a soul, not to feel the spirit of God within you? What could be an unfathomable trauma is prevented by the Holy Spirit that shall bathe every human in Love and the Consciousness of God. The Holy Spirit will take the place of souls and will be the guiding force to lead and mold Mankind in all things. The Holy Spirit connects Heavenly spirits and material beings of intelligence, such as Mankind, with the Love and Intellect of the

Father. These forces then are available for doing God's Will and accomplishing any task in Heaven. God's unlimited Will encompasses an infinite array of enterprises that do not include evil and all of these that are physically achievable will be possible for Mankind.

From the beginning of the Age of Redemption to its end, the angels had led Humanity from a state of primitiveness to an exalted state of advancement and accomplishment. In a time span of little more than 120,000 years, Mankind will have attained the equivalent of ten million years of natural evolutionary advancement of intellect and consciousness. At this level, he will be able to maintain this state and quickly begin advancements arising from his own great mind of intelligence and understanding. Angels that remain on Earth shall help humanity to transition into a sovereign state of self-governance and *unity* with the Earth.

There will be one profound difference from the previous Age of Mankind: there will be no evil influences to mislead, corrupt and destroy humanity. He will live in a world that is part of Heaven and will be under the guidance of Holy Angels and the authority of the Holy Spirit. It is difficult for a person living now to conceive of this, but there will be nothing that arises because of evil. Everything that Mankind does hereafter will conform to God's inviolable laws that govern the material and intellectual domain, uncorrupted with ill will, deception and untruth.

Mankind's unfettered, unspoiled intellect will find ways based on truth, logic, sensibility, fairness, imagination, and love to resolve all problems and to live as God intended upon the Earth. At some point Mankind will discover and join with intelligent life from other worlds. They will exchange the visions, ideas and products of their imaginations for the advancement and good of both worlds and to glorify their Creator. There shall be no wars or strife between worlds because this is Heaven, not some Godless universe.

The New Beginning

All heaven will now evolve with wonderful, awesome change, using new truths and even entirely new material creations of the angels. Willing souls can join with God and the angels of Heaven to make the Universe what it shall become. Shall the angels begin new themes of creation for the Earth and Galaxy? Yes, they will devise new themes for the NEW Heaven *and* the New Earth.

"Then I saw a new heaven and a new earth, for the first earth had passed away, and the sea was no more. And I saw the holy city, the new Jerusalem, coming down out of heaven from God, prepared as a bride adorned for her husband. And I heard a loud voice from the throne saying, 'See, the home of God is among the mortals. He will dwell with them as their God; they will be his peoples, and God himself will be with them; he will wipe away every tear from their eyes. Death will be no more; mourning and crying and pain will be no more, for the former things have passed away.'

And the one who was seated on the throne said, 'See, I am making all things new.'" The Holy Bible (NSRV), Revelations 21:1-5]

All angels, one of whom resides in each human being as its soul, can join God in His Heaven to help create the wonders of His Mind, forever and forever.

Death and Former Things
in the New Heaven and the New Earth

A long life marked with contentment and fulfillment is the dream of every human. Death prevents individuals from living forever in the material worlds. Humans deal with the challenges and expectations of life with awareness that life may end at any time, at any age, quickly or after a long struggle. So death is seen as a dark destroyer to be hated and feared, as though Death were the antithesis of God's Will, or an act of an anti-god. It is an affliction of all species for which God is accused and often someone will ask how can He love us and then give us death.

Yet, Life and Death are part of the Divine Plan for all creatures. If God is the giver of Life, can Death end it against His Will? Then what is Death? Is Death a destroyer, or a reformer? Humankind does not appreciate the benefits of natural death to his own species. Few recognize that death nourishes and sustains life in their world.

Death shall be experienced by every human and each shall meet it alone, but he shares it as a common experience of all living creatures. A person's life and death are intimately personal affairs and are his sacred engagements to experience the act of being. Through exercising the gift of conception, humans and all creatures can share the angels' powers of creation, to bring into being another creature that has his own likeness that shall be nourished through love and sustained by knowledge, to become his own replacement in an unbroken chain of perpetuity. Soon, he may die; but if he has achieved any goal of love or truth, he has fulfilled a purpose for being. Then death need not be a disappointment.

Humans hope for a "resurrection" through which their deceased bodies will be restored to life in a sublimely new and imperishable form. After dying, there is no consciousness in the body through which that hope is sustained; consciousness survives in the soul that alone continues to live and can cherish the hope of resurrection.

Death is not a final destiny even for creatures such as human beings, but is a transformation of form. Death is a process of returning a being of discreet material form to a widely disbursed form that sustains other living things. In time, the body of each human will return to the basic atoms, molecules and compounds from which all material creations are formed. Living or dead, everything is still part of God!

Now, oh Mankind, hear this message of Hope and Life *revealed for those whose angel souls attain eternal life. Your consciousness shall not die* even though your body returns to the dust of the Earth because the consciousness becomes part of the angel soul for eternity. Whereas, at death the angel soul captures the essence of the human's personality and records a summary of his life memories, and whereas such memories *become an integral part of the angel soul's being,* and whereas the personality and memories constitute consciousness, such consciousness will live forever within the angel that was your soul through life. Furthermore, this consciousness of your life will abide within the angel in company with the consciousness of all of its incarnations in past and future human lives, uniting your consciousness with those you never knew, but dreamed of knowing. Alas, those angel souls *who will not accept eternal life* with God their Father will die and so will the collective consciousness of all its human incarnations.

Just as death has different meanings for the body and soul in this Age, differences will remain for humankind and the angels beyond the end of the Age. A basis for understanding much about the eventual destinies of soul and body is provided in promises of prophecy in the Holy Bible, which asserts that, someday, there will be a "new heaven and a new earth". This promise shall be fulfilled for both the human and his angel soul in distinctly separate outcomes. What is the significance of this promise for Mankind?

Considering that the angel soul is either a fallen angel or an angel created anew within the earthly experience of Mankind, the "new heaven" has distinct meaning for all souls. Souls that are fallen angels have been denied a knowledge of the changing Heaven since they were isolated in Hades. Their memories of the former Heaven before that event is suppressed. Since Heaven changes constantly as new truths flow into it from the mind of God, the redeemed fallen angels will face a very different Heaven from the one from which they defected. To them, Heaven will seem "new" because it has changed.

The newly created angels, who have not seen Heaven, will encounter a sight that they could not have imagined, so very unlike the heavenly space they experienced between human incarnations. And to celebrate the triumph of Love and Truth, both new and fallen angels will be joined in a jubilee that shall leave all of Heaven with a glorious new theme.

This triumph of Christ, the Master and Redeemer, is victory for all these souls that overcame the temptations of corruption and disobedience to accept, instead, the patient love and mercy offered by the Father which abided to the end, the end that came only when there was not a single soul remaining to be saved. These shall share in the glory of Christ because they accepted his plea to fight and vanquish the evil that sprang into each of them from following the paths of deception and self-indulgence. Now Christ will share the fruits of this victory with all the angels of Heaven in the pleasure of the Father.

In the new Heaven, the Father will extend a new Will for all creatures of spiritual and material life. Christ, having lived and died as a man of flesh, understands the hopes and miseries and travails of humans and all creatures. Much shall change because of this. Heaven will display a new love for all creatures of Earth and other worlds of the universe: one creature shall not live only for the benefit of another or live at another's expense; all powers given to creatures are for their benefit and joy to share the gifts of love, truth and beauty that are given to all the Heavenly hosts. Nothing will ever occur in Heaven that is contrary to God's Supreme Purpose, and his approval shall sanctify all that is done by angels or humanly creatures.

Furthermore, we are promised that there will be no more death or sorrow in the new Heaven and earth. What does this mean for Mankind? At the end of the Age when God will end Earth's isolation from Heaven and He has dispensed Justice for all souls and fallen angels, no angel will ever again have to become infused into a human as its soul. There shall be no more souls from that time forward. Therefore, the angels will never again experience death with their human host and there will be no more pauses in the heavenly or hellish states to await a return to life. There will be no more death for the angels! This is the ultimate meaning of the promise of Resurrection, which is not restoration of a deceased body to life, but is the end of the angels' association with mortal flesh and is *salvation* of the angel from spiritual death for eternal life in Heaven.

To help understand what this promise means for the *human*, we can get a clue from Isaiah 65:17-20. A partial quote from these passages is as follows: "Behold, I will create a new heaven and a new earth ... be glad and rejoice in what I create, for I will create Jerusalem to be a delight and its people a joy ... the sound of weeping and of crying will be heard in it no more. Never again will there be in it an infant who lives but a few days or an old man who does not live out his years". Saint John echoes this promise in Revelation 21 in the account of his vision of the new Heaven and new Earth and the New Jerusalem: "...the home of God is among the mortals ... death will be no more; mourning and crying and pain will be no more, for the former things have passed away. ... See, I am making all things new". Isaiah's use of the words "infant" and "old man" and John's use of "mortals" assures us that their words refer to *humans* rather than to the angel souls.

When the new Earth is established, humans will no longer have souls and the angels will be free of this obligation. God's Spirit will dwell among humanity and they will be guided henceforth by the Holy Spirit. Mankind will have a *new* "spirit" which shall sanctify all his aspirations and endeavors. This spirit should not be thought of as a soul. Mankind's spirit will be derived from his awareness of Divine spiritual values and from interaction with the Holy Spirit. This spirit will be as ubiquitous to humanity on Earth as the Heavenly spirit is to the angels.

Humans will enjoy a new kind of life on Earth because many things will change due to the creative powers loosed by the Holy Spirit. Mankind's intellect and spirit will achieve continuous advancements in his cultural, social and physical spheres. God will take away many of the former things that have plagued humanity since his primeval appearance on the Earth.

Infants and children will no longer die of natural causes. They will grow into manhood and womanhood and look forward to a long, pleasant life in excess of one-hundred years. No parent need ever see their children die before them. They shall all live out their life expectancies and, when their time to depart has come, they will accept it without sorrow or fear. Humankind will have a new understanding of death, realizing that it is not the end, but a continuation of life because the residues of their bodies will eventually return to become part of many living things. Humanity will revere all life, because it is part of him and he is part of it. He will join harmoniously with this principle to become part of the life and beauty that adorn his spaces.

So the experience of death will vanish from the lot of the angels and will change dramatically for humans. Death will come at its appointed time for humans at the end of a full life and will no longer be cause for grief. Thus God's promise for humanity and the angels will be fulfilled.

The New Jerusalem will be the new Earth restored as a garden in the kingdom of Heaven wherein all angels, humanity and creatures live within God's Will and Grace, sharing things of love, truth and beauty forever. The fallen angels, expelled long ago from Eden for their sins against God and Earth's creatures, have led humanity from meekness to exaltation in their reach for redemption and salvation. Mankind will inherit the dominions of Earth to rule it in sovereignty, benevolence and charity. Then Earth will become the New Garden of Eden where no one will ever again be tempted to sin against God or his fellow being, causing him to descend into darkness, torment and death.

All of these things are the fruits of Christ's victory. Never again will Love be perverted, or Truth be corrupted, or Light be obscured, or Life be depraved. All angels and material creatures will forevermore abide in the peace and glory of a Universe created by the Father and ruled through his Supreme Purpose. AMEN!

EPILOGUE

A MESSAGE FROM CHRIST
TO THE SOULS AND MANKIND

Through the Love and Grace of our Heavenly Father, I, Christ, the first Son of God, add my message to the book that has been given to inform Mankind of His Truths. I address you in the flesh of humanity, for I am again with you as a child. It is from the boundless love of the Father that I am born among you once more, this time not to teach you, but to claim you all as the children of God and reward the righteous.

"I have come so that all the souls of Mankind can be shown the magnificent possibilities of a world in which the Laws and Will of God flow through every person in all that is done, unmolested by evil. While most of you are still in your present bodies, I shall begin the millennium of reign wherein the Will of the Father shall rule all human endeavors. All of Mankind will be able to see in themselves and all about them the power of Love and Truth to fulfill the aspirations of their minds and souls. Each person will live and work in harmony with his soul, individually and together as families, in communities and all institutions of Mankind, and in all nations to achieve a world that is beyond any description that you could accept from me now.

"As a child, I appear as any child would; yet, the Father has manifested powers in me through the authority of His Love and Intellect that have not been withdrawn from me during this sojourn in the flesh. Therefore, I am able to communicate with my messenger through the help of the angel Gabriel. As in my first human life as Jesus two thousand years ago, Gabriel was empowered to be my helper and to perform spiritual tasks which I am restrained from doing while in material form. Gabriel has been with me since the final month before my birth and he shall remain at my side until I am taken away. This is his sole capacity; he shall serve no other functions until I leave you. I tell you this because very few of you are acquainted with Gabriel, since Lucifer was

239

your archangel when you abandoned Heaven, and Gabriel had not yet been called.

"I greet you as a brother, for you are all my brothers and sisters in the Spirit of God. I am the first created by the Father and I came out of His supreme need to share Love with another Being. He made me from His own substance, just as each human is made from the flesh and substance of his mother. He then created the Holy Spirit and anointed his Kingdom with this Power.

"The Father taught me all that was in His heart about Love and Truth and how, from these, He planned to create a universe of majestic beauty and grandeur, and populate it with Life. He taught me the Laws inherent in His Being and how they work to rule all things of spirit and material form. Being with Him before the Universe was formed, I learned of the absolute necessity of Love for the existence of Life, and of Truth for Creation.

"Out of Love He created multitudes of additional companions in His image. Many of you now as souls were among these Heavenly angels created to fulfill His Love. He created you very much in resemblance to me, in the same way; but each of you is unique. I was the first, so I was His helper and assisted Him as He brought each one of you into existence, at first as part of Him, then a separate entity.

"Because of this and His Wisdom born of Truth, He gave me an honored place among you, in a capacity to serve you. I feel no power over you, but with you and in you. Love and Truth bind us all together as one body. You are my body, which is whole and strong and virtuous, and together we form the Son of God.

"From the moment you were isolated in the Earthly realm because you followed an errant deceiver out of innocent trust, you were made to forget your Heavenly past. It is for this reason that I now send my message to comfort you with assurances that your mistakes can be redeemed and you can be restored. I praise you now for the gifts you have given to Mankind through your redemptive efforts that have brought success to the Father's plan of redemption. He is well pleased, but not yet satisfied. All of you who so choose can reclaim your Heavenly birthright.

"Those souls who have been born anew in the Earthly realm shall receive the same blessings from the Father as the original angels. You are already part of the Heavenly Hosts. As with the original angels, I was the first to greet you when you were created as a spirit and when you became souls, and I am the last to comfort you when death takes your body of flesh. While I am in the flesh,

Gabriel will perform these visitations for me in the name and authority of the Father.

"I shall come to Earth once again, for the third time, at the end of the Age. I shall not be in the flesh then, for I am coming to take you out of the flesh. All souls living and dead who have chosen me and the Father shall return with me to Heaven and eternal life.

"Heaven shall be "new", and many things will not be as you recall them. But all of your beloved companion angels will meet you in greetings of love and great happiness, and they will reveal many surprising things to you.

"On Earth, Mankind will be governed by the Holy Spirit. Mankind's thoughts, deeds, accomplishments and destiny shall from there on be guided by and rooted in the powers of the Holy Spirit. He shall experience greater influence from the Spirit than from his angel soul. This is so because the Holy Spirit emanates from the Heavenly Father, whose power is greater than the power of the angels who, as souls, now influence the minds of humanity. Indeed, it is the Holy Spirit that empowers the angels to do the work of their Creator.

"There shall also be a "new" Earth. Many things will change. Mankind's numbers shall decrease to a level whereby he can live harmoniously with the resources of the Earth and its creatures. Earth shall be restored to a more pristine world of beauty and serenity. Many creatures that appear in the natural world as pests and poisons or overly savage shall disappear or be changed.

"The health of humanity shall improve, their problems shall be few. God shall take away the intractable diseases that cripple the body and mind. Mankind's ingenuity shall defeat or control many other diseases and illnesses that now mar, diminish or destroy his body. Venereal diseases will disappear because of righteous life styles. The effects of aging shall be delayed and minimized; life spans shall increase greatly.

"There shall be few things in Earthly living to despoil lives of happiness and satisfaction. Sorrow over death and misfortune shall be shallow and short-lived because the virtues of love and a new understanding are extensively and powerfully infused into the fabric of all families and communities.

"These are things of the future which lie beyond the end of your journey of redemption. I pity you all in your struggle with weakness and vulnerability to temptation and sin. But the Love and Mercy of our Father is always within easy access. You are His children, my brothers and sisters, and we work mightily to gather you in to safety so that we may hold you in our embrace of love once more, willing to forgive and forget the disobedience that led you into troubled waters. We can separate you from those who confuse and mislead and try to tear you from our safe berth. Only call to us and extend your willing hands.

"Come to us! Repent, have faith, share love with us, and leave the dark, treacherous waters. Swim to the Light on the Shore of the Living from which my voice calls to you! There you will find your Heavenly family and the Love and Safety of your eternal home.

"The Age of Redemption is almost over and most of you have achieved the goals of redeeming your original sins committed against humanity and Earth's creatures. You have not yet won the victory, but the power to do so is available to you now. See how far you have come since the Age of Redemption began! Progress now permits you to become truly partners with your human hosts. Together, you can achieve the victory, to win back Heaven for all the Earth.

"Oh, Mankind! Open your eyes and see what wonders can lie before you. Your angelic souls need your help. Join them now to help them complete their redemptive goals so that they may be free. Let human mind and soul work together so that all may be saved for the Father, can defeat the power of Satan's hold, and achieve a state of Heaven on Earth. Let the mind of each person yield to the soul that seeks God. Choose to live righteously, and let the Father's Love and Truth flow through you like a cleansing stream. It will transform you into instruments and expressions of Love. You can achieve a world far beyond Mankind's present dreams.

"You have come to that place where soul and mind are truly wed, where love can bind the two as one, together reaching for the stars where Heavenly angels abide. Soul, teach the mind of your human host God's Laws and Truths and the things of Love and Beauty. Mind of Mankind, accept your soul as the fountain and giver of all to which you aspire, and let it lead you into paths of righteousness and love. Then you will come as one into the Promised Land, a new creature before God that is both human and angelic. The holy Purpose of redemption for the fallen angels will now be clearly seen as Love and Beauty radiating from the Father's heart."

ABOUT THE AUTHOR

WILLIAM PLESS is the son of a Methodist minister. He grew up in Alabama with a sound Judeo-Christian heritage. He has been a life-long seeker of unwritten meanings of intellectual and spiritual truths. With a university education in physics, Mr. Pless spent his career in the aerospace industry, frequently describing his work in professional journals and handbooks. He helped establish the Lockheed Space Operations Company that performed a multi-billion dollar Space Shuttle processing project. After retiring, he turned toward a new purpose—dedicating himself to the Father's Will. *The Spiritual Nature of the Universe* is the culmination of work from a heavenly directive.

Printed in the United Kingdom
by Lightning Source UK Ltd.
9371200002B